The Economics of
Industries and Firms

We work with leading authors to develop the
strongest educational materials in economics,
bringing cutting-edge thinking and best learning
practice to a global market.

Under a range of well-known imprints, including
Financial Times Prentice Hall, we craft high quality
print and electronic publications which help readers
to understand and apply their content, whether
studying or at work.

To find out more about the complete range of our
publishing, please visit us on the World Wide Web at:
www.pearsoneduc.com

The Economics of Industries and Firms

Ken Heather

FINANCIAL TIMES
Prentice Hall

An imprint of **Pearson Education**

Harlow, England · London · New York · Reading, Massachusetts · San Francisco · Toronto · Don Mills, Ontario · Sydney
Tokyo · Singapore · Hong Kong · Seoul · Taipei · Cape Town · Madrid · Mexico City · Amsterdam · Munich · Paris · Milan

Pearson Education Limited

Edinburgh Gate
Harlow
Essex CM20 2JE

and Associated Companies throughout the world

Visit us on the World Wide Web at:
www.pearsoneduc.com

First published 2002

© Pearson Education Limited 2002

ISBN 0 273 65585 X

British Library Cataloguing-in-Publication Data
A catalogue record for this book is available from the British Library

Library of Congress Cataloging-in-Publication Data
Heather, Ken.
    Industrial economics / Ken Heather.
        p. cm.
    Includes bibliographical references and index.
    ISBN 0–273–65585–X (pbk.)
    1. Managerial economics. 2. Costs, Industrial. 3. Production (Economic theory)
4. Industrial organization (Economic theory) I. Title.

    HD30.22 .H43 2002
    338 5'024'658—dc21

                                                    2001040991

10 9 8 7 6 5 4 3 2 1
06 05 04 03 02

Typeset in 9.5/12.5pt Stone serif by 35
Printed by Ashford Colour Press Ltd., Gosport

Contents

Preface

Businesses do not operate in a vacuum. The microeconomic environment in which they function in part constrains and in part determines their decision-making processes. This book is designed to offer a concise overview of this important area. It attempts to be rigorous in its analysis. Yet the non-technical nature of much of the discussion enables non-specialist economists to follow the arguments. Many students who will read this text will not be taking a specialist economics degree. Many will be following business courses either at undergraduate level or in a master's programme. Whatever the course, the book assumes only a very basic knowledge of elementary microeconomics and any of the arguments can be followed with the most basic mathematical understanding, although widespread use of simple diagrams is made.

If you are not studying economics (or even if you are!) there may be some reluctance to believe that economists can make a significant contribution to understanding business behaviour. There are three areas of difficulty that are common. They can be expressed in the following statements.

1. *'I want to be able to solve business problems, but economists just look in general terms at the business world.'*

Economists also wish to contribute to the solution of business problems but an overview of the world of business is crucial. Imagine going to the specialist with a pain in your kidney. You have a specific problem that you want solved. The doctor has an ability to help partly because he/she has specialised in dealing with problems of the kind you have. However, that ability is partly determined by a more general medical training in which the doctor has seen your problem as part of your overall health. Studying how healthy bodies work enables an appreciation of what happens when things go wrong. It is this general perspective which is crucial for understanding your particular medical problem. Similarly, if you are to focus on business problems you will be much better able to do so if you have an overview of the functioning of industries and firms in which specific business problems occur.

2. *'Economists make assumptions that are not true of businesses.'*

A further problem arises in the minds of many students. They can find it frustrating that economists make assumptions that they perceive as invalid. You may have already thought this issue through in the context of a first principles course. I hope you there appreciated that those assumptions enabled you to focus on the essential relationships. Take the assumption that firms wish to maximise profits. Fritz Machlup once used a powerful illustration to consider this. Imagine a two-lane road, i.e. a single carriageway in each direction. Now imagine trying to model the decision of a motorist attempting to overtake. It would be hugely complex. One would need to consider, among other things, vehicle speed, lighting and weather conditions, the gradient of the road and the assumptions about the behaviour of other drivers. One might reasonably conclude that it is too complex for a driver ever to take a decision to overtake. Yet millions of decisions are taken every day, almost all of them correct. Similarly, economists will sometimes model a firm's behaviour assuming that its cost and revenue conditions are perfectly known. In practice they are not. Does that necessarily mean that the profit-maximising assumption is invalid? It does not. As with the driver on the road, so the manager of a firm takes decisions as if all the many variables affecting the decision are known. As with drivers so with businesses, they usually make the correct decisions. So making decisions on the basis of unreal assumptions can often effectively and accurately predict behaviour.

Nevertheless, we shall through the course of the book drop some key assumptions that economists sometimes make, in order to see what effect this has on decision taking. Thus, for example, a whole chapter (11) is give over to considering the possibility that managers do not seek to maximise profits. A large part of Chapter 10 is devoted to considering behaviour when demand conditions are not known.

You should therefore find by the end of the book that you are quite comfortable with the assumptions that are being made about industries and firms. They do not lead to unrealistic conclusions.

3. *'The technical language of economists is often not the language of businessmen.'*

Sometimes economists do use language that is unfamiliar to those whose behaviour they are describing. Decisions of consumers, for example, may be described in terms of marginal utility. Few people shopping in Safeway would use this terminology about their purchases, yet the economist's language of consumer behaviour enables clear thinking that reaches important conclusions about consumer demand. You may have watched a leading snooker player score a large number of points. A physicist may describe such behaviour in terms of kinetic energy etc. The snooker player may never have heard of the term even though he is a much better player than the physicist. Similarly, an economist may use language unfamiliar to business managers to describe their behaviour. This helps us towards the clear thinking that enables insights to be made into the operation of firms and industries. It does not make the economist a good manager. Nor is it supposed to. It does, however, give some powerful insights into the way in which businesses are organised.

I hope you will therefore feel that a book on the economics of industries and firms can play a valuable role in helping you to appreciate the business world.

An overview of the book

Chapter 1 outlines some key ideas on the profitability and efficiency of industries and firms. Chapter 2 introduces some competing perspectives on the way that industry is structured. Chapter 3 examines the important area of market concentration and discusses its relevance to firm behaviour. The fourth and fifth chapters focus on production costs and in particular the effects of technological change. In Chapters 6–8 we cover merger activity and its effects on the microeconomic landscape. Other forms of business relationships are also considered there. Three chapters, 9–11, are devoted to a central question of how business prices are set. As part of this analysis we consider the question of estimating the demand for the business product. Firms also compete on non-price variables. The most important of these is advertising, which forms the subject of Chapter 12. The final chapter draws the strands of the book together and considers them in the light of government policy towards firms and industries.

Features of the book

A number of features have been incorporated into the book in order to make things as clear as possible and to demonstrate its relevance to business decision making. These features are as follows:

Objectives and key results

Each chapter has introductory objectives and concluding key results. The objectives have two functions. They explain how the topic to be considered impinges on the behaviour of businesses. They also establish the learning objectives of the chapter. The key results summarise the key points that you should have discovered during your reading. They act as a checklist of the central themes of the chapter.

Articles from the business press

Each chapter contains two articles on business behaviour. They are an important part of the text. Each article, or part of one, is from the *Financial Times* or other economic journal chosen to illustrate a key idea in that chapter. If you still feel that the subject matter of the book is divorced from the real world of business, these articles, read in conjunction with the appropriate chapter, should go a long way towards changing your mind.

Questions and Web-based answers

The questions at the end of each chapter should stimulate your thinking on the issues raised. Other than the ones referring directly to the business press articles you can find help in your thinking from a website, **http://www.e-econ.co.uk**. You can also reach this website via **http://www.booksites.net/heather**. I will talk you through the main elements of the answers there. However, in order to maximise the benefit from this you should give careful thought to your answer *before* going to the Web. The Web address is also given after the questions at the end of each chapter.

Glossary of terms

Since the book introduces terminology, some of which is probably new to you, it may help to have a handy reference to brief explanations of their meaning separate from the chapter where they are first introduced. This is provided in a glossary towards the back of the book.

Further reading

Some economists' thinking towards this important area of study has developed in recent years. The major changes are reflected in this text although I have tried to keep the treatment brief. For students who need to study any particular aspect of the subject more fully the appropriate parts of some key books that are in print are recommended in the appendix. The most important *articles* are referenced in the bibliography.

Acknowledgements

Whilst writing this book I have been conscious that whilst it is my name on the cover, a whole variety of people have contributed to it. In particular I would like to record my gratitude to the following. David Bibby has been sharpening my thinking for more years than either of us cares to remember. He read through and commented on an original draft and the finished product is the better for it. Several people kindly contributed to the word processing. My thanks go to Caroline and Harriet Archer and to Rachel Armstrong. Rosie Booker not only typed some of the draft but also contributed in her own unique way to keeping my feet on the ground. Of course, any remaining errors, and I hope they are few, are my responsibility. The Media Development Centre team at Portsmouth does an excellent job in producing associated Web materials and I am extremely grateful for their enthusiastic support. The Pearson team is always a very professional one. Laura Prime has remained throughout the project and I have appreciated her constant professionalism and cheerfulness. Although Paula Harris was not quite able to see the project through to its conclusion, I am sure she has found her new baby, Ben, more than adequate compensation for the disappointment.

University of Portsmouth, February, 2002

Publisher's acknowledgements

We are grateful to the following for permission to reproduce copyright material:

Table 1.1 from T. Coelli and S. Perelman, Technical efficiency of European railways, *Applied Economics*, Vol. 32 (2000) pp. 1967–1976, Taylor & Francis Ltd., http://www.tandf.co.uk/journals; Table 1.2 and Figure 1.7 from E. Davis and J. Kay, Assessing corporate performance, *Business Strategy Review*, Vol. 1 (1990) pp. 1–16, © Centre for Business Strategy, LBS, Blackwell Publishers Ltd.; Table 1.3 from A Report on the Supply of Groceries from Multiple Stores in the United Kingdom, CMD 4842 (2000), Competition Commission; Table 2.2 from R. Rumelt, How much does industry matter?, *Strategic Management Journal*, Vol. 3 (1990) pp. 167–85, © John Wiley & Sons Limited, reproduced with permission; Figure 2.3 reprinted with the permission of The Free Press, a Division of Simon & Schuster, Inc., from *Competitive Advantage: Creating and Sustaining Superior Performance* by Michael E. Porter, copyright © 1985, 1998 by Michael E. Porter; Table 3.3 from H. Demsetz, Industry structure, market rivalry and public policy, *Journal of Law and Economics*, Vol. 16 (1973) pp. 1–10, © 1973 by The University of Chicago, all rights reserved; Figure 3.6 from M. Peteraf, The cornerstones of competitive advantage: a resource-based view, *Strategic Management Journal*, Vol. 14 (1993) pp. 179–91, © John Wiley & Sons Limited, reproduced with permission; Tables 4.2 and 4.3 from G. J. Stigler, The economies of scale, *Journal of Law and Economics*, Vol. 1 (1958) pp. 54–71, © 1958 by The University of Chicago, all rights reserved; Table 8.1 from G. Meeks, *Disappointing Marriage: A Study of the Gains to Mergers* (1977) Cambridge University Press; Table 11.1 from W. Hornby, Economics and business: the theory of the firm revisited: a Scottish perspective, *Management Decision*, Vol. 33 (1995) pp. 33–41, © MCB University Press; Table 11.2 from T. Burke, S. Maddock and A. Rose, How ethical is British business?, University of Westminster, Working Paper, Series 2, No. 1; Table 11.3 and Figure 11.10 reprinted from *European Management Journal*, 12(2), P. Doyle, Setting business performance and measuring performance, pp. 123–132, © 1994, with permission from Elsevier Science; Tables 12.1 and 12.2 from P. Nelson, Advertising as information, *Journal of Political Economy*, Vol. 82 (1974) pp. 729–54, © University of Chicago Press; Table 13.1 from D. Parker and S. Martin, The impact of UK privatisation on labour and total factor productivity, *Scottish Journal of Political Economy*, Vol. 42 (1995) pp. 201–20, © Scottish Economic Society, Blackwell Publishers Ltd.; Table 13.2 from C. Winston, Economic deregulation: days of reckoning for microeconomists, Journal of Economic Literature, September (1993) pp. 1263–89, American Economic Association.

We are grateful to the Financial Times Limited for permission to reprint the following material:

Box 1.2 from Enlarging the shop window, © *Financial Times*, 31 January, 2001; Box 2.1 from Competition rules apply, © *Financial Times*, 18 October, 2000; Box 2.2 from Activism among the mini-mills . . . , © *Financial Times*, 19 December, 2000; Box 3.2 from Dotcoms devoured, © *Financial Times*, 23 October, 2000; Box 4.1

from International banks ready to claim east European prizes, © *Financial Times*, 20 October, 2000; Box 4.2 from Ugly duckling swan into the middle ground, © *Financial Times*, 7 November, 2000; Box 5.1 from Economies of scale set the cranes nodding, © *Financial Times*, 19 January, 2001; Box 5.2 from Reasons to be venturesome, © *Financial Times*, 1 February, 2001; Box 6.1 from Living long in dangerous waters, © *Financial Times*, 29 January, 2001; Box 6.2 from Future Whitbread butterfly emerges from its chrysalis, © *Financial Times*, 20 October, 2000; Box 7.1 from Carmakers eye route to twin track revenues, © *Financial Times*, 28 February, 2001; Box 7.2 from Dealmaking pioneers must play a cool hand, © *Financial Times*, 5 July, 2000; Box 8.1 from Drug combination has created a potent mix, © *Financial Times*, 2 March, 2001; Box 8.2 from Slow road to merger, © *Financial Times*, 7 January, 2000; Box 9.1 from Little gold at the end of the spectrum, © *Financial Times*, 3 November, 2000; Box 10.2 from Labelled as the devil of the consumer society, © *Financial Times*, 25 April, 2001; Box 11.1 from Shares in the action, © *Financial Times*, 27 April, 1998; Box 11.2 from Business learns the value of good works, © *Financial Times*, 19 December, 2000; Box 12.1 from Fashion fails to find the silver dollar, © *Financial Times*, 18 October, 2000; Box 12.2 from Advertising takes off, © *Financial Times*, 21 July, 2000; Box 13.2 from Under attack from blame and claim, © *Financial Times*, 23 April, 2001.

We are grateful to the following for permission to use copyright material:

Box 1.1 from A nation of enthusiastic amateurs, *The Financial Times Limited*, 1 February, 2001, © Bob Bischof. The writer is Honorary Consul for Germany and has written this in a personal capacity; Box 9.2 from Fallacies and first movers, *The Financial Times*, 1 February, 2001, © Charles Leadbeater; Box 13.1 from When regulation fails, *The Financial Times*, 18 October, 2000, © John Kay.

We are grateful to The Economist Newspaper Limited for permission to reproduce in Box 3.1 an extract from "Antitrust: the new enforcers" published in *The Economist* 7th October 2000, © The Economist Newspaper Limited, London 2000.

In some instances we have been unable to trace the owners of copyright material, and we would appreciate any information that would enable us to do so.

Firm efficiency and profitability: some basic concepts

To an optimist the glass is half full, to a pessimist it's half empty. To an economist it's inefficient because the glass is larger than necessary.

Firms strive to make profits. Managers generally believe that to be successful they must be efficient. This chapter explores the meaning and importance of profits and efficiency and their significance for a market economy.

OBJECTIVES

After reading this chapter you should be able to:

- Understand the meaning of technical, cost and allocative efficiency.
- Know why monopoly power is often regarded as an inefficient market structure.
- Appreciate the links between consumer preference, profit and efficient resource allocation.
- Understand the link between profit and firms' added value.

Introduction

Since society's wants are great we must use efficiently the limited resources at our disposal. We have a limited amount of resources, so we can produce a limited amount of output, but the volume of demand that is made upon that output is limitless. Therefore we need the resources that we have to be used in an efficient way. Although there is a substantial government sector, most resources are consumed by firms and industries. So a key consideration for economists and firms is the efficiency with which they conduct their affairs. In this chapter we shall introduce some key ideas concerning efficiency that will be developed later in the book. We shall see that the concept of efficiency helps us to understand why firms exist at all. In doing this we shall explore the role of profitability both from the point of view of economists and also from the perspective of firms and industries themselves.

We begin by explaining what we mean by the concept of efficiency. There are two main elements to the idea. One is *productive efficiency*, and the other is *allocative efficiency*. Let us focus first of all on productive efficiency.

Productive efficiency

When firms produce output, do they do so at least possible cost? If they do, they are productively efficient. This idea of productive efficiency has two separate elements contained within it. One is technical efficiency and the other is cost efficiency. When firms are technically efficient, we mean that they are producing a given level of output with the minimum possible amount of resources. So if a firm is using some capital and some labour to produce output, and if that firm could not use less capital to produce that output, without compensating by more labour usage, then we would say that the firm is technically efficient. It is not wasting resources. There are various ways in which firms might be technically efficient. Some ways involve a capital-intensive method of production where they are using a lot of capital, but not much labour. Other methods are more labour intensive, where they use rather more labour but less capital. These can be a technically efficient means of output. But depending on the price of capital and the price of labour, some of these mechanisms of producing output may be cheaper than others. So cost efficiency is achieved if a firm picks the kind of technically efficient output that minimises the cost of producing output. So technical efficiency is not sufficient to give us productive efficiency, because technical efficiency tells us nothing about the cost of using resources.

We can illustrate cost efficiency in a firm in Figure 1.1. Here is a firm whose long-run average cost curve (LRAC) is given as shown. If this firm is to be cost efficient it means that at whatever level of output it has chosen to produce, it will minimise the cost of doing so. So if the firms picks X_1 as its chosen level of output, it will only be cost efficient if it keeps its costs down to C_1, the minimum possible cost associated with X_1 level of output. If it chooses to produce X_2 level of output, then to be cost efficient means only to be spending

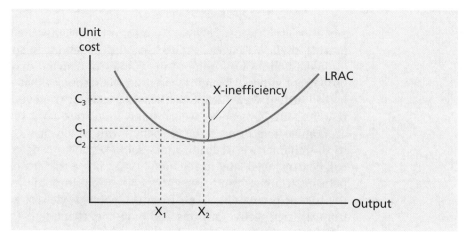

Figure 1.1 Cost efficiency for a firm

C_2 on resources. That is, it minimises the cost of producing X_2 level of output, and so on for any level of output that it has chosen. If, on the other hand, to produce X_2 output is at present involving the firm in a cost of C_3, it is producing at a cost greater than the minimum necessary. And that difference between C_3 and C_2 we refer to as X-inefficiency. If the firm is cost efficient, there is no X-inefficiency.

To summarise, then, productive efficiency is a combination of technical efficiency and cost efficiency. A firm is achieving productive efficiency if it is producing on its cost curve. If it is productively inefficient, it is producing with higher costs than necessary. The firm is, by definition, X-inefficient.

Are firms cost efficient? One way of answering that question is to examine the structure of the industry in which they operate. If firms are operating in an industry that is highly competitive, they are forced to be cost efficient. If they are not, they will not be able to make any profit, and they will simply die. So the structure of industry, if it is competitive enough, obliges firms to be cost efficient. What happens if we do not have a competitive structure? Suppose we have an industry where firms have a great deal of monopoly power. Are they cost efficient? The answer is that they might well be. If the firm's goal is to maximise its profit, then its goal is also to minimise the cost of producing its chosen level of output in order to maximise profits. However, it is possible that it may choose not to pursue the goal of profit maximisation. It may choose as part of its goal to have a relatively quiet life. Then it can afford to have some X-inefficiency, because the competitive pressures that it faces are not strong enough to oblige it to be cost efficient. So one can see that the structure of industry will help us to say something about the likelihood of firms being cost efficient, and therefore the question of how efficient society is in using its resources is linked to the question of the structure of industry.

Allocative efficiency

Are firms and industries using resources in order to meet the demands of consumers in an optimal way? Are they using resources in such a way that they produce the kinds of output that society most wants? We can use the opportunity cost curve in Figure 1.2 in order to see the link between cost efficiency and allocative efficiency. If as a society we are using all our resources in a cost-efficient way, we will maximise the amount of output that we can produce. So if all firms are cost efficient, society will be on the opportunity cost curve and might be at a point such as A, producing OF of output Y and OH of output X. However, society could be at some other spot on the opportunity cost curve. Any spot around the curve such as B or C will show us firms producing in a cost-efficient way. But it is possible that firms could be producing some output at minimum cost, but producing output that society does not value particularly highly. Cost efficiency says nothing about whether firms and industries are meeting society's preferences. Allocative efficiency, on the

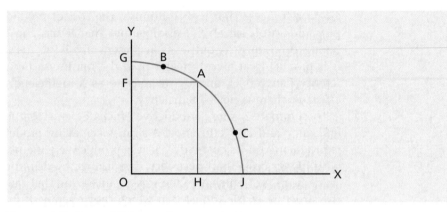

Figure 1.2 Cost efficiency for a society

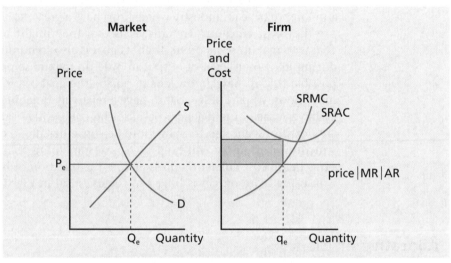

Figure 1.3 Perfect competition: short-run equilibrium

other hand, is about whether firms are using our resources in just those kinds of industries that consumers most wish. Which of these cost-efficient combinations gives allocative efficiency? We will examine this first in the context of a perfectly competitive industry.

Figure 1.3 shows a market that is perfectly competitive. In the first instance we will look at such an industry in the short run. The left-hand side of the diagram shows the market, where supply and demand determine the price at P_e. Each firm has to take the price as given to it. In perfect competition the firm is a price taker, quantity maker. How much output does a firm choose to produce? It chooses to maximise its profits, which means producing where marginal cost is equal to marginal revenue. So this representative firm chooses the appropriate level of output to make, which is quantity q_e.

Remember that the price that it charges is the price P_e, because it has no choice. It operates in a perfectly competitive industry with no control over price. From the firm's point of view, profit maximisation requires the firm to produce at q_e, where marginal cost is equal to marginal revenue.

Now consider this decision from society's point of view. How much output does society want this firm to produce? In order to see that, we have to remember two things. First of all, we have to remember that the demand curve reflects the value that society places on any given level of output. The demand curve tells us what society thinks each unit of output is worth. Secondly, we have to remember that the cost curve reflects the opportunity cost to society of using resources. If a firm's costs are at a given amount, they are spending that on scarce resources of land, labour and capital. But scarce resources have an opportunity cost. If the firm is producing this output using these resources, then these resources are not available for some other firm in some other industry. Private costs equal social costs. So bearing those two things in mind, if resources are to be used allocatively efficiently, society wants the firm to produce any unit of output that society values as least as much as the opportunity cost of the resources being used in production.

One important qualification to the above argument is that there are no externalities in consumption or production. Externalities introduce a divergence between private and social benefits or between private and social costs. An example of an externality in consumption is the smoking of cigarettes. The benefit to society is the benefit to the cigarette consumer, less the costs imposed upon others by passive smoking. The externality introduces a divergence between private and social benefits. An example of an externality in production is the dumping into a river of toxic waste as a by-product of some manufacturing process. The cost to society is not just the cost to the firm of manufacturing the product. It also includes the cost to society not borne by the firm, the dead fish stocks and so on. To say that social cost equals private cost requires that such externalities do not exist. Where externalities are present we would need to modify our argument accordingly.

Now return to Figure 1.3. In the absence of externalities in consumption the demand curve represents the value that society places on each of these units of output. The marginal cost curve, labelled SRMC, tells us, in the absence of production externalities, the extra cost to society of producing each additional unit of output. It tells us the amount of extra resources that are being used up, resources which have an opportunity cost. How much output does society want this firm to make? Society wants all the units of output where the marginal opportunity cost of resources is less than the value we place upon the output. So from society's point of view the optimum level of output is where the marginal cost is as great as the marginal value of the goods, represented by the demand curve. This is at quantity q_e, because that is where marginal cost is equal to demand. Allocative efficiency requires that output is where marginal cost equals demand.

So from the firm's perspective it wishes to produce where marginal cost is equal to marginal revenue. From society's perspective we wish the firm to produce where marginal cost is equal to demand. But in the perfectly competitive situation, demand and marginal revenue are the same. So what maximises the firm's welfare, maximising profit, is what maximises society's welfare since marginal cost is equal to demand. Given a perfectly competitive structure we are likely to get an allocatively efficient use of society's resources.

The role of profit

We now consider the role of profit in achieving efficiency. We can see this if we stay with the perfectly competitive structure. We will look at a non-perfectly competitive structure shortly. First we use the perfectly competitive structure to see the value of profit in allocating resources in an efficient way.

Thus far we have confined our thinking to the short run. Now let's think about a perfectly competitive firm in the longer term and we do that with the aid of Figure 1.4. Focus first of all on the market where we have a supply curve, S, a demand curve, D, and the equilibrium price is at P_e. The equilibrium output for the market is at Q_e. This is a price which means that firms are making profits. Price is higher than long-run average cost. When that is the case, and if there are no barriers to the entry of new firms, new firms will enter the market, seeking the profits that firms are currently making. As new firms enter the market the supply curve shifts right from S to S_1 and the equilibrium price falls to P_E. This process will continue until firms in the industry find that all their profits above normal have been eroded away, and each firm is producing a level of output where marginal cost is equal to marginal revenue. For this representative firm this is at q_e output. At that level of output, it is covering all costs, including opportunity cost, because its output X price (total revenue) is equal to output X average cost (total cost). Here we

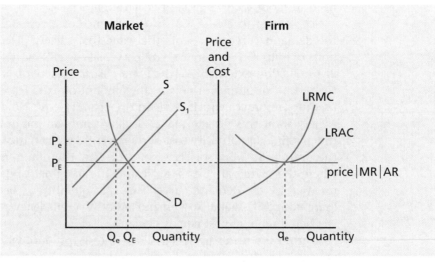

Figure 1.4 Perfect competition: long-run equilibrium

have a firm in long-run equilibrium producing an allocatively efficient level of output where marginal cost is equal to demand. It is willing to stay in the industry because the price is sufficient to cover all its costs, including opportunity cost. In other words, it is making a normal profit. Remember that we include all costs in the cost structure, including the normal profit that is represented by opportunity cost.

When we have a perfectly competitive system, profit is a crucial element of having an efficient allocation of resources. If we start off with an industry making normal profit, if demand rises, prices rise. If prices rise, profits are made in the short run. Those profits attract new resources into the industry. As new resources come into the industry, equilibrium in the long run returns, where firms are allocatively efficient producing where marginal cost is equal to demand.

We can now see why profit is so important. Profit is important in the short run, because when consumers wish more of a product and wish more resources to be allocated into an industry, they communicate that information to resource owners in the form of rising prices and therefore profits above normal. So when resources move into an industry they are moving in response to consumers wanting more resources in the industry. Profits in the short run are important because they act as an indicator to firms to respond to consumer preference.

Profits in the long run are important because such profits in a competitive industry will be normal profit, and normal profit is that income which covers all costs, including opportunity cost. Firms are thus willing to continue to produce the output that society wants. Without that normal profit firms would not produce output at all in the long run. So if we have a perfectly competitive structure we are going to get allocative efficiency. We are now in a position to see this, not just from one firm's perspective, but for the whole economy. Refer to Figure 1.5, where we return to society's opportunity cost curve. Anywhere around the curve is cost efficient, but if society's preferences

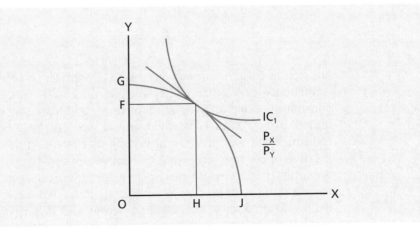

Figure 1.5 Allocative efficiency

BOX 1.1 Cost efficiency in British industry

Cost inefficiency is widespread in the UK, according to this view.

As Railtrack struggles to restore confidence in Britain's disrupted rail system, it may seem odd to reflect that it could have learnt a simple lesson from the Football Association. After Kevin Keegan had set a unique example by admitting he was not up to the job of England coach, the FA swallowed its patriotic pride, looked for the most skilled and experienced man it could find and hired Sven-Göran Eriksson.

Compare and contrast Railtrack. After Gerald Corbett, the chief executive, resigned, the company turned to Steve Marshall, finance director – one of the management team that has been unable to halt its descent. The fact that Railtrack's activities mainly involve engineering, technology and information technology – and, at present, remedying huge safety problems – seemed to be of little concern to those who offered the job to an accountant.

If the FA could conduct an international search for the best man for the job and find a Swede, why did the Railtrack board or the shareholders not insist on a professional railway man? A Swiss, for example. They seem to be able to run trains on time, have clean stations, charge less than half the fares and still turn a profit.

The Railtrack story is in some ways symptomatic of what still happens far too often in British business. The root cause is the self-confident Anglo-Saxon belief that anybody can, with a minimum of knowledge or training, turn his or her hand to anything.

Endearing and entrepreneurial as the I-believe-I-can-do-anything attitude may be, this bravado often hides a cavalier attitude to business. It is fearlessness born out of naivety and it produces little more than enthusiastic amateurism.

Problems are rarely tackled at a fundamental level. Instead, 'financial' solutions are put forward, often on the advice of consultants, whose knowledge is by the very nature of their occupation superficial and, more often than not, also financially oriented. The result is that companies or divisions are merged, sold or closed and complex processes made simpler by outsourcing. What is left of manufacturing is often merely assembly work.

Far from being a shining example of entrepreneurial excellence, the new economy appears to be 'no-knowledge-driven', at least as far as electronic commerce is concerned. Entrepreneurs have launched ventures in markets they know nothing about, with no competence in marketing, logistics and sales fulfilment, their amateurism aided by equally uninformed institutional investors who are now deserting the sector even faster than they entered it 12 months ago.

Fewer, better-prepared start-ups makes more sense than large numbers of no-hopers. And here, too, football can show the way: top British football clubs are abandoning 'kick-and-rush' tactics in favour of a 'continental' style of play, with its more patient build-up – and much better results.

Source: Financial Times, 1 February 2001   **FT**

are seen in this community via a set of indifference curves, then the highest indifference curve that society can get on is IC_1. This is feasible, given the constraints imposed by the opportunity cost curve, if we produce OF of Y and OH of X. That is the allocatively efficient level of output. Firms and industries will produce this, providing that relative prices are given by P_X/P_Y. Relative prices here are equal to relative opportunity costs, the slope of the opportunity cost curve. Since prices reflect opportunity cost, marginal resource owners have no incentive to reallocate productive capacity. So producers are willing to produce at this level of output and it is that combination which maximises society's well-being. Consumers are willing to purchase goods in these quantities at these relative prices. Consumers cannot improve their utility since marginal amounts of income bring equal satisfaction if spent on either good at this point. In other words, this satisfies consumers because the relative price is the same as the slope of the indifference curve, the condition for maximising social welfare.

Competitive selection

The perfectly competitive model on which the optimal efficiency model is based has been argued to be unrealistic. Its defenders point out that it is not a description of the world, simply an ideal against which actual market structures can be judged. They also point out that it is still a powerful model for predicting behaviour. If this is the case it has its place even if the assumptions are unrealistic. Recall that we addressed this issue in the preface.

However, it is possible to relax some assumptions, produce a more realistic competitive model and still have one that is an ideal allocator of scarce resources. Specifically, suppose that all firms are not equally efficient. Perhaps some have technology or superior managers not available to others. This would mean that the average firm makes a normal profit in the long run but some can do better. It also means that some are larger than others. The more cost efficient have lower marginal costs and therefore a larger output than the less efficient.

It has also been observed that there are new entrants into industry at the same time that others are leaving. The perfectly competitive model assumes that there are only entrants when price exceeds average costs, only leavers when price is below average costs, and neither leavers nor new entrants when price equals average cost. How do we explain this discrepancy between theory and observation? Despite the competitive assumption of perfect knowledge, not all firms have the same information. Existing firms have acquired information about their efficiency whilst they have been in the market. On this basis they may be deciding to leave. Potential entrants have to make assumptions about their likely efficiency level. They may believe that they can be profitable and therefore be willing to enter. Subsequent events will show them whether they have made a good choice but on the basis of their expectations they may be entering as others are leaving.

Notice too that by selection the 'exiters' will be the least efficient and thus smaller than the average firm. By selection the efficient remain. The entrants will also be smaller than the average existing firm, since those who remain are more efficient than average. Again this is confirmed empirically. See Jovanovic (1982) and also Hopenhayn (1992). This more realistic model of competitive selection still leaves us with an optimal allocation of scarce resources. Firms maximise profits where MC = MR. By assumption MR = AR = D so they still produce where MC = D.

Remember, though, that all this assumes an essentially competitive structure. What happens if we don't have a competitive structure at all? What if there is a considerable amount of monopoly power within the structure of an

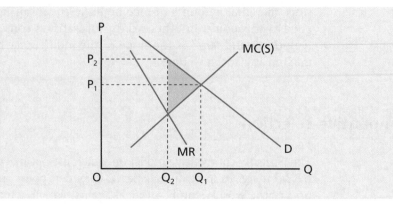

Figure 1.6 Monopoly power and deadweight losses

industry? Where does that leave the firm? Remember that with regard to cost efficiency we still get that if we assume that the firm wishes to maximise profit. If what the firm is seeking is to maximise profit, it will wish to keep its costs down to the minimum possible amount for its chosen output level. This is the condition for cost efficiency. But is it in a firm's interest to be allocatively efficient if we have monopoly power? The answer is no.

Monopoly power and allocative inefficiency

Figure 1.6 shows a firm with some monopoly power, facing a downward-sloping demand curve. The essence of monopoly is that the firm has some power over price. Then marginal revenue is less than demand. In order to increase output the firm has to lower price and so the extra revenue that the firm will get for one more unit of output is less than the price that it will be charging for the product. The appropriate level of output for the firm that maximises its profits is OQ_2, output where marginal cost is equal to marginal revenue. It is worth it to a firm to expand output to that level because until that point the additional cost of increasing output, marginal cost, is less than the additional revenue received, marginal revenue. What price does it charge? It charges the maximum price that it can get for that output. Remember it is constrained by the demand curve, so the price is P_2.

The allocatively efficient level of output, the optimum from society's perspective, is greater than the firm's optimum. Society wants all units of output made where the marginal cost of production is less than price. That is OQ_1 output where marginal cost is equal to demand. So an allocatively efficient level of output is OQ_1 output at P_1 price, whereas the firm's profit maximising level of output is OQ_2 output where demand is greater than marginal cost. This result contrasts with the perfectly competitive industry. Firms maximise profit where MC = MR. Society maximises its welfare when firms produce where MC = D. In perfect competition D and MR are the same. However, where monopoly power is present D and MR diverge. Hence the firm's optimum is a lower output at a higher price than society's optimum.

How much does society lose as a result of the allocative inefficiency of monopoly power? Remember that the demand curve reflects what society thinks each unit of output is worth. The marginal cost curve reflects the additional cost to society in terms of the scarce resources that these units of output are costing. So the difference between the two, the shaded triangle, represents the deadweight loss of value to society of this extra output, over and above opportunity costs. This is what society is losing, because the firm is restricting the amount of output that it produces below that social optimum level.

So again we have an argument that says that whether we use our resources in an efficient way depends upon the kind of structure of industry that we have. If we move out of the world of perfect competition into a world where firms have monopoly power, we may still get cost efficiency. But we are not likely to get an allocatively efficient use of resources, because what maximises the well-being of firms with monopoly power is different from what maximises the well-being of society.

Economists have tried to measure the extent to which resources are used efficiently and it is worthwhile considering briefly some of their results. Here we look at a study focusing on technical efficiency. In Chapter 2 we shall consider some studies concerned with allocative efficiency.

Railways and technical efficiency

European railways are largely publicly owned, with a degree of public funding and public accountability. However, they are still firms using scarce resources and so their efficiency is an important consideration. Coelli and Perelman (2000) attempted to measure their technical efficiency, measuring the level of inputs, staff, lines, rolling stock etc. against the volume of output of rail journeys achieved. The degree of technical efficiency varied widely between countries. However, when they considered the period 1988–93 and compared it with the period 1978–83 they found substantial improvements in all countries except Greece. A selection of their results can be seen in Table 1.1. TFP is Total Factor Productivity. It measures output against a weighted average of different kinds of inputs. A number equal to one would indicate no change over the two periods. So the UK achieved a 39.2% rise in TFP over the period against an average for European railways of 16.7%. The columns headed 'input changes' enable us to see where the improvements were concentrated. They were not primarily achieved by gaining more output from the same volume of inputs but from sharply reducing the inputs themselves. If marginal resources of labour, rolling stock and underutilised lines are shed, the average performance of the remaining resources will improve.

Table 1.1 Productivity change in European railways from 1978–83 to 1988–93

Railways	Country	Index of TFP change	Input changes (%)		
			Staff	Rolling stock	Lines
BR	United Kingdom	1.392	−32.4	−50.4	−5.2
CFF	Switzerland	1.289	−3.7	−2.2	2.6
CFL	Luxembourg	1.329	−17.2	−12.5	1.0
CH	Greece	0.830	17.8	11.6	0.9
CIE	Ireland	1.245	−15.6	−29.8	−1.5
CP	Portugal	1.180	7.9	2.3	−12.3
DB	Germany	1.179	−26.1	−14.9	−5.1
DSB	Denmark	1.388	−6.6	−23.1	12.9
FS	Italy	1.207	−18.0	5.4	−2.5
NS	Netherlands	1.120	8.0	−15.7	−3.2
NSB	Norway	1.051	−33.9	−7.4	−4.4
OBB	Austria	1.212	−10.4	8.6	−2.7
RENFE	Spain	1.078	−18.6	−0.1	−5.9
SJ	Sweden	1.021	−26.7	−35.5	−6.6
SNCB	Belgium	1.304	−22.2	−16.1	−18.5
SNCF	France	1.021	−18.9	−28.1	−2.6
VR	Finland	1.154	−44.4	−12.6	−3.2
	Mean	1.167	−15.3	−13.0	−3.3

Source: Coelli and Perelman (2000)

Efficiency, firms and transactions costs

The concern for efficiency helps to explain why we have firms at all. Why do firms exist? Take an example to illustrate. Why do travel agents exist? It would be perfectly possible for an individual to arrange a flight with the airline company and to arrange hotel accommodation when going abroad. And yet many people choose to use a travel agent, a firm, rather than use individual markets to achieve what they want. Once a firm exists, the way it allocates its resources *within* the firm is not of a market form. When people arrive for work in the morning, there is not a labour market to find who will do a particular task for the least reward. Within the firm resources are not allocated on a market basis, but on the basis of management decision. Once a firm is established, markets are not operating within the firm. If we look outwards from the firm at the way in which that firm relates to other organisations, we find relationships usually on the basis of markets. If we look inwards, markets are not being used. We say that *hierarchies* are the basis of resource allocation, not markets. So when firms exist, within the firm, markets are not being used to allocate resources.

How do we explain the existence of firms such as travel agents? Is such an arrangement an optimal use of society's scarce resources? One of the first people to address this problem was an economist called Ronald Coase (1937), who introduced the idea of transactions costs. His work has subsequently been developed and enriched by others, notably Oliver Williamson (1975). Transactions costs are the costs associated with the organising and arranging of exchanges. Going back to the example of the travel agent, I could organise a flight and a hotel, but I now have to have an exchange with the hotel. I need another exchange with the airline and so on. If I go to the travel agent, she does it just once for me, and does it for thousands of other people too. So she makes one exchange with, say, the hotel operator, which will replace a whole series of individual exchanges. So the number of exchanges that take place are considerably reduced by having the travel agent. Each exchange involves transactions costs. The existence of the hierarchy minimises the transactions costs and therefore is in that sense efficient. It may be more efficient to have a firm, even though resources within the firm may not be allocated on a market basis. If an organisational arrangement is less costly than the use of a market, firms will come into existence. So the existence of transactions costs is a key explanation of why firms exist at all.

A further example of transactions costs is provided by search costs. If I want to get the best deal for a hotel in Vienna where I want to go for the weekend, I can ring around all the hotels in Vienna. It will take a considerable amount of my time and it will not be cheap because I have to make the phone calls. The travel agent has an awareness of all these prices available to her. By having all that information she can economise on the amount of resources needed to get me the holiday. Because she is reducing the transactions costs, the search costs, the travel agent does it more efficiently than I do as she has more information available than I can easily acquire.

There is also a view that firms may exist, at least in some markets, because firms will also be more likely to engage in research and development, so that in the future costs are lowered. As an individual I am not in a position to engage in research which might reduce the cost of transport and the cost of hotel accommodation in future years. But in selling the skills, a key part of what firms are doing is not simply meeting consumers' current needs – they will also work out how to meet consumers' needs more effectively in the coming periods of time, by engaging in research. So the very existence of firms themselves can be partly explained by thinking through the nature of efficiency and by thinking through the nature of costs.

Bounded rationality and asset specificity

There are many other examples of transactions costs. We shall not provide a complete list of all such possible costs here but suggest a few others. We will also return to this subject in later chapters.

One explanation for non-market transactions is bounded rationality. This refers to a situation in which economic agents wish to act rationally, but the complexity of a situation, or uncertainty about the future, limits the extent to which rational decisions can be made. Is it better for a firm to buy a specialist's labour, a market transaction, or to offer him a job and manage his labour inside the firm?

At first a market transaction might be thought better. One can simply buy the specialist's services when needed, having negotiated a suitable contract. However, it might be that the first contract gives the specialist such an insight into the firm that he is the best person to employ in subsequent periods. He knows this and can use his 'monopoly power' in negotiating future contracts. It may thus be better to appoint someone inside the firm and manage that worker, rather than using the market solution.

When resources can produce only one kind of output and have no alternative uses we have asset specificity. Suppose a firm is uncertain whether to make the investment itself or allow another company to make it and buy the goods from that firm as a market transaction. Under these circumstances, agreeing the price will be difficult. This is a bilateral monopoly. Negotiating a contract, and in subsequent periods renegotiating it, could prove expensive. There are high transactions costs which may encourage a firm to make its own investment rather than rely on a market exchange.

If resource owners are efficient, they will wish to minimise costs. Sometimes this is achieved by market exchanges. At other times it is worth establishing a hierarchy and incurring the costs of organising such an arrangement. Which is cheaper is a question that can be answered by considering transactions costs as well as costs of production.

Profits in action: the search for added value

We have seen the significance of profits as a means of allocating resources and achieving efficiency. In this last part of the chapter we illustrate this with reference to UK supermarkets.

From a firm's perspective the rationale for its existence is the search for what John Kay (1993) calls 'added value'. Firms have costs to meet. These include the purchase of inputs from other industries, whether domestic or foreign. On top of that they have the costs of buying resources such as capital and labour. These we refer to in Figure 1.7 as input costs. But firms try to organise production and distribution in such a way that the value of their output, their turnover, is greater than input costs, including purchased inputs. That difference is the value added to these inputs which enables them to make economic profit. But we need to think carefully about the nature of added value. Costs that firms incur are not simply accounting costs, purchased inputs plus labour costs, but also opportunity costs. The capital resources they use could have been put to use elsewhere.

So added value is the market value of a firm's output less all the costs of inputs. In other words, it represents the costs to the economy if the company

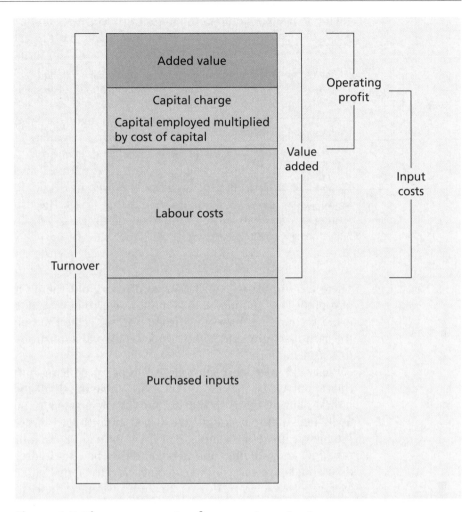

Figure 1.7 The components of corporate output
Source: Davis and Kay (1990), p. 11

were to disappear and its resources were used in the next most valuable area of productive activity. Added value is *not* the accounting concept of operating profit. Operating profit is the difference between the value of output and the value of labour and material inputs. It does not take account of capital costs.

We take one particular example of the search for added value by using a key article of Davis and Kay (1990) that comes from the supermarket industry at that time. We think through industry profitability at that time. Subsequently we consider what has been going on in that industry in the last 10 or 15 years which will shed further light upon the nature of the market system.

What we are looking for is the extent to which firms succeed in adding value. The first supermarket in Table 1.2 is Sainsbury's. At this particular time, Sainsbury's according to the accountants declared a profit of £369 million. This is operating profit. But now look at *all* the costs incurred to produce that.

Table 1.2 Assessing the performance of UK supermarkets

1988/89 results	Operating profit £m	Operating assets £m	Cost of operating (at 10.8%) £m	Added value (rents) £m	'Input' costs £m	Rents divided by inputs (%)
Sainsbury	369	2624	283	86	889	9.7
Tesco	274	1908	206	68	678	10.0
Gateway	205	1669	190	25	587	4.2
Asda	156	1508	163	−7	429	−1.6
Argyll	156	1081	117	39	487	8.1
Kwiksave	58	287	31	27	110	24.6

Source: Adapted from Davis and Kay (1990)

There were input costs of labour and so on, but there's an opportunity cost of capital. They required £2624 millions worth of capital assets. That is to say, if the accountants have got it right and we value the buildings, the trolleys, the cash machines and so on correctly, the value of those capital assets came to £2624 million.

We could say that if Sainsbury's stopped producing output and sold off all the capital assets, they would have been able to sell all those assets for £2624 million. But by tying up that amount of these assets, Sainsbury's were giving up income that they could have earned in putting those assets into some other productive use. For example, had they not had £2624 million tied up in cash machines and buildings and so on, and they had put it into government bonds, they would have earned some income. Now the long bond rate over that period averaged 10.8%. So in this next column we have the cost of operating, £283 million, 10.8% of £2624 million. This is what Sainsbury's had to give up as income they could have earned on this operating asset, in order to sell super-market food etc. That loss of income is a cost. So we can say that the amount of income that Sainsbury's earned in excess of all their input costs was not £369 million, but only £86 million. This is added value or what economists call rent, or profit above normal.

Look down the list of other supermarkets. One that is particularly interest-ing is Asda, who at that time declared an operating profit of £156 million. But if we take into account the opportunity cost of the assets, Asda's share-holders would have done much better if those assets had been sold off and put into government bonds. The profit was not enough to cover all oppor-tunity costs, and the rent, the profit above the normal, the added value, was actually negative.

This way of looking at profitability throws light on the extent to which firms make a contribution to the economy. It is the extent to which they add value. If we simply look at this column of rents, the greatest achiever would appear to be Sainsbury's, who made far more than anyone else. At the bottom we have Kwiksave, making a mere £27 million. On the other hand, the amount of inputs that Sainsbury's required to make this amount of rent was far greater than the input costs that Kwiksave used to make their added value. So in the last column of Table 1.2 we divide the rents by the inputs. This gives what Davis and Kay call the 'intensity' with which value added is created. How much does each firm add to each unit of output that it uses? By doing this we can see that Kwiksave was the most successful of all the six supermarkets in that year. £1 of inputs in Kwiksave was sold for £1.25, whereas for Asda it was £0.78.

Changes in markets over time

We have seen the structure of one industry at a particular time. There is within that industry a considerable variation in performance. In later chapters we think more about how companies organise themselves, in an attempt to try to explain why there is such a variation in performance between firms, even within the same industry. But for now we will consider how things can change over time. Market economists claim that where firms make profits in excess of normal, there will be new entries into the industry, increasing the quantity of goods and services, depressing prices and reducing profits to normal. Is there any evidence that that there have been new entrants into this industry over the last 10 or 15 years? There *is* some evidence to suggest that. For example, the rate of return made by supermarkets in the UK tends to be higher than the rate of return made by supermarkets in Continental Europe. Continental supermarkets have an interest in setting up in Britain, where the returns are higher than they are in their own market. This has happened. Aldi from Germany opened their first store in the UK in 1990. Lidl, also from Germany, started in the UK in 1994 and within five years had 170 sites. The Danish firm Netto also opened its first UK store in 1990 and had 120 by August 1998. They were looking for a share in the rents, the profit above the normal that established firms in the market had been making.

We also see changes with the firms within the UK. Some companies such as Argyll have disappeared and their assets have been taken over, because the market decided that these firms were not cost efficient. How has Asda survived, given that by our understanding of rents they were making a loss? The answer is that their share price fell very sharply in the early 1990s. Asda was under significant pressure. They responded by becoming more cost efficient. Their performance as a company improved considerably in the later 1990s. Recently there has been a major new entrant into the market from the USA. Wal-Mart has become a major presence, not by opening up new stores but by purchasing Asda. At the present it is not renaming stores under its own label but retaining the Asda name.

So a market is not static. It changes over time, and some economists wish to argue that wherever you have a market where profits above normal are being made, we might expect that in the absence of significant barriers to the entry of new firms, other firms will enter those markets and erode away the profit. As we will see in a subsequent chapter, not all economists are convinced that markets do operate in this way and we shall examine some evidence to see the extent to which this does happen.

For now, let us summarise. From society's point of view efficiency is important, both cost efficiency and allocative efficiency. We want resources to be used in a most efficient manner. Profit seeking by firms may well give us cost efficiency, although we might think that the structure of industry will determine the extent to which we get allocative efficiency. Profitability is properly measured by the extent to which firms add value. Profit is a key indicator of how resources are allocated, because it is the profits that firms generate that is the attraction for new firms to enter markets. So resources are allocated to markets where consumers value them most highly.

Economists, therefore, do not see the quest for efficiency and profitability as harmful to society's interests. On the contrary, they are legitimate aims for business. That quest plays a crucial part in meeting people's needs.

KEY RESULTS

1 Efficiency is crucial for maximising social welfare.

2 Cost efficiency means producing any given output at minimum cost.

3 Allocative efficiency requires that resources are allocated to maximise consumer satisfaction. In an individual market MC = D.

4 Where monopoly power is present there may be allocative inefficiency.

5 Resources respond to consumer preference through profits.

6 Properly measured, profits are the extent to which firms add value.

Questions

1* Why would a firm stay in an industry a) in the short run and b) in the long run if it could only just break even?

2* Refer back to the section in the chapter where we considered efficiency and the railways. How do you think *government policy* affected efficiency in the rail industry in Europe?

3* Some data from the Competition Commission Report on multiple stores is given in Table 1.3. The report also gives evidence about the number of stores that each supermarket has. There is also evidence about their market shares in each UK region. For example, Tesco has 46.5% of sales in Northern Ireland. Sainsbury's has 35.5% in London. Safeway is the largest in Scotland with 28.4%. Would their geographical distribution be important to their degree of monopoly power?

4 Consider Box 1.1. Is the argument correct? If it is, how do such inefficient businesses survive?

5 Refer to Box 1.2. What does the Internet do to entry barriers for industries that trade heavily there?

* *Help available at http://www.e-econ.co.uk*

Table 1.3 Shares of grocery sales from the
largest UK stores, 1998/9

Tesco	24.6
Sainsbury	20.7
Asda	13.4
Safeway	12.5
Morrison	4.3
	75.6
Somerfield	8.5
M&S	5.0
Waitrose	3.3
Aldi	1.3
Lidl	0.9
Netto	0.5
Budgens	0.4
Iceland	0.1
Booth	0.1
Co-operatives:	
CWS	1.5
CRS	1.3
Local co-ops	1.4
	100.0

Note: Numbers do not sum perfectly due to rounding errors

Source: Competition Commission (2000)

BOX 1.2 Profitability attracts a new entry into diamond jewellery

Profits attract new entrants into a market. Two large organisations are to operate a joint venture to enter the diamond jewellery sector. Who will be the winners and who the losers?

If the recent De Beers and LVMH statement about their new joint venture were anything to go by, then Tiffany, Cartier and Bulgari, its rivals in the diamond jewellery sector, should be jumping up and down with excitement.

The deal, which sees the world's largest luxury goods company joining forces with the world's most famous diamond brand to develop flagship stores is, according to the companies, 'expected to create long-term value for both groups and will become a catalyst for brand competition in the sale of diamond jewellery'.

The theory is that the arrival of a new and formidable entrant will shake up the sleepy sector and boost the market. In practice, it is unlikely that the champagne corks will be popping in Place Vendôme or Fifth Avenue over the prospect of a new competitor.

The announcement comes amid increasing consolidation in the luxury sector. Many smaller companies have been partly or wholly swallowed by conglomerates that are better placed, through their marketing and distribution might, to propel brands into the big league.

In couture, businesses such as Kenzo, the Japanese designer, and Italian design houses Emilio Pucci and Fendi have linked with LVMH. Gucci, the Italian house, has recently taken a 51% stake in the Alexander McQueen label and snapped up Yves Saint Laurent. And in the watch sector, Richemont, which owns Cartier, has bought up a host of smaller manufacturers and jewellers, including Van Cleef & Arpels as well as Les Manufactures Horlogères, which includes the Jaeger LeCoultre brand.

Bain & Company, the management consultants that engineered the tie-up between De Beers and

▶

BOX 1.2 continued

LVMH, has called this phenomenon 'the Starbucks effect'. When companies increase what Bain calls the perceived 'premiumness' of a product by means of product innovation, branding, marketing or delivery, the entire category can reap higher prices and profits.

'When a new entrant joins the market it can have a halo effect on the whole category,' says Cyrus Jilla, a partner with Bain & Company, who worked on the LVMH and De Beers joint venture. 'It . . . may encourage other players, such as [the US jeweller] Zales, to invest in their premium brands.'

Gucci, which considered a tie-up with De Beers but decided against it, believes there is little reason to think the new venture will provide a wake-up call for the jewellery business.

'We felt the best opportunity for us was to go after that business with our own brand names,' says Domenico De Sole, chief executive of Gucci. 'Three years ago, there was no jewellery business at Gucci; last year, we did close to $50m and now we view this business as expanding very rapidly.'

Compelling though this is, there are some who feel that such a move could be detrimental even for the best-known operators.

Carlo Pambianco, president of Pambianco Strategie Impresa in Milan, the luxury goods consultancy, says: 'I think they will see strong rates of growth in the market but this may be at the expense of the other players such as Cartier, Tiffany and Bulgari and some of the medium-sized companies, which are perhaps more vulnerable.'

Mr Pambianco does not think the top-end players are happy that there are now more competitors. 'I think they'd say that if the market were going to grow anyway, we'd rather have a bigger share of that market between three than share it out between four.'

Mr Jilla believes the deal between De Beers and LVMH may also affect independent retailers, which may be prompted to look at how they might modernise merchandising or step up expansion or marketing activities.

Mid-market companies such as Zales and Signet, formerly Ratners, could examine how to bring their brands and their retail offering more up to date.

Some observers are critical of diamond jewellery sellers who have let the changes in retailing – such as modern stores and funky presentation – pass them by. This, they think, may be the catalyst for change. But others, which are unable to compete, will either wither or be swallowed up.

Source: Financial Times, 31 January 2001   FT

The structure of industry and the performance of firms

When something works in practice an economist is one who asks 'but will it work in theory?'

The context in which firms operate is important for their ability to be successful. This chapter explores key ideas in the link between market structure and the performance of business.

OBJECTIVES

After reading this chapter you should be able to:

- Describe the structure–conduct–performance approach to the economics of industries and firms.
- Appreciate the major criticisms of SCP.
- Understand the contestable markets hypothesis.
- Know why the Chicago school believes that markets bring about an outcome close to perfectly competitive equilibrium.
- Appreciate the Austrian school approach to industrial economics.
- Understand Porter's five forces model and industry S-curves as tools for business decision making.

Introduction

We reviewed some basic concepts concerning the operations of markets and the role of profit in Chapter 1. Now we explore some relationships between the structure of industry, the behaviour of firms, and firms' performance in terms of, for example, efficiency and profitability.

A structure–conduct–performance approach

One common way of looking outward at these relationships is to use what is known as a *structure–conduct–performance approach* (SCP). In this approach we begin by looking at the structure of industry and how industry is organised into different kinds of markets. Then we argue that firms' conduct, or behaviour,

Table 2.1 Some illustrative relationships

Structure	Conduct	Performance
Perfect competition	Profit maximisation No advertising	Allocatively efficient
Monopolistic competition	Profit maximisation Advertising	Allocatively inefficient
Oligopoly	Possible profit maximisation Advertising and other non-price competition	Allocatively inefficient
Monopoly	Possible profit maximisation Some advertising	Allocatively inefficient

in terms of prices and so on, is determined by the nature of the industrial structure. Then, given the way in which firms behave, we can analyse their performance. Take an example from a typical first year introductory economics course. If we look at perfect competition, this is an example of a given industrial structure. It defines a certain number of firms, the nature of the product, the level of barriers to entry and so on. Flowing from the nature of that structure, we get a particular conduct in terms of the way in which firms behave. This includes the way in which these firms make pricing and advertising decisions and so on. Coming out of that conduct, that behaviour, there is a particular performance, in terms of the extent to which firms are able to make profits, how cost efficient they are, and how allocatively efficient they are.

Now look at monopoly. This is a different structure. Because there is a different structure, firms behave in a different way. There is different behaviour in terms of pricing. Unlike perfect competition they may well advertise. That different behaviour leads to a different performance in terms of profitability and how allocatively efficient that particular industry is. One might then conduct a similar analysis of monopolistic competition and oligopoly. Different structures give rise to different conduct, which gives rise to a different performance. The main relationships are described by Table 2.1. The number of variables that we are looking at there in terms of conduct and performance is somewhat limited. There are a wider number of these things that we might want to think about. So a typical SCP approach might look something like Figure 2.1.

The top box shows a wide variety of possible elements of market structure, many of which we consider in detail in later chapters.

- *Seller concentration.* How many or few firms are there in the market? (See Chapter 3.)
- *Buyer concentration.* How many firms or consumers are buying the product?

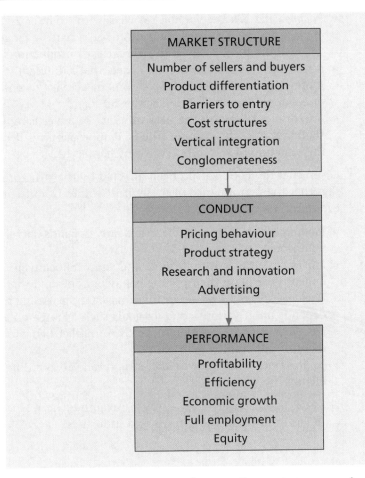

Figure 2.1 The structure–conduct–performance approach

- *Product differentiation.* Are firms producing an identical product, or are they differentiating their products from what other companies are producing? (See Chapters 9 and 12.)
- *Entry barriers.* How easy or hard is it for new firms to join the market? (See Chapters 9, 10 and 12.)
- *Cost structures.* What is the nature of the relationship between output and cost? Are there significant economies of scale? (See Chapters 4 and 5.)
- *Vertical integration.* Do firms in the industry control production from raw materials to final consumer? Or do they concentrate on one part of the production process, buying inputs from other firms and selling their output to other firms too? (See Chapter 7.)
- *Conglomerateness.* Do firms concentrate on just one product or a whole variety of products? (See Chapter 6.)

The SCP approach is to look at these elements of the structure of the industry. We can predict from this the conduct of firms in terms of the variables in the second box.

- *Pricing.* That is a key variable, as we saw in Chapter 1. (See Chapters 9–11.)
- *Product strategy.* Do firms concentrate on a narrow range of products or are they willing to diversify into new areas of production? (See Chapter 6.)
- *Research and innovation.* Can we expect that a different structure will produce more or less research and development activity to enhance the prospects of economic growth? (See Chapter 5.)
- *Advertising.* What are the determinants of advertising expenditure? As we shall see in a later chapter, the SCP approach says it can be explained by the structure of the industry. (See Chapter 12.)

Given that the conduct has been affected by the structure, the SCP approach says that the performance of these firms comes from their conduct. Consider the third box of Figure 2.1.

- *Profitability.* How profitable firms are depends largely on their pricing behaviour.
- *Efficiency.* How cost efficient and how allocatively efficient firms are depends partly on their pricing behaviour and on other aspects of conduct.
- *Economic growth.* How successful firms are in increasing real output over time depends upon various conduct goals such as research and innovation.
- *Full employment.* Do different kinds of market behaviour make the attainment of full employment easier?
- *Equity.* Does a different market structure lead to a different distribution of income?

The SCP approach gives us a way to examine the relationship between key variables in understanding firms and industries.

Criticisms of the SCP approach

This structure–conduct–performance approach has been criticised by many economists. We now consider the major criticisms that have been raised to see why, to some, it is not a particularly powerful way of analysing firm behaviour.

The direction of causality

To many, the direction of causality is much more complicated than implied so far. SCP implies that the direction of the causality is from structure – how many firms are there and so on, to conduct – how the firms behave, to performance – how efficient and so on is this outcome. So there is a clear direction of causality from structure to conduct to performance. But there is a strong case for saying that the links are not as simple as that. The causality is more complex and the links can actually go the other way. We give three examples. Look at Figure 2.2. This reproduces Figure 2.1 with these added possible causal links.

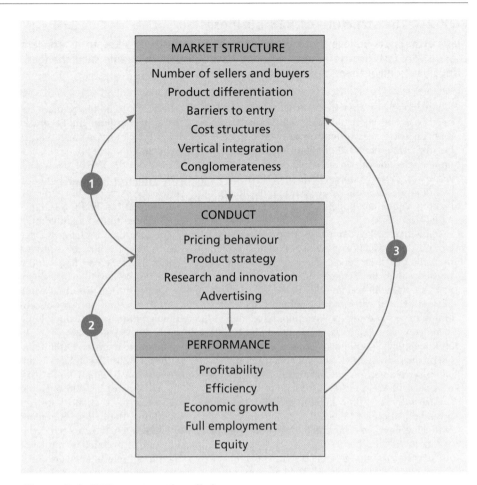

Figure 2.2 SCP: some other links

First, from the diagram, we have the possibility that the conduct can affect the structure. Second, we can consider the possibility that the performance of an industry can affect the conduct of the industry. Third, it is possible that the performance of an industry might have a direct effect on the structure of the industry. So the direction of the causality might well go the other way from what we have so far considered.

Let us look at each of these possibilities in turn. First we consider the link from conduct to structure. One of the features that we had in our list of conduct features was advertising behaviour.

Suppose a company decides to increase the volume of advertising. If it advertises successfully it attracts sales away from its competitors' products. But if it is successful in doing that it increases its share of the market. If it grows and becomes more dominant in the market, that advertising behaviour, the conduct, has changed the structure of the industry in terms of seller concentration. So the link is not from structure to conduct, but rather from conduct to structure. Similarly, if a firm engages in more research and development activity, it takes a decision to change its behaviour. If it is successful, and it

BOX 2.1 The structure of B2B business

Many economists believe that the structure of an industry is a key to its efficiency. Some industries change very fast. If governments will not leave markets to handle such changes, they find it difficult to control them.

B2B marketplaces are websites where buyers and sellers come together to buy or sell products and services. There are two main types, vertical and horizontal. Vertical B2B marketplaces are based on a single industry or industrial sector, such as aerospace, motor vehicles or chemicals. The most common are those set up so that manufacturers can buy all the components they need online at a one-stop shop.

Horizontal B2B marketplaces are organised around the products and services provided rather than the industries served. They are horizontal in the sense that they serve a wide range of industries. They specialise in products that are used in every business, things such as office supplies, spare parts, airline tickets and services (commonly referred to in procurement jargon as MRO – materials, repair and operations – goods).

The dividing line between collaboration and collusion is a narrow one. Companies which cross it because of B2B ventures face serious sanctions – the European and US competition authorities have the power to cancel proposed B2Bs and impose swingeing fines, opening the door to court action by aggrieved third parties seeking damages.

The competition regulators do not want to discourage B2B marketplaces. They recognise the potential of industry collaboration to improve trading efficiencies and hence cut costs.

However, the prospect of powerful erstwhile rivals sharing information and pooling market power inevitably raises regulatory eyebrows. Sheila Anthony of the Federal Trade Commission, the US antitrust regulator, has likened competition concerns about B2B marketplaces to a 'serpent in the garden of efficiencies'.

Rulings on B2B deals will be decided on a case-by-case basis by the regulators and the usual competition tests will be applied. But lawyers highlight two areas of potential concern to the regulators which anyone contemplating a B2B needs to consider.

The first is the risk that the sharing of information by competitors which is crucial to the operation of most exchanges could lead to price fixing or other anticompetitive behaviour.

'It seems to be the primary concern of antitrust authorities in both the EU and the United States,' says Alex Nourry, a partner at Clifford Chance, the law firm.

To avoid the risk of such collusion, B2Bs need a clear policy on information disclosure and internal security systems, such as firewalls, to prevent confidential information leaking back from the marketplace to its parent companies.

The organised exchange of data from named or identifiable firms, such as production and sales figures, prices, credit terms and discounts, will 'generally be illegal', Clifford Chance warns. Swapping information that would normally be classed as a trade secret is also likely to run into trouble with the regulators. But historical data is much less sensitive.

The other main potential regulatory sticking point for B2B marketplaces is any restrictions set on who can take part or on what other exchanges the participants are allowed to join.

So far as the regulators are concerned, the fewer such limits the better. As a general rule, according to Clifford Chance, 'to achieve their much touted pro-competitive effects, most B2Bs will need to be open to all relevant buyers and sellers (at the user, as opposed to ownership, level at least) on a fair and non-discriminatory basis'.

But there may be markets where such completely open access does not make any commercial sense. 'Initial success may require a more aggressive and exclusive approach on the part of the exchange owners, which will entail a certain regulatory risk,' says Mr Lewis.

'Because the balance of risk to reward will be different for each exchange depending upon the market structure, B2B marketplaces will find it necessary to court the ire of regulators to different degrees,' Mr Lewis adds.

Incurring the watchdog's ire may be a painful prospect. But the lure of B2B is such that few experts believe any regulatory threat will deter the big industry players. Mr Busby says he thinks the B2B model for the future 'will be owned by industry at large and run at arms' length'.

Source: Martin Brown and Jean Inglesham, *FTIT*, 18 October 2000

develops one or two new products that it can differentiate from its rivals, it can build up a degree of monopoly power in the production of that product, perhaps some new pharmaceutical drug. Again the result is that the structure of the industry is affected by the behaviour of the firm. The link again is from conduct back to structure.

But there is a second possible reverse link. Figure 2.2 shows not only a link from conduct to structure, but from performance to conduct.

Suppose that some firms in an industry look at their performance in terms of their profitability, and decide that it is inadequate. What might they do about it? One possibility is that they might seek to reduce the competition amongst themselves by forming a cartel. A cartel is an arrangement between firms to cooperate on some aspect of their behaviour, usually price. It is often illegal. Here their conduct, their behaviour in terms of the way in which they set prices, is affected by their performance. The performance in terms of profitability affects their conduct in agreeing as a group to raise prices. So again the link is different from the way in which we first suggested. It is from performance back to conduct.

Now we consider a third possible reverse link. There might be a feedback from performance directly to structure. Take one possible illustration. Again let us suppose that companies are doing poorly in terms of profitability. We have said that they might decide as a result to form a cartel. Alternatively they might decide to merge. If they merge their businesses they might be able to get economies of scale. But what they would also be able to do is to have a larger share of the market, which would enable them to control price and output decisions better. The link now is from performance, poor profitability, to structure, in terms of seller concentration. As a result of the poor profitability seller concentration rises.

So the link between structure, conduct and performance is, in the view of many economists, not a simple one. It is not simply from structure to conduct to performance, but the structure and the conduct and the performance are all seen as being determined simultaneously because of these complex links between one another.

Contestable markets

The next criticism of the structure–conduct–performance approach comes from the work of W.J. Baumol (1982), who introduced the concept of what he called a contestable market. Remember that a key link in the structure–conduct–performance view is the link from seller concentration to market pricing behaviour to performance in terms of whether firms make profits in excess of normal. However, Baumol wishes to argue that seller concentration is not significant in terms of the ability of a company to make profit above normal. Whether a firm can do that depends not on seller concentration, but on the degree of contestability of a market. Contestability means the ease with which new firms can enter the market, and the ease with which firms in the market can leave if they regard their performance as inadequate. To illustrate the significance of this we will assume that a market is perfectly contestable. There are no costs to firms joining a market if they see profits being made above normal. And there are no costs in leaving the industry if they feel that their performance isn't enough to cover their costs. Firms operating in the market at the present time cannot charge a price more than sufficient to cover opportunity costs. They know that if they do so, they will simply attract new firms into the market. There are potential rival firms who can operate a 'hit and run' policy. They can come into the market if prices appear above opportunity costs, and leave without cost should prices return to that level.

In practice, markets are unlikely to be perfectly contestable, but they could come close. Let us take two examples of markets to see how this might work. Take first the UK banking industry. There was a period of time when a relatively small number of banks dominated the UK market. During the 1980s legislation changed to enable building societies to enter that market and begin to offer chequeing accounts. The costs to these building societies of coming into the market to compete with the banks for chequeing accounts were relatively small. The huge costs of entry were the capital costs associated with setting up a branch network on the high streets. But building societies were already there, operating in a related market where they were serving customers by way of arranging mortgages. The additional costs of operating chequeing accounts were really quite small. It was a fairly contestable market. Given that they were already in the market of selling mortgages, if they entered the market of the banks and began to operate with chequeing accounts, and then subsequently found that it was not profitable, it was relatively costless to leave. It did not mean selling up all the branches. They were going to stay on the high street in order to be able to sell mortgages. So banking became to some extent a contestable market. The fact that the banks were fairly concentrated and a relatively small number of banks dominated the market would in Baumol's view be largely irrelevant. Banks would still have to behave as though there were many firms in the market. What counts is not seller concentration but how contestable the market is. In recent years the rise of Internet banking has allowed other entrants into the market without the cost of establishing a branch network. This can be argued to make banking still more contestable. That said, the rate of return on capital in the UK banking sector remains high.

An alternative example is the market for airline services. Suppose that there is a service operating between two airports, and then prices rise and the airlines begin to enjoy substantial profits. The cost of a new aircraft enabling another company to compete with the existing firm is immense, but the cost of transferring an aircraft from one route to another route is relatively small. The cost of producing the aircraft is a 'sunk cost'. Whatever happens, the cost is irretrievable. The marginal opportunity cost of switching from one market to another, however, is much less. So the airline market is a contestable market. When profits appear, another company diverts one of its airlines to that particular route. If prices then fall again, it simply removes the aircraft from that route and returns to the route that it was on before. Again, exit is relatively costless.

Much of the original research into the applicability of contestable markets was done with the airline industry. Subsequent research has found that the market is less contestable than might be supposed. The reasons for this include the following. First, to attract passengers to a new airline service requires substantial advertising. This is not a sunk cost. It is only incurred upon entry. Second, new entry is difficult. There are limits to the number of landing slots available. These tend to be in the control of the incumbent. Third, the existing firm can easily lower its prices. Knowledge that this is so is probably enough to deter most threats of new entry.

In principle, however, a market may be contestable. Its significance can now be seen. The structure–conduct–performance view has, as a key link, seller concentration determining behaviour which determines performance. That link is undermined if seller concentration is no longer significant, and that what is significant is the degree of contestability of a market.

So to some economists the contestability hypothesis does a great deal of damage to the structure–conduct–performance approach. To other economists it does much less damage. Others would say that there is indeed a link between structure and conduct, and one of the elements of structure that we are interested in, which affects conduct, is the question of entry barriers. It is a simple modification to add to that the idea that it is not only entry barriers, but exit barriers which are also important. So it has not destroyed the SCP view. We simply need to modify slightly our understanding of the structure box in Figure 2.1 as we seek to understand the link from structure to conduct to performance. Thus the seriousness of Baumol's criticism is still open to debate.

The Chicago school

The next criticism of the structure–conduct–performance view comes from the work of a group of economists known as the Chicago school. The term comes from an influential group of economists originally at the University of Chicago, although its followers are spread through universities worldwide. Perhaps its best known member is Milton Friedman.

Once more we are looking mainly at this key link from structure in terms of seller concentration, and its effect on firms' conduct and hence on performance. One central idea of the Chicago school is to say that, aside from government policy, there is no significant degree of monopoly power which will exist in a market. In the long term markets will bring competition in the absence of government intervention. There is nothing that ultimately stops other companies from replicating what a company with monopoly power might do. If a firm has substantial monopoly power, that is a short-term idea. If firms are using that power to make profits, other firms will see those profits and find ways of entering the market and compete that way. So monopoly power is not really significant. If you look at markets where there is monopoly power, it is always those markets to which power has been granted by the state. In the UK the Post Office has monopoly power in the delivery of letters costing less than £1. The reason is that by government edict, new firms cannot enter that market. There are many firms providing competition in the delivery of parcels. They are excluded from doing that with the delivery of letters. So a monopoly exists, not because it is the inevitable way in which markets operate, but because governments grant firms monopoly power. Another way in which governments do this is by patent rights. Why do some drugs companies have monopoly power in the production of certain pharmaceutical drugs? It is because of patent laws that are simply government-granted monopoly rights. Governments prevent new firms entering that market. The only other examples are government-owned industries. New firms are prevented from entering by law in order to retain the state's monopoly. So, according to the Chicago school, if we move out of the realm of markets where governments have decided to make monopoly power, monopoly is not of any great significance in the long run. Once more, if the Chicago school is correct, it undercuts an important element of the structure–conduct–performance approach. We no longer see seller concentration and the development of monopoly power as an important element in the process. Monopoly power is simply a short-run concept. Before long new firms will enter that market, so our best way of understanding how the economy operates is to see it as a long-run matter where it is competition in all markets that prevails, aside from government choice to create monopoly power. All this leads to an important conclusion for the Chicago school. In the absence of resource misallocation through government intervention we can use the perfectly competitive model as a close approximation of market price and output in the long run, even where the conditions for perfect competition do not exist. So, for example, the Chicago school accepts the reality of advertising even though advertising does not exist in perfect competition. However, firms will choose the ideal level of advertising. If they chose more, other firms would enter the market, advertise less, charge a lower price and capture market share.

The Austrian school

The last criticism of the structure–conduct–performance approach that we are going to look at comes from another group of economists called the Austrian school. The name comes from its beginnings in Vienna rather than the nationality of its current proponents. It has some views in common with the Chicago school. In particular, both utilise the marginalist approach in which consumers maximise welfare by allocating limited incomes so that marginal utility equals price for all goods. Firms are also presumed to maximise profits such that marginal cost is equal to marginal revenue. Both schools are critical of government intervention as a means of improving resource allocation.

However, the Austrian school of economists differs from the Chicago school in an important respect. To the Austrian school, monopoly power is a reality, and that monopoly power can exist for quite a long period of time. It is an important idea. But to the Austrian school the existence of monopoly power is a good thing. This is because it is the fact that firms are able to enjoy monopoly profits that gives them the incentive to produce in a cost-efficient way. It also provides the incentive to innovate in order to improve the way in which output is produced, and over time create a growing national product. If it were known, according to the Austrian school, that monopoly power could not exist for very long, there would be no incentive to innovate. Why does a pharmaceutical drugs company spend millions of pounds in research and development in order to try to produce some drug that may alleviate cancer or some other disease? Why would they do it? Not for the good and well-being of society, but because they see that if they can do it, they can make very considerable monopoly profit. So monopoly profit is important as an incentive for firms to produce and innovate. We can see that best by referring back to Figure 1.5.

In the last chapter we examined the concept of allocative efficiency and saw that anywhere around the opportunity cost curve is cost efficient. However, if society's preferences are given by a set of indifference curves, including IC_1, the allocatively efficient level of production is OH of X and OF of Y. How do we get this allocatively efficient level of output? We only get it if we assume perfect competition, where prices reflect opportunity costs. So a perfectly competitive structure gives us allocative efficiency. We have seen that where there is monopoly power present, price does not reflect opportunity costs at the margin, so we do not get an allocatively efficient level of output. To the Austrian school this is not really very important. To them, the key is how fast we can move the opportunity cost outwards over time so that society grows and gets better and better off. The means of moving the opportunity cost curve outwards is research and development, and research and development comes from firms being willing to do it, because they are seeking monopoly profit.

So the criticism of the Austrian school is that this structure–conduct–performance model is too static. It assumes that we have a given volume of resources, and the key question is how efficiently those resources are used. To the Austrian school there is a much more important question. The question is 'How fast can we grow the amount of resources that we have?' That requires the incentive to research and innovation. That incentive is the possibility of monopoly power profits. So once more the structure–conduct–performance model is weak. It is weak in the Austrian school's view because it is interested in the static concept of equilibrium, rather than in the more dynamic question of how fast we can shift outwards the opportunity cost curve. We shall develop these ideas more fully in a later chapter.

Studies on allocative efficiency

One key part of the Austrian school approach, then, is that allocative inefficiency is not very significant. There have been many studies to try to estimate the extent of this kind of inefficiency for a whole economy. We shall examine two such studies to see if they support the Austrian view. In Chapter 1 we thought about studies examining technical and cost efficiency. Remember that here we consider allocative efficiency. The first study conducted was that of Harberger (1954). He estimated for the US economy the deadweight loss of Figure 1.6 for each market. His estimate came to just 0.1% of gross corporate product. Clearly, this is a result which strongly supports the Austrian contention. Other studies have been conducted since then, for the US and for other economies, using his approach. All have produced similar low estimates of the deadweight loss of monopoly power.

However, the Harberger approach has been criticised for making assumptions that tend to underestimate significantly the size of the problem. We mention just a few. There may be other costs of monopoly power not picked up in the Harberger approach. For example, monopolists may well consume resources attempting to protect their monopolistic position. One might also argue that advertising expenditure is wasteful and should be part of the monopoly loss to society. Remember that in perfect competition there is no advertising since the firm cannot differentiate its product from other firms in the industry.

Harberger also had to estimate the elasticity of demand for each industry. He assumed that it was unitary. It has been pointed out that this is unrealistic. If there is monopoly power, demand tends to be inelastic. This means that Harberger has underestimated the deadweight loss.

Other studies have been conducted correcting for these and other assumptions. One such study was undertaken by Cowling and Mueller (1978). As one might expect, the estimate is substantially higher. The percentage of gross corporate product lost according to their method was between 4% and 13% for the USA. The comparable figure for the UK was in the range 3.3–7.2%. Generally other studies using their approach have found much higher estimates than found with the Harberger method.

The results of such studies, then, are not conclusive for the Austrian school view. One has to decide which are the more realistic assumptions when considering the evidence of these different studies.

Strategic decision making

Some economists would argue that not only are there reverse linkages in the SCP paradigm but that the *predominant* one is from conduct to structure. The starting point of an understanding of firms and industries is not focusing outwards on the industrial structure but inwards on the way in which firms organise themselves. To some this is a substantial criticism of the structure–conduct–performance model. In the view of many economists, the key link is not from structure to conduct to performance. The key link is from conduct to structure. If we want to understand the way in which firms and industries are organised the starting point is the strategic decisions that firms make. Those strategic decisions affect everything, including the structure of industry.

Strategic decisions include their external relationships – how they set prices for their customers and so on. This kind of approach is sometimes called the New Industrial Economics, which sees as the very starting point of our understanding, strategic decision making by firms. As we shall see in the chapters on pricing behaviour, the emphasis is on imperfect markets, especially oligo-poly. This view is quite inconsistent with the Chicago view with its emphasis on competitive equilibrium.

But in the view of many economists strategic behaviour is determined by more than the structure of an industry. It also includes internal relationships, the way in which they organise themselves. Let us focus now on some key ideas about the internal structuring of firms, what is sometimes called the archi-tecture of a firm.

Remember from Chapter 1 that firms aim to produce added value. We can begin to understand *how* firms add value when we see how they produce an internal architecture. That architecture will include a number of key things. It will include how the firm allocates authority within its structure, so that decisions get made in an appropriate way. It will include how the company evaluates performance, so that people can be rewarded appropriately for their contribution. It will include how the firm organises itself in terms of reward-ing people for their performance and this will include not only remuneration, but also promotions strategy and so on. So this architecture, this organisation within a firm, is as important as its external relationships to other firms and its customers. Now those that see the architecture of firms as an important element in the process of determining how markets operate see architecture as something that, if the firm is to be successful, must be something that can-not be simply repeated by other firms.

Suppose we have a company that organises itself in various ways and appoints good people to its organisation, so that these people contribute suc-cessfully to the firm and are an important part of what the firm does in order to add value. Is the presence of those people themselves the key to under-standing firm architecture? No. It is relatively easy for other firms to replicate that simply by offering sufficient to attract those key people out of the organ-isation where they are now. There is nothing in the nature of hiring excel-lent people that constitutes a specific architecture that cannot be reproduced by other firms. Furthermore, the presence of potential competition means that the existing firm has to pay outstanding people the full opportunity cost of their services in order to retain them. If there is to be a specific non-repeatable architecture, the whole has to be greater than the sum of the parts. Consider some football teams who do well because they are in a position to pay high salaries to attract the best footballers. Other clubs can compete by offering even higher salaries to those people and attracting them away from that club into a new club. But some clubs seem to be able to perform and achieve results that are better than would be suggested by the contribution of each indi-vidual player. It is not simply that they have bought good players, but the structure of the club enables it to get more out of those individuals such that the team performance is greater than the sum of the individual contributions. Similarly, if a firm can create an architecture which enables that company to achieve that, they have something which is non-repeatable. Then they can get added value, and that added value will not be eroded away because other firms cannot repeat the kind of architecture they have. What is true of a foot-ball team can be true of a firm seeking added value.

An example of a firm with such an architecture that is often quoted is Marks & Spencer. This firm has been thought to have the kind of structure within it, and the kind of structure of relationships with its suppliers, which has enabled it to earn good profits and be successful over a period of years. So to some people this is a very important part of our trying to understand the structure of industries and firms. We are no longer focusing on the structure of industry and asking how many firms there are in the market and so on. We are not looking outwards at the industrial structure. We are looking inwards at the nature of firms' organisational architecture, and seeing that the way in which they are organised will itself affect the structure.

If we simply look with some casual empiricism at what is going on, we can see companies who for a long period of time have indeed been successful in creating added value. Their competitive advantage has not been eroded away. The industrial structure is determined by the way in which such firms organise themselves. So there is a case for saying they have managed this because of the specific architecture they have created. However, we can quote counter-examples. In the last few years Marks & Spencer has had serious problems and seen its profit levels and its market share decline quite dramatically, first in its clothing sector and subsequently in its food sector, such that now the company is struggling in all areas. In 2001 it announced that it intended to cease trading outside the UK entirely. Some would say that their declining profit levels are unsurprising. It is not possible to create an architecture that other firms cannot replicate. One can do it in the short term, but whatever one does as a company, it is not impossible for someone else also, given time. So looking at the architecture of a firm is not some brilliant new insight in trying to understand the structure of industries and firms. It is simply a matter of minor interest, in that all we are looking at is the attempt by some firms to create barriers to the entry of new firms. These barriers to entry tend to be short-run things because in the end, new firms can enter the market and erode away the profits of existing companies, just as Marks & Spencer has found.

Empirical evidence for the SCP approach

Some attempts have been made to test whether changes in company profitability can be explained by the structure of the industry or whether these changes are firm specific. As so often, we find that different researchers apply different methodologies to different data sets and come to radically different conclusions. Schmalensee (1985) concluded that industry factors were the strongest explanation of variations in profit and that explanations based on firm-specific factors were very weak. Rumelt (1991), however, came to the opposite conclusion. Some of his important results are seen in Table 2.2. Not all the variations were explicable but of those that were, only a small part could be explained by 'industry effects'. However, it is reasonable to argue that cyclical factors are largely industry effects. When an economy enters a recession some industries are much more affected than others. In that sense these are

Table 2.2 Contributions to the explanation of profits variance in business

Corporate	0.80
Industry	8.28
Cyclical	7.84
Business unit	46.38

Adapted from Rumelt (1991), pp. 167–85

industry specific. Even so, according to Rumelt, easily the biggest amount of variation is attributable to company-specific behaviour. In the rest of the book we shall be open to the possibility that either of these views could be correct.

Porter's five forces and the decision-making process

One economist, Michael Porter (1980), has used the SCP approach to suggest how firms can analyse their markets. The basic idea is contained in Figure 2.3.

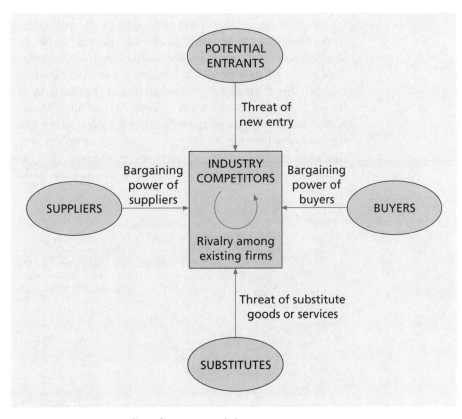

Figure 2.3 Porter's five forces model
Source: Porter (1980)

Porter argues that the business unit must find a position in its industry where it can best defend itself from competitive forces or seek to influence those forces to its own advantage. This structural analysis is the fundamental underpinning for formulating competitive strategy. The elements are:

- *Rivalry among existing firms.* How many competitors are there and how powerful?
- *Threat of new entrants.* How easy is it for new competition to spring up?
- *Bargaining power of buyers.* If, for example, the firm is relying on just one customer for its sales it is in a weak position compared with a firm with many customers.
- *Bargaining power of suppliers.* The firm can more easily secure added value if it is in a strong position to negotiate terms with the suppliers of its inputs.
- *Threat of substitute products or services.* Clearly the firm has more monopoly power if there is no threat of a close substitute for its product.

Just as some have criticised the SCP model, so others have criticised the Porter model. One criticism is that it is essentially static. It tells a firm how things are at a moment of time. It does not say much about how things may alter in future. As a result, some firms use such an approach in conjunction with an S-curve of the kind described by Figure 2.4. This purports to show how a typical industry evolves over time. When the product is new and relatively unknown, sales are growing slowly. The growth phase shows the period when industry sales grow rapidly. The market is still young. Maturity and the likely appearance of new products leads to a negative growth in sales. The S-curve enables the company to make planning decisions according to where it is on the curve. Even the S-curve approach is open to criticism. For example, McGahan (2000) has pointed out that life cycle phases are difficult to see, and that industry boundaries are not as precise as implied here. She has also argued that there are substantial differences in the way that industries evolve. Thus the S-curve has limited value as a tool for decision making.

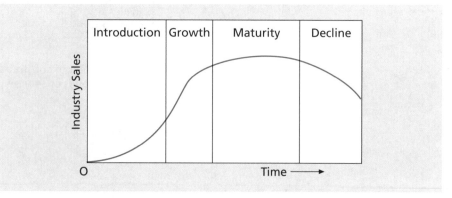

Figure 2.4 An industry S-curve

Conclusion

Some argue that an analysis of industry structure is the basis of understanding the economics of industries and firms. Others have questioned this and made alternative suggestions. In the rest of the book, we shall assume that the structure of industry *is* an important determinant of the way in which markets operate, and so we shall spend some time looking at aspects of the industrial structure. However, we shall also be open to the view that other schools of thought offer considerable insights. Hence we shall return to these concepts throughout the rest of the book. In particular, we do need to focus on the structural architecture of firms because there is a powerful link from the way in which firms organise themselves and take strategic decisions to the way in which the industrial structure is determined. So we shall not decide that one or other school of thought is correct, but we shall be open to the possibility that each school can contribute to our understanding of the way in which industry is organised.

KEY RESULTS

1 The structure–conduct–performance (SCP) approach argues that the behaviour and therefore the performance of firms is determined by the industrial structure in which firms operate.

2 Many economists have challenged the SCP approach since there may well be reverse causal links.

3 Major criticisms of SCP have also come from the theory of contestable markets, from the Chicago school and from the Austrian school.

4 Contestable markets theory says that firm behaviour is determined by the size of entry and exit barriers to and from an industry, *not* the number of firms that operate in it.

5 The Chicago school suggests that there are no long-term obstacles to competition in an industry unless they are raised by governments.

6 The Austrian school also believes that markets maximise welfare. They see monopoly profit as an important spur to innovation and hence economic growth.

7 Businesses sometimes use Porter's 'five forces model', a development of the SCP approach, and industry S-curves as tools for decision making.

Questions

1* In the chapter we gave examples of possible reverse links in the SCP approach. For each one, think of another example.

2* Use Porter's five forces model and the S-curve to consider the prospects of a major supermarket chain such as Tesco or Sainsbury. Remember that we considered this industry in Chapter 1.

3* Do you agree with the Cowling and Mueller view that advertising is an example of allocative inefficiency? Why might Harberger and others disagree?

4 Consider Box 2.1. Is the advent of B2B likely to improve or reduce allocative efficiency?

5 Consider Box 2.2. What are the costs and benefits to steel consumers and producers of following a protectionist policy?

* Help available at *http://www.e-econ.co.uk*

BOX 2.2 Competition in the steel sector

Some economists believe that monopoly power is temporary. Monopoly profit always causes other firms to climb barriers and enter the market, unless governments prevent it. In this case the competition is from abroad.

For more than a decade Nucor, the steel mini-mill, has been the most successful steel company in the US. It has also been a thorn in the side of the large integrated steel producers.

While Bethlehem Steel, LTV, US Steel and others regularly paraded to Washington seeking trade measures to block imports, Nucor stood aloof while its long-time president, Kenneth Iverson, lectured his US competitors on the evils of protectionism.

No more. Last month Nucor and several smaller US steel mini-mills took the lead in seeking to curb imports of hot-rolled steel from 11 countries, alleging that steel is being dumped in the US market below cost. Hot-rolled steel is the largest single class of steel product, used in carmaking, construction and pipe and tube manufacturing.

The action was a significant shift in Nucor's approach to trade issues and one that is likely to reverberate in Washington as the US steel industry faces yet another serious crisis.

The new activism adopted by Nucor could bolster the industry's case for some kind of comprehensive import protection at a time when US spot steel prices have hit their lowest level in 20 years. The outgoing Clinton administration has been meeting the steel companies and the steelworkers' union to consider broader measures. In the past, steel importers would single out Nucor to make the case that demands for import relief by the large, integrated steel producers were little more than old-fashioned protectionism by companies that had lost their competitive edge.

But Dan DiMicco, Nucor's chief executive, says the company's growing vulnerability to import competition and continued trade barriers in steel markets abroad forced 'a change of paradigm'.

Nucor, which pioneered the mini-mill technology of fashioning steel from industrial scrap rather than

melting ore in blast furnaces, has gone in a decade from being a small player in specialised markets such as structural steel to becoming the second largest US steel-maker.

Nucor's growth has pushed it into segments such as beam, flat-rolled steel and hot and cold-rolled products that are highly import sensitive. But Mr DiMicco says that Nucor's new aggressiveness is mostly the result of a steel market in which even the lowest-cost US producers are having a hard time making money. Share prices of many of the large integrated producers have fallen almost into the penny stock range over the last year.

Nucor has fared considerably better, but even so its shares have slid to less than $40 from more than $60 (£41) in early 1998, before the onset of the Asia financial crisis diverted huge volumes of steel into the US market.

'For Nucor to get involved, things must have really gotten out of whack,' says Mr DiMicco. He took over as chief executive earlier this year and was the architect of the shift in Nucor's attitude towards trade protection. Previously he was chief executive of Nucor-Yamato, a joint venture mill in Arkansas with Yamato Kogyo Steel of Japan. Last year Nucor-Yamato, with the blessing of the Nucor board of directors, won an anti-dumping case on steel beam imports, which rose from about 300,000 tons in 1997 to 1.6m tons in 1998 as a result of the Asia crisis.

'Our Japanese partners helped us to understand that no matter what we did there was no way we were ever going to sell steel into Japan,' says Mr DiMicco.

'They control the distribution channels, they can let your steel sit on the docks for ever [and] they can change specifications to keep product from coming in.'

Nucor's foreign competitors are less charitable about the company's change of heart. 'Nucor has been the most profitable steel company in the world and they're pretending they're Geneva Steel,' says David Phelps, executive director of the American Institute of International Steel, which represents US steel importers. Geneva Steel, a US producer, declared bankruptcy last year, one of several smaller US steel producers to do so.

Indeed there is little in Nucor's bottom line to indicate that the company is suffering the same financial disaster afflicting many of the older US steel companies. It had record earnings per share in the first two quarters of 2000 and even its third-quarter earnings were only slightly below the record high of 1997.

Mr Phelps charges that Nucor is engaging in little more than 'the use of trade laws to manipulate the US market'. By spending a few hundred thousand dollars on lawyers, he says, a company 'that has never lost a nickel' may win import duties that earn it millions of dollars by forcing up domestic prices.

But Mr DiMicco says that in the current steel market the company has little choice but to use every weapon at its disposal, including the full arsenal of US trade laws: 'It's not in the best interests of our employees or shareholders to sit on the sidelines any more.'

Source: Financial Times, 19 December 2000

3 Concentration and profitability

Mathematics has given economics rigour, but alas, also mortis.
ROBERT HEILBRONER

The ability of a firm to make profits over a sustained period could be the outcome of the industrial structure in which it operates. Alternatively, it could be a function of the unique nature of the firm itself and the way it is organised. In this chapter we consider both possibilities.

OBJECTIVES

After reading this chapter you should be able to:

- Understand what is meant by market concentration and how it can be measured.
- See the problems associated with any measure of concentration.
- Appreciate the possible links between market concentration and firm profitability.
- Use Peteraf's model of competitive advantage to analyse firms' ability to make profits.

Introduction

In the first two chapters we looked at the possibility that there was a link between the structure of industry and the behaviour of firms and hence its performance. We also saw that not all economists are convinced that this is a crucial link. In this chapter we assume that industrial structure *is* important. We focus on one aspect of industrial structure, namely seller concentration. What, exactly, does it mean? How concentrated is market power? How is it linked to profitability?

The meaning of concentration

There are two different ideas associated with concentration; one is called overall concentration, and the other is called market concentration. Overall concentration is concerned with the output produced by the top, say, 50 or 100 firms in an economy. What proportion of the economy's output is concentrated in the hands of those particular firms? It does not matter in what particular industry these firms are operating. Our interest is simply seeing how few firms there are, controlling a given proportion of society's output. But we are concerned with the behaviour of individual firms and industries, so we focus on the other aspect of concentration, *market* concentration. We look at any particular market and see how much power resides in the hands of firms there. We do this because market concentration, at least in the view of many economists, will help to determine how prices are set in that industry, how much profit is made, how advertising behaviour is determined, possibly how much research and development activity takes place, and how efficient is that industry.

Measuring market concentration: the concentration ratio

There are various ways of measuring market concentration and the first and the simplest way is based on what is called the concentration curve. At any one moment in time, any individual market or industry will have such a curve. Table 3.1 shows the distribution of output between the largest firms in a number of hypothetical industries. Figure 3.1 shows how a concentration curve is constructed for each industry from such information.

Along the horizontal axis we measure the number of firms in the industry, *cumulated from the largest*. The vertical axis measures the proportion of the industry's output. For industry A, the largest firm has 60% of the market. Since the second firm has 20% of the market, the total amount of output in the hands of the top two is 80%, and so on. In this case we have information about all the firms in industry A. We can see that the top five firms have 100% of the market between them.

Table 3.1 Concentration ratios for five hypothetical industries

Percentage share of	Firm 1	Firm 2	Firm 3	Firm 4	Firm 5	CR3
Industry A	60	20	10	5	5	90
Industry B	30	30	25	15	–	85
Industry C	80	5	5	5	5	90
Industry D	30	30	30	10	–	90
Industry E	30	30	15	15	10	75
Industry F	25	25	25	25	–	75
Industry G	70	10	10	10	–	90
Industry H	50	20	10	5	5	80

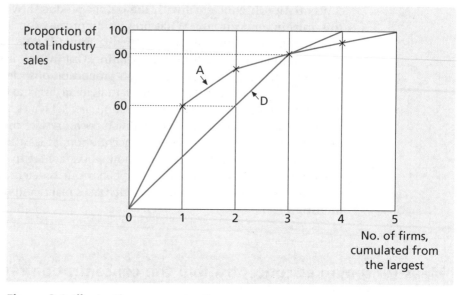

Figure 3.1 Illustrative concentration curves

Industry D's concentration curve is also plotted on Figure 3.1. The top three firms each have 30% of the market, so that the top one has 30%, the concentration curve shows the top two having 60%, and so on. Because there are only four firms in this industry, the curve reaches 100% before that of industry A. If an industry had more than five firms, the concentration curve would not reach to the top right-hand corner of the diagram in Figure 3.1, since only the largest five firms are considered in this example.

We can draw a concentration curve for any particular industry at any moment in time if we have the information. From that concentration curve, we can develop the concentration ratio. The ratio is a very simple measure. We pick an arbitrary spot on the concentration curve and ask: 'What is the proportion of industry output in the hands of the largest n firms?' For the UK the usual number for n to take is either three or five. For the American market it is nearly always four that is chosen. By picking an arbitrary spot on the curve we can see how relatively concentrated industries are.

Table 3.1 shows eight different industries, two of which, industries A and D, we plotted on the concentration curve. The last column of the table shows the concentration ratio for the three largest firms, the CR3. For industry A the top three firms have got 90% of the market, for industry B the top firms have got 85% of the market, and so on. So the CR3 is useful in giving us a simple idea of how concentrated an industry is. By using proportions of output rather than values, we can also make comparisons with other industries. Unfortunately, its simplicity is also what makes it difficult to use. By simplifying in this way we are looking at only one spot on the curve, so the summary measure may miss some important information.

We can see that if we come back to the concentration curves in Figure 3.1. It is perfectly possible for two concentration curves to cross. If they cross, we can see how arbitrary the concentration ratio is. Industries A and D could be regarded as equally concentrated, since both industries have a CR3 of 90%. But if we look at the four-firm concentration ratio, we can see that industry D appears to be more concentrated than industry A, having a CR4 of 100%.

This problem does not arise if the concentration curves do not cross. Consider, for example, industries A and H. We could say that industry A has a higher absolute degree of concentration than industry H, since A's curve lies entirely above that of H. But if the curves cross, which industry is more concentrated is somewhat arbitrary. So if we are interested in looking at, say, the relationship between the degree of concentration and industry profitability, the point on the concentration curve that we select will be crucial in determining the relative concentrations of the industries that we are trying to consider. Nevertheless, for all the problems associated with it, it is a measure which is widely used, because it is simple, easy to understand, and contains information which is relatively easy to obtain. Thus in many studies that look at the relationship between concentration and other variables, the concentration curve and its associated concentration ratio is used to measure market concentration.

One other problem about the concentration curve and the concentration ratio we can see with reference to Figure 3.1. Both markets A and D are equally concentrated in the sense that both of them have 90% of the market in the hands of the top three firms. But this tells us nothing about the distribution of power *between* those three firms. For industry D the distribution of power between the three firms is even, each with 30% of the market, but the distribution of power within industry A is rather different with the largest firm having 60% of the market. The pricing or advertising behaviour in industry A might be rather different when one firm dominates the market, compared with industry D where those three firms are all of equal size.

Measuring market concentration: the Gini coefficient

A second way to measure concentration is to use to what is called the Lorenz curve, and from the Lorenz curve to develop what we refer to as the Gini coefficient. Unlike the concentration curve, in order to be able to construct a Lorenz curve, we need information about *all* firms in the industry. Consider Figure 3.2.

Along the horizontal axis is plotted the percentage of firms cumulated from the largest. Up the vertical axis we plot the percentage of total industry sales/output. Clearly the curve is going to start from the bottom left corner, since 0% of the firms have 0% of the output, and it always finishes in the top right corner, since 100% of the firms will have 100% of the output. If we have an

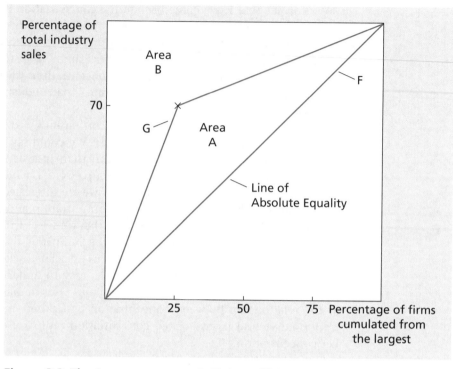

Figure 3.2 The Lorenz curve and Gini coefficient

industry where all firms are of the same size, then we have the line of absolute equality: 20% of the firms will have 20% of the output, 50% of the firms will have 50% of the output and so on. This, for example, is true of industry F from Table 3.1. Suppose now we have an industry where all firms are not of the same size, then we have a Lorenz curve which bends away from the line of absolute equality. For example, Figure 3.2 shows industry G from Table 3.1. The more uneven the size distribution of firms, the further from the line of absolute equality the Lorenz curve for a given industry will be drawn. At the extreme, we will have a very small percentage of the firms in the industry producing all of industry output.

   This idea of focusing on the extent of inequality of firm size is in essence what the Lorenz curve is all about. But we can take the idea further and develop a summary measure of an industry's market power. This is the Gini coefficient.

   As we have seen, the further away from the line of absolute equality the Lorenz curve goes, the more uneven is the distribution of firm size. So if we take the Lorenz curve for industry G, then the shaded area A represents the extent to which the Lorenz curve has departed from the line of absolute equality. So if we take area A as a proportion of the whole triangle, A plus B, then we have a measure of how uneven is firm size. That we refer to as the Gini coefficient. If we have a monopoly industry, so that one firm has all the industry's output, then that area, A, would be the same as area B. So A as a proportion of B gives us 1.

If all firms are of the same size, then area A is 0. So the Gini coefficient is always between 0 and 1. The more uneven is the distribution of power in the industry, the closer the Gini coefficient is to 1.

There are various formulae for calculating the Gini coefficient. One is given by:

$$G = \frac{1}{N} \sum_{i=1}^{N} (N - 2i + 1)\, Si$$

where N is the number of firms and Si is the share of the ith firm in terms of sales of the industry.

We work the formula through in terms of industry F where we assume that all four firms have 25% of the total market each. So given what we have been saying, we should find that the Gini coefficient is 0. Assume in this case that market output is £4m so that each firm's output is £1m.

We take the first firm, the ith firm, and set i equal to 1. We have four firms in the industry. So:

$$(4 - 2 + 1) \times 25 = 75$$

Now take i and set it equal to 2. That is, i is now the second firm in the industry. So now for this firm we have

$$(4 - 4 + 1) \times 25 = 25.$$

We then set i equal to 3. Thus

$$(4 - 6 + 1) \times 25 = -25$$

Then, finally set i = 4. So

$$(4 - 8 + 1) \times 25 = -75$$

So we have taken each of the firms in turn and now we sum them. This comes to 0. Finally we multiply that by 1/N, which here is $^1/_4$. This gives us 0. In this case the Gini coefficient is zero since all firms are the same size. Note also that the result is independent of industry size.

So the Gini coefficient comes from the idea of a Lorenz curve. But remember that in order to be able to use a Lorenz curve and thus develop a Gini coefficient, we will need information about *all* the firms in the industry, not just the larger ones.

Measuring concentration: the Herfindahl-Hirschmann index

The next measure we consider is known as the Herfindahl-Hirschmann index (HHI). In the view of some, one of the problems about concentration ratios is that it does not give enough emphasis to the larger firms. A large firm might

Table 3.2 The Herfindahl-Hirschmann Index for some hypothetical industries

Percentage share of	Firm 1	Firm 2	Firm 3	Firm 4	HHI
Industry A	50	50	–	–	$50^2 + 50^2 = 5{,}000$
Industry B	80	10	10	–	$80^2 + 10^2 + 10^2 = 6{,}600$
Industry C	25	25	25	25	$25^2 + 25^2 + 25^2 + 25^2 = 2{,}500$
Industry D	40	20	20	20	$40^2 + 20^2 + 20^2 + 20^2 = 2{,}800$

dominate a market, and have the power to set whatever price it chooses, constrained only by the demand curve. Other firms will then follow. The amount of power in the hands of the large firm is out of all proportion to that which is implied by the concentration ratio. So, in the view of the proponents of the HHI, what we should be doing is finding some way of emphasising the importance of the large firms. This index does that by squaring the market shares of each firm in the industry. By squaring the market shares of all firms, the larger firm is given a much greater prominence in the data.

The formula H for the HHI is given as:

$$H = \Sigma(^{S_i}/_s)^2$$

where S is the sales of the industry, and Si is the sales of the ith firm. Consider Table 3.2. In industry A we have two firms, each with 50% of the market. Remember that what we are doing is to square the market shares of each firm and then sum them. So $50^2 + 50^2$ gives us 5000.

Now we look at industry B, where we are assuming that one firm dominates the market. If we square the market shares of each of these three firms and add them up, we get 6600.

So the HHI is saying that industry B is much more concentrated than industry A, even though on a three-firm concentration ratio basis we would say that these two industries are the same. How do we get this larger number for industry B? It comes because by squaring the market shares, it is emphasising the importance of the largest firm in the industry. What is the index for monopoly, and what is the index for perfect competition? For monopoly, if there is one firm with 100% of the market, 100 squared gives us 10,000. For perfect competition, where each firm is infinitely small, then squaring an infinitely small amount and adding them will give 0. So the HHI lies somewhere between 0 and 10,000. The key to understanding the number's significance is that the formula is emphasising the significance of the larger firms.

One of the reasons why this particular index is of interest is that it is the basis for US antitrust policy. Although it does not meet with the approval of the Chicago school, the American authorities look at large mergers to decide

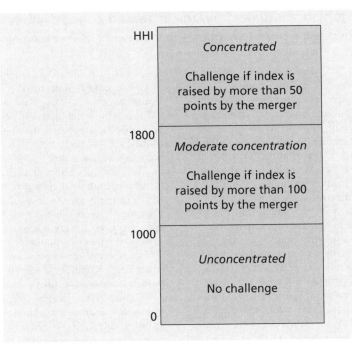

Figure 3.3 The HHI and US antitrust policy

whether they think they are in the public interest. The most important thing that they consider is whether a merger will increase market power. Will it give a more concentrated industry, and would the increase in concentration be significant enough to have a detrimental effect on consumers? The basis for that decision is what would be happening to the HHI.

If the number is between 0 and 1000, this is regarded as an industry that is unconcentrated, and so a merger between two firms is going to be left unchallenged. If the index lies between 1000 and 1800, this is regarded as a moderately concentrated industry. So the authorities then look to see, as a result of the merger, whether the HHI is raised by more than 100 points. If it is, then the merger will be challenged. If the index in an industry is already above 1800, then a merger will be challenged, even if it raises the index by no more than 50 points. This is summarised in Figure 3.3.

We have considered just a few measures of market concentration. It is not the case that there is a measure of concentration that is right, and that other measures are wrong. It is a question of thinking through what some particular measure is showing us, and then deciding whether that is appropriate or not in any individual instance. In the case of the US authorities, their decision is that they want to emphasise the significance of the large firms. Hence the HHI is the basis for anti-monopoly legislation.

We have considered only a few of the many possible measures of concentration. For other possibilities, consult the further reading.

BOX 3.1 Government attitudes towards increased concentration

The Economist considers the current US attitude to increases in market concentration and offers some criticisms.

America's antitrust enforcers are working weekends in the pursuit of what they believe are substantial economic benefits for consumers. Are they right? Adam Smith famously noted the tendency of businessmen to take any opportunity to conspire against their customers, but felt that there was little the state could do to stop them. Most other economists were dubious about the effectiveness of antitrust policy until the early 20th century. More recently, the profession has been split over its merits. There is general agreement that competitive markets benefit consumers. The debate concerns whether or not the government is able to keep markets appropriately competitive, and what the costs might be if it intervenes inappropriately. Milton Friedman, for example, started as a supporter of antitrust; but he turned against it in part because he thought that the possibility of being the victim of a mistaken antitrust action might deter good businessmen from attempting worthwhile new things.

The trust-busters' biggest difficulty is deciding whether or not a market is (sufficiently) competitive. Traditional legal definitions of market power, which look at the number of significant firms in a market, are viewed with increasing scepticism by economists, who prefer to look at how easy it is for more efficient new firms to enter a market. The Herfindahl-Hirschmann Index, which measures the degree of concentration in an industry by squaring the market shares of firms in the industry and adding up the total, is nowadays dismissed as irrelevant, except as a preliminary screening device. Yet antitrust lawyers still give much weight to it.

Judging the ease and likelihood of new entry inevitably involves speculation, especially about how market structures change over time. For instance, new entry tends to occur because incumbents are earning bigger profits than they need in order to stay in business. It is the sight of excess profit that eventually attracts new competitors.

Those who worry that America's trust-busters are going too far argue that they have used definitions of markets that are far too narrow and static. Many markets under scrutiny are small enough for it to be likely that, if serious monopoly profits were being made, another company would enter. In one recent case, a merger of two of the three biggest baby-food makers was blocked. But Wal-Mart, among others, already makes soft drinks. Can apple sauce be much harder?

Nor are there any obvious large barriers to entrepreneurs opening a supermarket or to banks putting an ATM in a store, for example. Local radio stations face intense competition, not least from rivals delivering via the Internet. The airline industry, subject to numerous antitrust actions, is notable for its meagre profitability, hardly a characteristic typical of the abuse of market power. The case against MasterCard and Visa, which operate in the apparently highly competitive credit-card industry, may repeat a common 1960s error of protecting not competition but a particular competitor, in this case American Express.

Two big oil mergers, Exxon/Mobil and BP/Amoco, have been challenged over the past two years, and allowed to go forward only after numerous concessions were made, including massive divestitures of service stations. Years ago, this may have been important to maintaining competition. More recently, however, petrol pumps have appeared in front of numerous stores that use the stuff as a draw to sell expensive crisps and sweets to jaded motorists. Another merger, BP Amoco's with Arco, was challenged because both firms had large reserves in Alaska, and BP had used its market power 'to maintain higher prices on the west coast by exporting crude oil to the Far East.' This conclusion seems to reveal an anti-trade bias and, odder still, to assume that oil prices are not set on a global basis.

Source: 'Antitrust, the new enforcers', *The Economist*, 7 October 2000

Problems with concentration measures

We now consider some of the main problems implicit in using concentration data.

Concentration or dispersal of power?

Imagine that you have five firms in a particular industry. The largest three have 25% of the market each, the fourth largest firm has 15% of the market and the smallest firm in the market has 10%. Now let us imagine that the two smallest firms merge. How much of an increase in market power has taken place? If we look at, say, the CR4, we can see that before the merger took place the top four firms had 90% of the market between them. Now the CR4, as a result of the merger, has increased to 100%. At first we might say this is clearly an increase in concentration which has come out of the merger. But now let us remember what we said about the Gini coefficient.

When we looked at the Gini coefficient we saw that it was giving an indication of how evenly sized firms were. By this measure, as a result of the merger of the two small firms, all firms in the industry are the same size. The Gini coefficient has actually been reduced to zero. According to this measure we have a *decrease* because the merger evened up the size of the firms in the market.

With the first measure, it is the concentration of power in which we are interested. In the second case it is the dispersal of power. Let us take an example to see how a competition authority might be in a dilemma when it comes to a merger between two smaller firms in a market. In 1987 two large ferry companies, P&O and Sealink, dominated the cross-Channel market from Dover to Calais. During 1993 the Channel Tunnel opened, operated by Eurotunnel. In terms of the capacity to carry cars and passengers across the Channel, Eurotunnel became the hugely dominant firm in the market. As a result of this new entrant, P&O and Sealink asked the competition authorities in Britain if they could merge their interests in order to be in effective competition against Eurotunnel. A merger could be seen as an increase in concentration, thus reducing competition. It could also be seen as reducing the Gini coefficient, thus making competition more effective. At first the authorities refused the request but later acceded to it. This kind of scenario always exists when two smaller firms in a market consider a merger.

Defining an industry

A second problem is defining what is meant by an industry. If a firm makes biscuits and another crisps, are they producing different products or are they competitors in the snack-foods industry? The wider our definition of industry, the greater the number of firms and the less the apparent concentration.

Economists normally say that two products should be regarded as being in the same industry if they are close substitutes. Formally, the cross-price elasticity of demand should be high. This does not really solve the problem in that there is no cut-off point that determines how high is 'high'. What *does* help is that the European Union has a set of definitions of what constitutes industries and product groups. Although the boundaries are somewhat arbitrarily drawn, this at least means that it is possible for researchers to make consistent comparisons of market concentration levels across EU countries.

The problem is further compounded by the fact that most companies are multi-product organisations. As a result, the output of most firms does not fall neatly into one particular product group or industry.

The presence of imports

A further problem occurs where data fails to pick up the importance of imports as a source of competition. Often a CR3 of 80%, for example, will mean that the three largest firms in the industry produce 80% of UK production. But the total market may be much larger if there is a significant volume of imports. The industry may be very competitive even if concentration levels appear high. If one is aware of the problem and the data is available, the problem is readily solved. Instead of calculating concentration as CR3/Q, where Q is domestic production, we can calculate CR3/Q+M, where M is imports. Readjusting concentration data for imports will be very important for some industries and for some countries like the UK, where trade is very open.

The choice of variable

One minor problem is worth a mention. We have spoken of concentration as being measured by industry sales. One could do the same calculations by employment. What proportion of total industry employment is in the hands of, say, the three largest employers? One might also use value added, the difference between industry output and the total of inputs from other industries, whether domestic or foreign. It is also possible to use capital assets. Of these, the most common variables are industry sales and employment. Employment data tends to produce slightly lower levels of concentration. This is because large firms tend to be more capital intensive. However, the difference in the data obtained from using different variables is not large.

Potential or actual power?

There is one more problem about the use of concentration data to consider. Are we interested in the actual power of firms or their potential power? Are we looking at what it is possible for firms to do by raising prices above costs or are we more interested in what they actually do? When we look at concentration data we are considering potential power that firms have.

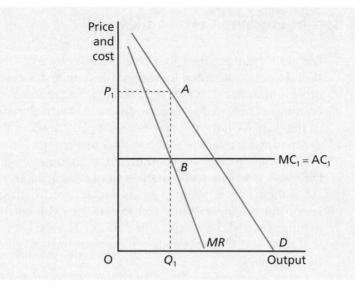

Figure 3.4 The Lerner Index

An alternative way of looking at market power is not to look at concentration data but to look at the actual market power that firms use. How might we do that? One measure is the Lerner Index. Think about a perfectly competitive industry. Here price does not exceed marginal cost at all. Rather, price reflects marginal cost of production. But now if we look at a monopolistic firm we can see that what a firm does is to charge a price in excess of marginal cost. Consider Figure 3.4. Here is a firm with some monopoly power. It is faced with a downward-sloping demand curve. Thus marginal revenue is less than average revenue. For simplicity, assume that the marginal cost and the average cost curve are constant so that MC = AC. If we further assume that this is a profit-maximising firm it produces where MC = MR at output OQ_1 and charges price P_1. Because it has some market power the price that the firm charges is in excess of marginal cost. The Lerner Index attempts to measure that excess in order to give us an idea of how much power the firm is actually using.

We take the price, in this case P_1, minus the marginal cost and that difference is the extent to which the firm raises price above marginal cost (AB). Then we express that as a proportion of the price, p1. So the Lerner Index is

$$P - MC/P$$

What the Lerner Index is measuring, then, is the extent to which firms actually use their power to raise prices. This is different from measures such as the concentration ratio, which measure the extent to which firms have the power to raise price above marginal cost. So we have to recognise that the concentration curve and the concentration measures represent an attempt to say what is the *potential* for raising price rather than the extent to which they actually do it.

Concentration in European economies

For most countries there is a considerable range in the degree of concentration that exists between industries. Some industries are highly concentrated, other industries much less so. We can take an example of this from the British economy. The CR5 for tobacco products is virtually 100%. At the other end of the scale we have the processing of plastic, where the largest five firms in the market have only 8% of the total market.

Over time, market concentration has changed significantly. In the UK in the 1960s it was increasing fast in most industries, levelling off in the 1970s. Since then it has fallen in many sectors whilst increasing in others. One reason for the fall in some sectors has been the much higher level of competition from abroad, especially Europe. However, there is some indication that since the 1990s there may have been further increases in concentration in many markets.

Why are some industries so much more concentrated than others? One common explanation given is economies of scale. If in the long run firms find that by increasing their output average costs of production fall, there is a tendency for those firms to engage in merger activity. Alternatively, they may simply increase the size of output that they produce in order to take advantage of those economies of scale. So we expect a relationship between the degree of concentration in an industry and economies of scale. (We shall have much more to say on economies of scale in the next two chapters.)

The link between concentration and profitability: two views

As we have seen, many economists would take the view that we should be concerned about the build-up of monopoly power, even though it has its advantages in creating economies of scale. This is because it has the potential to exploit consumers. We saw that this is the view that is taken by the US authorities. If the index rises beyond a certain level they are inclined to say they won't allow the merger to take place even though it may be the case that the merger would result in economies of scale. In Europe a more *ad hoc* view prevails. Each merger proposal is treated on its merits, with the authorities trying to decide the net advantages to society. But where this view is held, the concern is that increases in concentration allow prices to rise above costs, increasing profits to firms. If these profits are greater than opportunity costs, there is no gain to society. The link is from concentration to profit.

So far we have suggested that as firms get greater concentration (although they may gain economies of scale) it will enable them to raise prices above marginal cost and exploit consumers. There is an alternative view that says this is not the case. The causal link is not from concentration to profitability. The link is from efficiency to concentration and from efficiency to profit. This view is associated with an American economist by the name of Demsetz (1973).

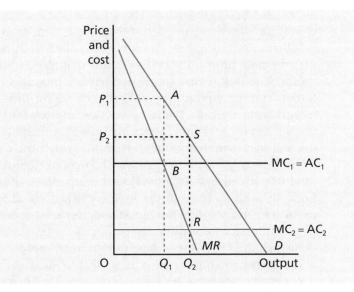

Figure 3.5 The Demsetz view of monopoly power

In Figure 3.5 we revisit the firm we met in Figure 3.4. We assume that there are constant unit costs, so we have no economies or diseconomies of scale. Hence, marginal cost equals average cost. Now let us suppose that there are a number of firms in the industry and each firm faces a downward-sloping demand curve so each firm restricts output and raises price above marginal cost and charges a price of P_1. This firm makes abnormal profits. It produces OQ_1 output at a price of P_1. Then $OQ_1 \times AP_1$ represents total revenue. Total costs to the firm are given by output times average costs, $OQ_1 \times Q_1B$, so the rectangle $OQ_1 \times AB$ is the profit above the normal that this firm makes.

Now, says Demsetz, suppose that this firm improves its cost efficiency. Perhaps it engages in some research and development and it comes up with a new technique to produce output at a lower cost. For now, we will assume that other firms in the market have not got this process available. The firm now has a lower cost structure than other firms. Originally, costs were given by $MC_1 = AC_1$. Now their costs are lower. Their marginal cost curve is still equal to their average cost curve but now at $MC_2 = AC_2$. The profit-maximising position of the firm is now at a greater output. Marginal cost equals marginal revenue at OQ_2. The price it charges is P_2.

The effect of the superior efficiency is that it makes a larger volume of output. But there is another important effect too. It also makes more profit. Now the total profit is $OQ_2 \times OP_2$. Notice what that means. The superior efficiency of the firm has caused it to be able to produce more output and therefore have a higher proportion of the total market. The industry is more concentrated and it also makes greater profits.

The first view sees a link from concentration to profits. Demsetz disagrees. He argues that what has enabled them to increase their profit is superior efficiency. This superior efficiency makes possible profits but it also leads to an increase in concentration. The superior efficiency of this firm has increased concentration in the industry because this firm is now producing a higher proportion of the industry's output than before. It is also at the same time making more profits, so the link is not that more concentration equals more profits. The link is that superior efficiency produces both increased concentration and more profits. Profit is the reward for increased efficiency.

Furthermore, in the Demsetz view, technology will, over time, be diffused throughout the economy. So the increased profitability that this firm is enjoying will be a temporary one; the profits which the firm is now making will attract new entries into the market. The new entries into the market will be the ones who are also able to develop the superior techniques. So over time we finish up with all firms in the industry being forced to use the newer, better technology that this firm has introduced. Increased concentration, in the absence of government intervention, is temporary unless the firm with market power keeps its prices to a level where only normal profit is earned.

The increased concentration is good, the increased profitability is good. It is not that consumers are being exploited. The increased efficiency that the better firms have used will benefit all consumers in the long run. Clearly this is a much more relaxed view about the link between concentration, profitability and market power.

Now has Demsetz evidence to support his contention? Consider Table 3.3. Because he is an American economist he tends to focus on the CR4 so we have a number of industries here with different degrees of concentration.

The rates of return to firms of various sizes are given for each group. For example, for those 14 industries where the CR4 is between 10 and 20% the rate of return on assets to the smallest firms (R1) averaged 7.3%. Note that for a CR4 of over 60% there were only three such industries. In general, with

Table 3.3 Average rates of return in US industries by concentration and size

CR4	Number of industries	R1 %	R2 %	R3 %	R4 %	R %
10–20	14	7.3	9.5	10.6	8.0	8.8
20–30	22	4.4	8.6	9.9	10.6	8.4
30–40	24	5.1	9.0	9.4	11.7	8.8
40–50	21	4.8	9.5	11.2	9.4	8.7
50–60	11	0.9	9.6	10.8	12.2	8.4
Over 60	3	5.0	8.6	10.3	21.6	11.3

CR4: four-firm concentration ratio measured on industry sales in 1963.
R1: firms with assets < US$500,000.
R2: firms with at least US$500,000 assets but < US$5 million.
R3: firms with at least US$5 million assets but < US$50 million.
R4: firms with assets > US$50 million.

Source: Demsetz (1973) p. 6, Table 2.

the relatively unconcentrated industries the variation in the rate of return as firm size increases is quite small. However, as we move towards a more concentrated structure, the difference between the rate of return made by the small firms and the rate of return being made by the large firms is getting greater.

There are two ways to explain this finding. One possibility is that larger firms in more concentrated industries are gaining these additional profits by the use of their market power, perhaps the establishment of some kind of agreement or cartel among themselves. Large firms are using their power to exploit consumers by agreeing prices above cost and eliminating competition between them. The second possibility is that it is the superior efficiency of the larger firms driving down costs, causing both an increase in concentration and an increase in profitability. Which of those explanations is the correct one? Demsetz argues it must be the second. It cannot be the first one because if the large firms were getting together to agree prices and driving price above costs, the smaller firms would benefit also. The higher prices, which the large firms establish, would enable the smaller firms to raise their prices as well and so the smaller firms' rates of return would rise as well. We can only conclude that the higher rate of return, the greater profitability being made by the larger firms, is not a result of collusion, but the result of superior efficiency.

We should not worry about the potential of high concentration for exploiting consumers. The reason for this increase in concentration and this increase in profit is the result of superior efficiency by the large firms, a process from which firms and consumers will gain in the end.

Not all economists would accept the Demsetz argument. Other economists such as Scherer (1970) have pointed out that this evidence is consistent with an alternative view. The alternative view is simply that the higher rates of return of the larger firms are from the economies of scale being made in the industry. Thus, according to Scherer, the link from concentration to profitability is still more convincing than the Demsetz alternative.

The sustainability of profits

Whether or not the activity of large firms is benign can partly be addressed by asking whether such profits are sustainable in the long run.

If, as the Chicago school maintains, new firms will always climb over entry barriers where it is profitable, the existence of high profits is not a concern. The market is doing its job. If, however, profits persist over time this is clearly a matter of concern. Many studies have been conducted to determine the extent to which profits persist. We consider two of them in more detail in a later chapter. In general, they tend to show that profits do get eroded away over time to some extent. They also show that the degree to which they persist varies considerably between industries. Even where they persist, this does not entirely negate the Chicago school view. It can be argued that persistent profit is a reflection of firms driving down costs and charging low prices so that consumers benefit, even though new competition is kept out.

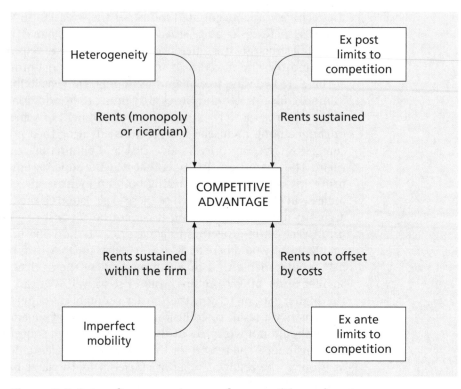

Figure 3.6 Peteraf's cornerstones of competitive advantage
Source: Peteraf (1993)

Peteraf's cornerstones of competitive advantage

Wherein does a firm's ability lie in sustaining profit over the long term? Whilst society would prefer that resources are optimally allocated, firms are more interested in seeking not only profit but the ability to maintain it. One model that enables us to see how firm advantage is served is that of Peteraf (1993). Figure 3.6 summarises her view that there are four cornerstones of competitive advantage.

- *Heterogeneity*. In perfect competition all firms are identical and have identical resources. A key argument of Peteraf's is that this is not so. In this respect she follows the model of competitive selection that we met in Chapter 1. Different firms have different factor endowments, some of which are superior to others. If competition is strong the average firm will achieve only a normal profit. The superior firms will achieve rents, that is, profit in excess of normal.
- *Ex post limits to competition*. The difference in resource endowments enjoyed by the superior firms will be short lived if subsequent to its gaining a superior position there are no forces to limit competition for the rents.

The two key things which limit such competition are imperfect substitutability and imperfect imitability. Imperfect substitutability is important. As we saw with Porter's model, if firms can produce substitute products, the power to achieve rents is limited. Imperfect imitability occurs where it is not possible for other firms to imitate what the superior firm is doing. There are many possibilities here. They include imperfect knowledge by other firms of how the superior firm is organising itself and property rights to scarce resources.

● *Imperfect mobility*. This refers to the tradability of resources. If the factors giving a firm its superiority are tradable the rents may not be captured by the firm but by the owners of the resources. A restaurant may enjoy a superior position but make no rent. The site owner may capture the rent by charging the restaurant a high price for the use of the land and building.

● *Ex ante limits to competition*. Prior to establishing a superior position there must be limits to competition for that position. Return to the restaurant example. Clearly if there is competition to obtain the advantage of the location and knowledge of its value is clear, the advantage of the site will be competed away from the restaurant to the site owner.

A great advantage of the Peteraf approach, it is claimed, is that it may well help to explain why profitability varies in ways not explained by the nature of the industrial structure. Such rents can be made, given the four conditions above, in relatively unconcentrated industries.

Conclusion

Economists once debated whether sustained profit was a function of market power or the result of superior efficiency. This debate still continues. However, more recently a further element of the discussion has gained prominence. Some now claim that it is less important to look at the industrial structure at all. The place to focus attention is upon the unique nature of the individual business. These schools of thought may not be mutually exclusive. Possibly both have something to contribute to the overall explanation.

KEY RESULTS

1 There are various ways of measuring concentration in industry. Some focus on concentration of power, others on its dispersal.

2 Each measure has its problems and therefore the interpretation of concentration data needs care.

3 It can be argued that higher concentration leads to greater profitability.

4 It can be argued that greater efficiency leads to both higher concentration and greater profitability.

5 Peteraf's model of competitive advantage focuses on heterogeneity, ex post limits to competition, imperfect resource mobility and ex ante limits to competition.

6 Peteraf's four cornerstones determine the extent to which firms can make and retain rents.

Questions

1* Five firms in a market have percentage market shares of: 25, 25, 25, 15 and 10 respectively. Calculate the CR3, the CR4, the Gini coefficient and the Herfindahl-Hirschmann Index. Suppose the two smaller firms propose to merge. How would such a merger change the value of each of the concentration measures? Comment on your results.

2* How would you react to the merger proposal of question 1 if you were a member of a government body charged with checking that merger proposals were in the public interest? Consider in particular the question of imports. According to the Competition Commission Report (2000) we considered in Chapter 1, the HHI in UK supermarkets was 1506. On a regional basis it was highest in Northern Ireland at 2935 and lowest in the East Midlands at 1266. How would you assess the benefits to society of a merger between two of the top six?

3* Overall concentration has risen substantially in many countries in the last 60 years, measured as the share of output of the largest hundred firms. The share of output of the largest hundred plants has grown relatively little. What conclusions can you draw from this?

4* Standard microeconomic theory suggests that where there are barriers to entry firms may well make rents. What does Peteraf's model say that is more than this?

5 Consider Box 3.2. Comment upon the three paragraphs beginning 'In the old economy, a company . . .'.

* *Help available at* ***http://www.e-econ.co.uk***

BOX 3.2 Concentration in Internet trading

Will competition always exist unless governments prevent it? Some believe that without government intervention concentration in some markets will increase until only one firm remains.

The internet shake-out is getting brutal.

As dotcom companies burn up their cash and fundraising opportunities evaporate, it seems certain the rout will continue. But less clear is where it will stop. Could it end with just one internet leviathan dominating the business-to-consumer market? A Yahoo.ebay.Amazon.com that serves all the consumer's needs?

The internet is often regarded as the most open and entrepreneurial market in history. In theory, there are few barriers to entry: almost anyone can start a business, without the need for large amounts of capital or a big factory. So as some companies die, others should spring up in their place, offering new features, better service or lower prices.

Yet as the business-to-consumer market develops, there are signs that it is becoming an online version of the winner-takes-all society: one in which two or three companies at the top take a vastly disproportionate share of the market, making it difficult for others to thrive.

In the old economy, the business world has already become familiar with the winner-takes-all phenomenon. It results from the greatly increased competition brought by globalisation.

When markets were small, separate and nation-based, there was limited competition across borders. Even big, multinational companies tended to have separate headquarters and factories in each country, so their size did not give them much of an advantage over smaller companies.

Globalisation, together with improvements in transport and communications, has changed that by allowing big companies to treat large regions, or even the world, as a single market. This has given them economies of scale in production, distribution, marketing and management that smaller companies cannot match.

You see the result on supermarket shelves. There are far too many consumer products for the space available, so retailers give priority to the biggest brands. This further increases the sales of these brands, giving their manufacturers even greater economies of scale – and so on, in a virtuous circle.

Recognising this, old-economy companies have been scrambling to establish scale before it is too late. Almost every industry, from advertising to telecommunications, is in a race for global domination. According to Thomson Financial Securities Data, the value of mergers and acquisitions announced last year rose 24 per cent to a record $3,029bn.

If scale is important in the old economy, it is even more significant in the new. This is because the products of the 'weightless' economy are more often intangible information or ideas than tangible objects that are manufactured and distributed.

In the old economy, a company can benefit from scale by spreading its fixed costs over a larger output, but its variable costs will increase as sales go up. In the digital economy, a company may incur high costs in developing and marketing an idea: but because its output is intangible, the incremental cost of distributing it to a wider customer base may be zero, yielding vast economies of scale.

Another aspect of the internet's scalability is the so-called network effect, which holds that products or services become disproportionately more valuable as more people use them.

If people want to go to an auction website, for example, they want the one that attracts the most users: that way, buyers get the widest choice of products, and sellers get the most bidders. So there is a natural tendency towards monopoly, and an almost insurmountable barrier to new entrants.

The same could be said of Amazon.com, which makes much of its ability to recommend products based on other people's purchasing habits ('Customers who bought this book also bought . . .'). The more people who use the site, the better these recommendations become, giving Amazon.com an advantage over retailers with fewer customers.

To get down to practicalities, it is becoming increasingly uncontroversial to argue that in the business-to-consumer sector only a handful of the very largest dotcom companies have the scale or strength to survive in their present form.

Source: Financial Times, 23 October 2000   **FT**

4 Understanding long-run costs

Economists are people who work with numbers but who don't have the personality to be accountants.

ANON

A key element of business behaviour is production costs. How can we establish the relationship between output and costs? What effect does this relationship have on decision making?

OBJECTIVES

After reading this chapter you should be able to:

- Know the different techniques available for measuring the long-run average cost curve.
- Describe the difficulties implicit in each measure.
- Understand the significance of the learning curve and its effects on firm cost curves.
- Understand how to show that the long-run cost structure affects firms' strategic decisions.

Introduction

We have already studied the concept of seller concentration in industry and its relationship to economies of scale, and we have seen that economies of scale are an important indicator of how concentration develops over time. In this chapter we look more closely at production costs and economies of scale and in particular we focus on how economists actually measure the cost curve. How do they get this evidence about the shape of the cost curve in industry? We shall see that this is important not only for economists interested in the industrial structure, but also for firms and industries taking output decisions.

Some basic definitions

Remember that we have a distinction between the short run and the long run. In the short run we are referring to that period of time where, if a firm increases its output, it must do so with the existing volume of capital. In the long run there is a long enough period of time, such that if a firm wants to change its output, it can change both its inputs of labour and materials but also its volume of capital as well. There are no fixed factors of production.

In the short run firms find that at first, as output increases, average costs tend to fall. This is because the fixed costs can be spread over greater output. That is, average fixed costs fall. However, there are also variable costs to meet. As firms increase output by working an existing volume of capital harder, there are diminishing returns to the variable factor. This makes marginal units of output ever more expensive to produce. This increases short-run average costs. Eventually this cost increase swamps the fall in average fixed costs so that short-run costs will inevitably rise at some output level. This explains why short-run cost curves are almost invariably U-shaped. In this chapter, however, we are focusing on the long run, working out the shape of the long-run average cost curve, LRAC. To do this we need to examine economies of scale.

Economies of scale are strictly a long-run concept. It is as firms change the scale of operations, as they alter the volume of capital that they use, that we observe what is happening to long-run costs. So as we see how economists go about measuring the long-run cost curve and whether there are significant economies of scale, we are focusing on a long enough period of time for firms to adjust the volume of capital. What is also important is the distinction between internal and external economies of scale. Internal economies may occur as a firm increases its output. The firm moves along its LRAC. External economies occur when an industry's output increases. This industry output increase causes the cost curve of each firm in the industry to move downwards. Internal economies of scale, then, are a function of a *firm's* output and external economies are a function of an *industry's* output.

Now there are four basic ways in which economists have set about trying to measure long-run costs. Each of them has its advantages, but each of these techniques has its disadvantages. So we look at each of the four in turn.

Cross-sectional measures

The first way of trying to estimate the shape of the firm's long-run average cost curve is called a cross-sectional technique. What we want to know is what happens to a firm's long-run average cost curve when its output changes, assuming everything else remains constant. If a firm's output increases, will its average costs fall because there are internal economies of scale, or will it rise, because of diseconomies of scale? We will often find that different firms within the same industry are operating at different output levels. Now we can plot the costs of each firm against its output and use that to establish the structure of the cost curve. Figure 4.1 shows the relationship between the output of an industry and the long-run average cost. Suppose a firm has q_1 as its current level of output and average costs are c_1. But we have found other firms of different sizes. Another firm has q_2 output and its costs are c_2, another firm at

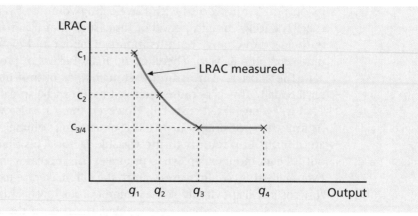

Figure 4.1 Cross-sectional measure

q_3 where its costs are c_3, and the largest firm in the industry produces q_4 output. For illustrative purposes assume that this particular firm has the same average costs as the smaller firm at q_3. If we know the average costs in the industry at different levels of output we can join these points up to create a cost curve. The industry's average cost curve in this case falls up to q_3 and then is constant at a level of output beyond q_3. That is quite a simple way of trying to work out the cost curve and providing there are firms of varying sizes in the industry it's a feasible method.

Although it is a simple way there is a significant problem. We may find that the implied cost structure is quite different from the actual cost structure. The problem can be seen in the following way. What are we actually measuring when we look at a cost curve? We are measuring the lowest possible cost of producing any given level of output. The long-run average cost curve does not tell us the costs that firms actually experience. It represents the least possible cost that, given the present state of technology, one could have to produce any given level of output. It is a boundary between what is possible and what is not possible with regard to unit costs. But what is measured with the cross-sectional technique is not the least possible cost. What we have measured is the costs that firms at the moment are currently experiencing. We can illustrate why we may have the wrong shape of cost curve by using this technique.

Figure 4.2 reproduces Figure 4.1 but shows also what actual costs may be. 'LRAC measured' is the curve obtained from asking firms about their costs. But suppose some of them have costs higher than they need be because they are not cost efficient. If a firm's costs are higher than they need be, the extra costs that they actually experience above what they need to experience is known in the language of economists as 'X-inefficiency'. Here is one possibility. Could it be that the larger firms have grown to be large because they are cost efficient? They are cost efficient, in that they have got their costs down to the minimum so that at q_3 and q_4, their actual costs are the same as the minimum

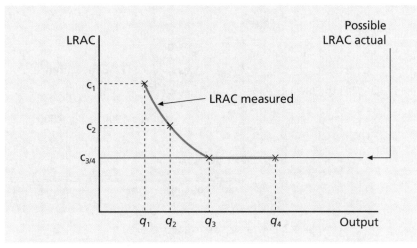

Figure 4.2 Problems with the cross-sectional measure

possible costs. It is also possible that firms producing q_1 and q_2 are small and have not grown to be as big as firms represented by q_3 and q_4 because they are X-inefficient. It is feasible that the minimum possible cost of producing q_1 is c_3, and that the minimum possible cost of producing q_2 is c_3. So we could have a situation in which the actual long-run average cost curve is horizontal. However, we have implied it to be a different shape, a falling long-run average cost curve, because instead of focusing on what is possible, we have focused on the actual. So the use of the cross-sectional mechanism for measuring the cost structure has a problem. We are not measuring the cost curve itself, we are measuring actual cost. If this industry has firms in it which are not cost efficient then we may be assuming that the cost structure is not actually what it is. Nevertheless, the cross-sectional technique has been used to try to establish the shape of the cost curve.

Time series estimation

Now we look at a second measure that overcomes the previous difficulty to some extent but unfortunately raises other problems. This is known as the time series measure. We do not look at a whole series of firms producing different levels of output at one time period. Rather, we focus on what is happening to firms' costs over time. We may be able to do it by just considering one firm and asking 'how much output was produced in, say, 1970 and what were average costs? When it grew to be a larger firm by 1980, at that larger level of output, what were average costs? By 1990 if it had grown again, at that larger level of output, what were average costs? By the year 2000, if it had grown again to a larger level of output, what were average costs?'

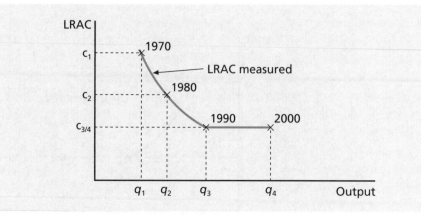

Figure 4.3 Time series measure

Suppose we plotted that information on a diagram; we might have something like Figure 4.3. In 1970 the firm produced q_1 output and its costs were c_1. In 1980 it had a larger level of output and lower average costs. In 1990 there was a still larger level of output and still lower costs. At q_4 in 2000, we assume that their average costs were the same as in 1990 and so we have a constant long-run average cost beyond that level of output, q_3. So again by looking at the actual data that firms have given to us we have been able to plot the information and construct a cost curve.

Over that period of time price levels will have changed; in most societies the average level of prices will have risen. So we do need some way to deflate those numbers by some suitable price index to produce a constant price series enabling us to compare like with like. But even if we do that we still have a problem in establishing the cost curve from the data that is given.

Recall again what a cost curve tells us. It is the least possible cost of producing any level of output. Furthermore, the cost curve is a curve that exists at a moment of time. A cost curve is a series of spots relating output to potential minimum costs, which exist at the same time. It is the cost curve that exists at one moment with given technology. But over time technology changes. Technology may enable a firm in 1980 to produce at a lower level of costs than it could have produced in 1970; in 1990 at a lower level of costs than in 1980; and in 2000 at a lower level of costs than it could have produced in 1990.

Look at Figure 4.4 to see what effect that has on the shape of the cost curve. We assumed that the cost curve must be of the shape given by 'LRAC measured'. But now here is another possibility. The cost curve in 1970 may have been horizontal. Whatever level of output used, the minimum possible cost would have been c_1. The firm producing q_1 output has its costs down to the minimum possible. It is not X-inefficient if it is producing at c_1 cost. Now assume that by 1980 it had expanded its output to q_2 and its costs were c_2. But during that period of time the cost curve fell; there is a lower level of possible costs because of improvements in technology. The firm is in a different

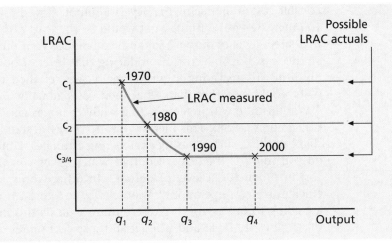

Figure 4.4 Problems with the time series measure

position than it was in 1970. The cost curve is still horizontal but lower. Similarly, in 1990 the possible cost curve, the minimum cost of producing, is at c_3. So we assumed that the cost curve had declined up until q_3 and then stayed constant, but that it hasn't changed over that period. It is possible that what has actually happened is that we have found one spot on three or four different cost curves as the cost curve shifted over time. If that is true, the shape of the cost curve that we've assumed may well be the incorrect one. The great problem then is that the whole cost curve may well shift whereas we've had to assume that the cost curve remains constant. So as the firm's output increases, we assumed that we are looking at different points on the cost curve, whereas in fact what we are looking at is a series of spots, each on a different cost curve. So both the cross-sectional and the time series measures for establishing the shape of the cost curve have a problem because we are looking at actual data whereas what we are actually interested in is the minimum possible level of costs.

Engineering estimates

A third way of trying to establish the cost curve, which overcomes the difficulties we have encountered so far, is the use of what is known as engineering studies or engineering estimates. This is quite a different approach; this time we get the answers that we are looking for with a questionnaire. Firms are asked: 'With the level of output that you are at present producing, what do you think would be the least possible cost to you of producing that output?' The questions are not solely based on what firms' costs are at present. They might be using processes that are not as efficient as others they could use. The idea is to get an estimate of what firms believe to be the least possible cost of producing that level of output. Now one can ask them: 'Suppose you increase your output, what would be the least possible cost of producing that larger level of output? Suppose you reduce your output, what would then be the least possible cost of producing that level of output?' Thus, by engaging firms in answering a questionnaire, we get their estimate of what their costs would be rather than what their costs actually are.

We illustrate with reference to a study that was conducted in this form by C.F. Pratten (1988). This method has become the standard for measuring the shape of the cost curve using engineering estimates. Pratten asked firms: 'What do you think is the level of output which gives you the minimum possible cost of producing a level of output?' In other words, what is the minimum efficient scale of operations? Another way to express it is to ask: 'If your costs are going to fall as you increase output, what is the smallest level of output that you could be at and still get all those economies of scale?' Then Pratten asked, 'Let us suppose you produce at only half that level of output, how much higher would your average costs be now that you're not getting all the economies of scale available?' And so by asking a series of questions related to what the engineers estimate costs to be at different levels of output one can produce a cost structure.

Let us look at Table 4.1, which gives figures produced by these engineering estimates. Focus first of all upon the relationship of output to costs within the UK. We have a number of different products here and in column two we see what is the minimum efficient scale, as a percentage of production of UK output. A firm in cellulose fibres would need 125% of UK output in order to get all the economies of scale and produce it in one plant. But in other industries the situation looks quite different; for bricks, for example, we would only need to produce in one plant 1% of UK output in order to get to minimum efficient scale. The equivalent figure for shoes is just one-third of 1%. For the European market the numbers are obviously much smaller. So, with beer, although you'd need 12% of UK output to get to minimum efficient scale, you'd only need 3% of EU output to achieve the same result. In the third column we have further information to help us to infer the shape of the cost curve. If the firm were only at half the MES level of output, one can see how much more unit costs would be. So for cellulose fibres, if the firm produced

Table 4.1 MES as a percentage of production: plants

Product	UK	EU	% additional cost at $\frac{1}{2}$ MES
Cellulose fibres	125	16	3
Electric motors	60	6	15
Beer	12	3	7
Bricks	1	0.2	25
Shoes	0.3	0.03	1

Adapted from: C.F. Pratten (1988)

at half minimum efficient scale average costs would be 3% more. That is a measure of the disadvantage to the firm if it produces at less than minimum efficient scale. Now consider bricks. If the firm were to produce at half MES the cost disadvantage would be much higher; 25% higher costs as a result of being half the size is clearly a substantial handicap.

This is an interesting way of attempting to measure the cost curve because, although it doesn't tell us every point on the cost curve, it does give us a good idea of the shape of the curve. It tells us where minimum efficient scale is. We also have an idea of the shape of the curve from zero to minimum efficient scale. We know too that beyond minimum efficient scale average costs are either constant or rising. They are not going to fall any further because by definition, the level of output that we found is minimum efficient scale. So this is an alternative way of working out the shape of the cost curve, not by looking at actual data but by surveys.

It overcomes the problems that we met by looking at the other two techniques. Unfortunately it introduces another problem. One is now relying upon people's guesses as to what costs would be at different levels of output. Remember this is not actual output data. This is someone's best guess as to what costs would be. So the data is only accurate as far as the engineers are accurate in guessing what the costs are. There is one other problem in using engineering studies of this kind. The people who are making the estimates are not economists. They are looking at actual costs. How much are labour costs? How much are capital costs? However, they are not thinking about opportunity costs. What are the costs in alternative uses of these resources? Because the economists' concept of costs is somewhat different from the engineers' concept, we are not sure that we are getting estimates from the engineers that accurately reflect the economists' understanding of the long-run average cost curve.

For example, suppose a firm buys raw materials at £50,000. Suppose further that there is a sharp increase in the price of such materials so that they would now cost £75,000. The engineering cost estimate is likely to be based on the purchase price of the raw material costs, whereas to the economist the correct cost is the £75,000 that reflects their cost in alternative usage.

A further illustration relates to the important concept of sunk costs. A sunk cost is one which has no opportunity cost at all. Suppose a firm has spent money on a specific piece of capital equipment. Suppose further that the demand for the output that the firm produces now falls. Should the firm continue to produce the output? One could argue that since the capital was expensive the costs of production are high. However, the economist would argue that the capital cost is irretrievable. It is a sunk cost. Decisions should be made upon opportunity cost.

Almost all costs are sunk if the time period is short enough. What is the cost of a car journey? Since the insurance and road tax have been paid one might say that they do not figure in the calculations. They are sunk costs. But if the car is full of petrol, the petrol too has no opportunity cost. So the problem of sunk costs is difficult for economists. But it is a particular problem if non-economists, whose understanding of costs may be different, make the cost

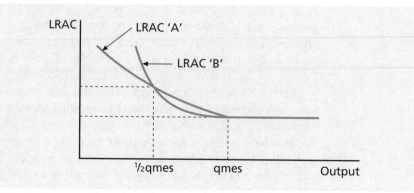

Figure 4.5 Engineering estimates

estimates. We shall consider the importance of sunk costs in later chapters when we analyse pricing decisions.

One other problem with this approach is that the measure will only give a rough idea of the shape of the LRAC. On the basis of the information in Table 4.1 we can construct an LRAC such as LRAC 'A' in Figure 4.5. However, the same information allows us to plot LRAC 'B'. The difference could be significant. Suppose, for example, a potential entrant thought of starting up at just 25% of MES. The disadvantage suffered is much greater if LRAC 'B' is a correct representation of the position.

Despite the problems these estimates are widely used and widely quoted when economists ask the question: 'What is the shape of the long-run cost curve?'

The survivor technique

There is one more measure of the cost curve, which is rather different from the ones we have looked at so far. This last approach to its measurement is known as the survivor technique. It was developed by J. Stigler (1958). Stigler's argument is that the shape of the cost curve can be inferred by looking at an industry at different moments in time and seeing which sized firms are the ones that survived best. If a firm is producing output that is not the level that minimises its costs, it will not be profitable. Because its costs are higher than they should be, its prices will be too high and the firm will find that it simply cannot sell the product. All such firms then will either have to change their output to a level of output at which they do minimise their costs or they will simply go out of business. So if we look at an industry at different points of time we can see which are the firms that have survived the best and ask the question 'what level of output are they producing?' From this information we can infer the shape of the LRAC.

Let us look at some evidence that Stigler produced to see how his survivor technique can be used in practice. Table 4.2 contains some data which Stigler

Table 4.2 Distribution of petroleum refining capacity by relative size of company

Company size (per cent of industry capacity)	1947	1950	1954
1. Per cent of industry capacity			
Under 0.1	5.30	4.57	3.89
0.1 to 0.2	4.86	3.57	3.00
0.2 to 0.3	2.67	2.16	2.74
0.3 to 0.4	2.95	2.92	1.65
0.4 to 0.5	2.20	0	.89
0.5 to 0.75	3.04	4.66	5.05
0.75 to 1.00.	.94	0	1.58
1.0 to 2.5	11.70	12.17	10.53
2.5 to 5	9.57	16.70	14.26
5 to 10	45.11	42.15	45.69
10 to 15	11.65	11.06	10.72

Source: Stigler (1958) p. 68

produced for one particular industry, the petrol refining industry. He divided up all the firms in the industry into different-sized categories, so the smallest firms have less than 0.1% of the industry's total output, the next category of slightly bigger firms between 0.1 and 0.2% of industry output and so on. Stigler then asked what percentage of the industry's capacity was produced by firms of different size classes. So, in 1947, we know that 5.30% of industry capacity was in the hands of the very smallest firms, and 11.65% of the industry's capacity was controlled by the very largest firms. Then he looked again at the industry in 1950 and 1954 and saw how things had changed.

Look at the 1954 data. Notice that if we take the smallest firms, the proportion of industry capacity that is in the hands of the smallest firms has declined. For the next category of firm size, the proportion of output in the hands of those firms has also fallen. But now if we look at what we might refer to as the medium-sized firms, those with 0.2 to 1% of capacity, the combined output of this group as a proportion of the total is actually rising over time. Now if we look at the largest firms, what do we notice? Over time the proportion of output in the hands of the largest firms is declining. Why is it that the smallest firms are finding that they are producing a lower proportion of industry capacity than they were some years ago? Stigler's answer is that their costs are too high. Market forces will discipline them. These firms will either have to expand and become bigger firms in order to gain advantages of economies of scale or they will simply go out of business. So the fact that the smaller firms have a smaller proportion of industry capacity than they had previously implies that there is a falling long-run average cost over that range. These firms have to grow in order to take advantage of the economies of scale and survive. Focus now on the largest firms. The proportion of capacity in their hands has also declined. The argument is that they are too big.

These firms are experiencing diseconomies of scale. They will be forced by the market to reduce their output and move to a more optimum size. That means moving towards minimum efficient scale. Table 4.3 shows the same industry at the same time periods. The distribution here is by size of plant rather than firm. Again note how the smallest and largest plant shares have declined over time. Firms will move to an optimal size of output with an optimal plant size. So, says Stigler, from this data, we can infer the shape of the cost curve. We do it in Figure 4.6.

Those firms that produced such a small part of the market were finding that the proportion of their output was tending to decline. This is because their costs were higher than the larger firms. They could not compete and survive. Some of them died, some of them grew and moved down their cost structure to a more optimally sized level of output. But we also know that at the very large levels of output the long-run average cost curve rises. How do we know that? The largest firms found that their output as a proportion of industry

Table 4.3 Distribution of petroleum refining capacity by relative size of plant

Plant size	1947	1950	1954
	1. Per cent of industry capacity		
Under 0.1.	8.22	7.39	6.06
0.1 to 0.2.	9.06	7.60	7.13
0.2 to 0.3	6.86	4.95	3.95
0.3 to 0.4	5.45	4.99	7.28
0.4 to 0.5	4.53	6.56	4.06
0.5 to 0.75	9.95	10.47	11.82
0.75 to 1.0	5.35	7.07	8.33
1.0 to 1.5	12.11	10.36	13.38
1.5 to 2.5	17.39	23.64	22.45
2.5 to 4.0	21.08	16.96	15.54

Source: Stigler (1958) p. 69

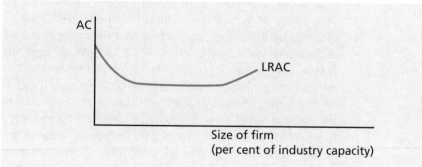

Figure 4.6 Implied cost structure: using the survivor technique

capacity was declining. They were forced to reduce their output because they had a cost disadvantage through being so large. They experienced diseconomies of scale. Over time the survivor technique shows us the level of output, or the range of output, at which firms minimise their unit costs. This can be seen in Figure 4.6.

So, according to Stigler, we can work out the shape of the cost curve by observing the change in the industry structure over time. The market will see to it that firms will move to an optimally sized level of output, the level of output that reflects minimum efficient scale. That enables us to infer the shape of the curve. It is a beautiful idea, but it does have substantial problems that we need to recognise.

The first problem lies in the assumption about markets. Is the market as powerful as Stigler assumes? Why is it that firms are forced to change their output to minimum efficient scale? In Stigler's view it is because the market is so powerful as a means of allocating scarce resources that firms that are not optimally sized simply cannot survive. So if we have a view that says markets do work, and that they work very efficiently, they will force firms towards that optimum level of output. In this case we have a great respect for Stigler's view. However, we may be of that school of thinking that suggests that markets are not that powerful as a means of allocating resources, and that firms can survive at a non-optimum level of output. They can control markets in various ways, isolate themselves from competition, raise entry barriers and so on. Then we may have more doubts as to whether the Stigler technique is as useful as he claims. This is because what underlies the Stigler view is a belief in the power of markets to drive firms to an optimal level of output. In other words, the technique makes Chicago school assumptions.

There is a second problem associated with the Stigler technique. And that is, of course, that we are not measuring the actual cost curve at all. We are inferring the shape of the curve from the data. Nothing in the data enables us to say that, if a firm produces at that level of output, its average costs will be €20 per unit or whatever. It simply enables us to say that the structure of the cost curve is such that it will decline and then rise, for example. It only tells us the shape of the cost curve, it doesn't tell us exactly where the cost curve is.

However, to Stigler this is no disadvantage at all. As economists we don't really need to know where the cost curve is. All we need is a confidence in the market to drive firms to the right level of output to minimise costs. If we believe that markets do that, we don't need to know where the cost curve is. We may have an interventionist view of the economy such that we need to know what the shape of the cost curve is. We may want to undertake industrial policies which push firms to that level of output. We may believe that we need to look at small firms and encourage them to merge in order to take advantage of economies of scale. We may believe that we need to look at large firms and control their market power and limit the output that they produce in order to push them towards a more optimal level of output. Then it becomes very useful for us to know exactly where the cost curve is. But Stigler is of the Chicago school. Monopoly power cannot survive. Markets are effective.

Government intervention is unnecessary. Knowledge of the exact location of the cost curve is information that is entirely unnecessary.

Similarly, markets will see to it that small firms will merge to gain advantages of economies of scale. Large firms will find that they simply can't survive with all the attendant disadvantages of diseconomies of scale. The market will drive firms to the optimal level of output. We simply do not need to know that information, we can have confidence in markets to do better. What governments do they will only do badly. So the Stigler technique is very interesting, but how enthusiastic we are about it as a means of measuring costs depends crucially on how confident we are in the power of markets to organise resources to move in the direction of those firms who minimise production costs.

Box 4.1 'Critical mass' for scale economies in European banking

In banking, as in many industries, there are economies of scale, especially of low output levels. European banking is one such industry.

In the past decade, scores of international banks have fought for market share in the emerging economies of the former communist bloc.

The winners of this bruising battle could emerge in the next year or two as the dominant players in central and east European banking.

The three largest international banks in the region – Germany's Hypovereins-bank, which recently completed a €7bn ($5.9bn) merger with Bank Austria, KBC of Belgium and Italy's Unicredito – already have nearly 30 per cent of the foreign banks' share of the regional market.

With these banks among bidders in coming privatisations in the Czech Republic and Slovakia, their share is likely to grow further.

As Zdeňek Bakala, chairman of Patria Finance, a Czech investment bank affiliated with KBC, says: 'Consolidation will sweep financial services across the region.'

The likely changes should accelerate the spread of modern banking to people who still carry out most of their transactions in cash.

It should also help integration with the European Union because most international banks active in the former communist bloc are EU-based.

For the banks, the great attraction in the ex-communist countries is the potential growth of markets, which by western standards are still undeveloped.

The region's total bank assets (excluding Russia's) are only half those of Austria.

The largest bank, Poland's PKO BP with assets at the end of 1999 of €14.6bn, would not make the top 30 in Germany. Even in relation to gross domestic product, the former communist states are far behind, with assets equivalent to 69 per cent of gross domestic product compared with with a euro-zone average of 254 per cent.

Within banking, the greatest expansion is likely to be in retail markets, which are the least developed. Credit cards are treated with suspicion and consumer finance is in its infancy. As Herman Agneesens, a managing director of KBC, says: 'There is everything to play for. It will be 10–20 years before the level of development reaches EU levels.'

The likely winners in the region are international banks. German and Austrian banks have taken advantage of their geographical proximity and historical ties to penetrate central Europe. Similarly, Scandinavian banks have come to dominate the markets of the Baltic states.

Among the most aggressive investors in eastern Europe have been west European banks based in smaller countries, such as ING, KBC and Portugal's BCP. Faced with consolidation within the EU, these banks have gone east in search of the critical mass needed to compete with big country rivals. As Mr Agneesens says: 'Eastern and central Europe is our big opportunity to build a bigger base. This can be our second home market.'

Source: Financial Times, 20 October 2000   **FT**

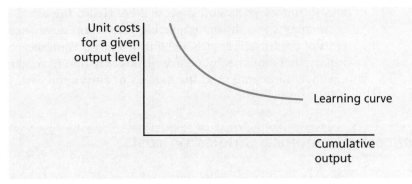

Figure 4.7 A typical learning curve

Two further problems of cost measurement

A further problem of cost measurement is that costs cannot always be assigned easily. Few firms today are single-line producers. Since most firms are multi-product firms, there is a further complication that some costs such as management overheads will have to be allocated in a rather arbitrary way between the various products. We shall return to this problem in Chapter 6.

A second difficulty, which is important in some industries, is what is called learning economies. Where a process is complex, a firm will often learn better and cheaper ways of producing simply by engaging in production. So, for example, when a new aircraft is produced, a great deal is learned in making the first few, which reduces the costs of producing subsequent units. It is likely that such learning effects will be largely exhausted at some point. We can show this diagrammatically in Figure 4.7. Notice that the horizontal axis does not show output but *cumulative* output, which is the total amount produced by firms in all previous production periods.

The learning curve, however, will have an effect on the LRAC. This can be seen in Figure 4.8. The more a firm has produced, the more it has learned

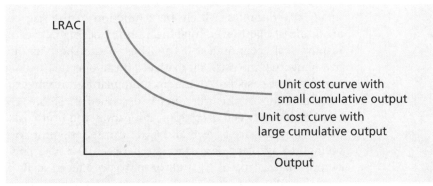

Figure 4.8 Learning effects and economies of scale

and so the lower its unit costs will be. Hence the effect of gaining learning economies is to shift the whole LRAC function downwards. This means that costs of production are not determined just by output levels but by cumulative output. Firms established in a market may thus have substantial cost advantages over newcomers, raising barriers to entry.

A summary of empirical studies on costs

Notwithstanding the difficulties we have encountered, many attempts have been made to establish the shape of the LRAC. The most typical result is that found by Pratten (1998) to which we referred earlier. Unit costs fall as firm output is increased but these are exhausted at some point. Beyond this level average costs are constant. A number of studies have reached other conclusions for particular industries. Drake (1992) found only small evidence of economies or diseconomies of scale in UK building societies. Unit costs are fairly constant. McAfee and McMillan (1995) argue that managerial diseconomies will be important in many industries.

It is important to remember that evidence is also time specific. Over time technology changes. Such changes may well alter the shape of the whole unit cost curve.

Cost curves and firms' location decisions

Clearly knowledge of the cost structure is valuable to firms in making long-run decisions about output levels. Part of a decision to invest and increase output will depend upon the effects this will have on unit costs. It is also crucial for making pricing decisions. We examine this important topic in later chapters. It will also have an effect upon location decisions, in particular whether to operate a number of plants across the country or whether to centralise production in one large plant.

Most scale economies are at the plant level. There may be some, such as financial economies, which are a function of the size of the *firm*, but most are found at plant level. Imagine a firm choosing between one large plant and reaping scale economies. It then has to transport its output to its markets, involving itself in costs. Alternatively, it can operate three separate plants, reducing transport costs but giving up some plant economies of scale. One possible representation of this dilemma is described in Figure 4.9, which shows the relationship between geographical location and unit costs. If it operates three plants of equal size at A, B and C we can see the unit costs of producing and selling at any place. For example, between D and E it is cheapest to supply output made at plant B. If all output is produced at B, plant economies are such that unit costs at point B are lower. However, transport costs will be more significant when selling, for example, beyond A and C. In this case, though, transport costs are small relative to scale economies and it is cheaper to build

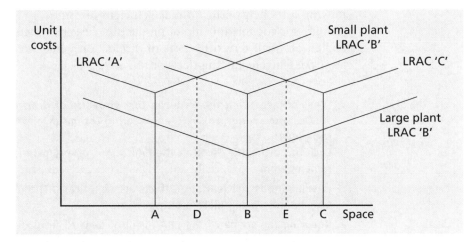

Figure 4.9 Location decisions and scale economies

one plant. Clearly whether this is so in any particular instance depends upon the relative costs of production and distribution.

Cost forecasting

Understanding how costs can be calculated is critical for firms entering into contracts to supply over a period of time. During the life of the contract costs will probably change. In particular, there are three areas for a business to consider.

- *Factor productivity.* Over the longer run new techniques will alter the productivity of capital and labour. It will be impossible to forecast such changes with certainty but past changes in the industry may well prove the best guide.
- *Factor prices.* The prices of capital and labour will probably change. Part of this change is because of rises in the price level. However, relative prices may well change too with its effects on costs. Again, past trends can be used as the starting point of the estimation.
- *Learning effects.* In some industries learning effects are important. The level of expected output combined with knowledge of the size of learning effects in the industry provide valuable clues as to how costs might change over time.

Conclusion

Costs are crucial in understanding the economics of industries and firms. We have seen the four ways in which measuring costs can be done, and have considered the problems in doing so. We have also seen one of the ways in which knowing costs helps firms to make efficient decisions. In the next chapter we shall develop the relationship of production costs to structural change. In later chapters we shall return to costs of production when we consider how firms can make efficient pricing decisions.

KEY RESULTS

1 Ways of measuring the long-run cost structure of firms are: cross-sectional studies, time series analysis, engineering estimates and the survivor technique.

2 Each has difficulties so that the limitations of any estimates need to be remembered.

3 In some industries learning effects are significant. These shift the LRAC downwards as cumulative output rises.

4 Knowing the shape of the LRAC is important to firms. Strategic decisions on output, mergers, and location can be affected by such considerations.

Questions

1* A. Noulas *et al.* (1990) found evidence of economies of scale in the US banking industry for assets up to $3 billion, and diseconomies for assets in excess of $6 billion. What might these economies and diseconomies be? Comment on the fact that the largest US banks have assets over $100 billion. Would you use these figures if you were asked to investigate a merger between two European banks? Would you be concerned by them if you were an executive of a large European bank?

2* Marvin Lieberman (1984) studied the chemical processing industry. He estimated that doubling the cumulative volume of output reduced unit production costs by 27%. Doubling plant size reduced unit costs by 11%. Indicate these results on a diagram similar to Figure 4.8.

3* Consider Figure 4.9. Redraw it for a firm with high transport costs and limited plant economies. Show why the firm will prefer to operate with a number of plants rather than to centralise production. Would your decision be affected if the firm's geographical spread of customers were to be uneven?

4* Most European countries' brewing industry is dominated by a handful of large producers. What does this suggest about scale economies? How do small brewers survive and in some cases flourish?

5 Refer to Box 4.2. How can smaller pharmaceutical companies save on research costs by buying the rights to produce products that are ready for the market? Will not the price they must pay for such rights reflect the costs of their development?

* *Help available at http://www.e-econ.co.uk*

Box 4.2 Optimal size in the pharmaceutical sector

Pharmaceuticals is a market where there are considerable economies, especially since research and development costs are high. However, there are means by which smaller firms can survive.

The pharmaceutical industry is undergoing a profound structural shift. Big drug groups have been getting even bigger because of mergers such as that of Astra with Zeneca and, most recently, Glaxo Wellcome with SmithKline Beecham.

At the other end of the scale, dozens of mainly loss-making biotechnology companies have sprouted to help supply the corporate giants with technology and drug candidates for tomorrow's blockbusters.

That leaves a space in the middle. It is a niche being exploited by a new corporate beast: the speciality pharmaceutical company.

Also known as emerging pharmaceuticals, the group – which includes Shire, Galen, Bioglan Pharma and, on some definitions, the Irish company Elan – has had an unglamorous image.

Acquisitive, pragmatic and nimble, they pride themselves on marketing niche drugs considered too small by 'big pharma'. Unlike flashier biotechs, they do not waste money on speculative, long-term research that may never bear fruit. Rather, they concentrate on maximising sales and profits.

Shire is typical of the new breed. Under Rolf Stahel, chief executive, it has acquired six companies and a comprehensive sales infrastructure in just a few years.

Among its strategic coups has been the acquisition of Richwood, a US company that owned Adderall, an obscure drug to treat hyperactivity in children. Sold by a young, highly incentivised, salesforce, Shire has transformed the drug's performance, piling on sales quarter after quarter.

Adderall is marketed to a limited number of specialist doctors rather than to a plethora of GPs. As a result, Shire has a US salesforce of 270, compared with the 4,000-plus typical of big pharma.

Mr Stahel describes Shire's strategy as 'search and development', a truncated version on the research and development conducted by others. Shire engages in no basic research, but picks up products that are on, or near, the market.

Bioglan Pharma has pursued a similar strategy, carving out a niche in skin care, pain control and drug delivery. Terry Sadler, chief executive, says it is 'constantly looking for niche opportunities, where we will not run into heavy competition from big pharma'.

Once Bioglan has detected an interesting market, it approaches large companies with an offer to buy products whose sales are falling because they are not being actively marketed. Last month, it bought several skincare products from Novartis, the Swiss drugs giant, to add to similar ones bought from AstraZeneca.

The key test for any acquisition is whether Bioglan can revive its sales through aggressive marketing, says Mr Sadler. 'If you can't reverse the decline in sales, don't buy it.'

So far, the strategy has paid off: the company has marketing teams and products in many European countries, while profits and sales are growing sharply. Its shares have nearly trebled since flotation two years ago, even though some investors have trouble distinguishing Bioglan from its biotech counterparts.

'We are always at pains to differentiate ourselves by explaining that we are a high-growth, profitable company with a healthy cash flow,' says Mr Sadler.

John King, executive chairman of Northern-Ireland-based Galen, has encountered similar troubles. Like Shire, Galen has a secondary listing on Nasdaq. Like Shire, too, much of its sales are in the US, where fund managers are more accustomed to the speciality pharma model.

'In the UK, investors still talk to us about cash-burn [like biotech companies] and I have to tell them: "Look, we are a profitable company with products on the market",' Mr King says.

Such difficulties have not harmed Galen's share price, which has risen nearly eight-fold in three years.

Galen has developed its stronghold in female hygiene through acquisitions of both products and companies. Two of its main products – a vaginal cream and an oral contraceptive – were bought from Bristol-Myers Squibb, a big US drugs group. Last month, it completed a £351m all-share takeover of Warner Chilcott, a US rival that will give it access to the important North American market.

It is a measure of how attractive the speciality pharmaceuticals model has become that other companies are now comparing themselves to the once-derided group. Paul Drayson, chief executive of PowderJect, until recently one of the most favoured biotechnology stocks, let it be known last week that his company deserved the speciality tag.

For now at least, the ugly ducklings of the drugs business have become its glamorous swans.

Source: Financial Times, 7 November 2000 **FT**

5 Scale economies, scope economies and technological change

Is it progress if a cannibal uses a knife and fork?

STANISLAW LEM

Businesses operate in a rapidly changing environment. Changes in output levels, the mix of output and changes in technology all affect costs. This chapter considers changes in costs and how they affect industries and firms.

OBJECTIVES

After reading this chapter you should be able to:

- Understand the link between minimum efficient scale and industry output.
- Explain how technological change affects market concentration.
- Know what economies of scope are and how they can affect the structure of industry.
- Appreciate how stochastic factors can influence structural change.
- Understand the links between the structure of industry and the incentive and ability to innovate.

Introduction

In this chapter we begin by examining the key factors that can cause changes to the structure of industries, including the shape of the LRAC, innovation and technological change. Later we consider the way in which the industrial structure can itself influence the speed of technical change. So there is a possible two-way causal relationship: a) from costs and cost changes to the industrial structure, and b) from the industrial structure to cost changes.

Economies of scale and the industrial structure

First, we consider what the shape of cost curve LRAC suggests about the likely industrial structure. In the last chapter we saw some work that has been done in attempting to establish the typical shape of the cost curve. Figure 5.1 shows

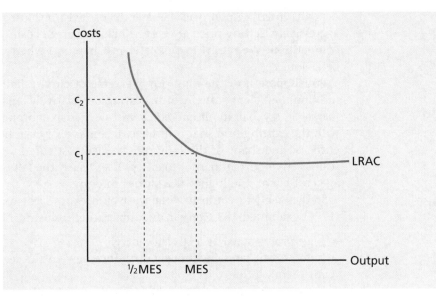

Figure 5.1 Economies of scale and concentration

a typical long-run average cost curve. As output increases average costs fall, reaching a minimum at minimum efficient scale, MES, which gives the firm a unit cost of c_1. We would expect that firms in any industry would grow until they reach at least that size so that they can take advantage of the economies of scale. Growth might be external, through merger activity, or internal via organic growth.

Thus we would expect that minimum efficient scale, as a proportion of total industry output, would be a key determinant of how concentrated the industry is because the industry will tend to increase in concentration until firms have reached minimum efficient scale. However, it is not only MES itself that is important. A further consideration is the shape of the cost curve from zero until MES.

How quickly does the long-run average cost curve fall and why is that important? We have seen that some studies showed not only what minimum efficient scale is but also what the cost disadvantage is as a result of being at half minimum efficient scale. In Figure 5.1, if a firm is at half MES, its costs are higher at c_2. How much higher is c_2 compared with c_1? The answer is important in helping to determine the structure of the industry. Suppose the cost curve is falling but very slowly, so that the long-run average cost curve is virtually flat to minimum efficient scale. It is relatively easy for new firms to enter the market if the existing firms are charging prices well above costs and making large profits. A firm can enter the market, starting up at a fairly small level of output, because it has a minor cost disadvantage compared with existing firms. This disadvantage may not be serious, especially if its product is differentiated in some way from the existing firms. It can build up some brand loyalty and survive long enough to be able to grow into a larger firm. The argument that new entry occurs relatively easily under these conditions depends partly upon the behaviour of existing firms. They may price aggressively, setting price at or even below average cost, in order to keep out competition. We return to this later in Chapter 9 when we focus on pricing behaviour.

But suppose now the long-run average cost curve is falling very quickly to minimum efficient scale. A firm starting up relatively small, coming into the market at, say, half minimum efficient scale, has an enormous cost disadvantage with the existing firm so it is unlikely to survive, or even be willing to attempt entry. So the shape of the long-run average cost curve to minimum efficient scale is an important barrier to entry. The steeper the fall of the long-run average cost curve, the higher the barrier to entry.

Studies tend to confirm what we would expect. For example, Schwalbach (1991) examined 183 German manufacturing industries. He found that:

- high profits acted as a spur to entry;
- high growth rates encourage entry since new entries feel that there is room for them;
- but entry was discouraged where economies of scale presented high barriers to entry.

Studies also tend to confirm what we might expect about the size of new entrants into the market. The average size of the new entrant is much smaller than the average size of the established firm. Cable and Schwalbach (1991) studied eight different countries. The average size of new entrant into UK industry is 44.9% of the average size of existing firms. Interestingly, in the USA it is only 6.7%. This is mainly because the typical market size is so much larger there. The size of new entrants in relation to established firms varied in the other countries between the figures for the UK and the USA.

Technological change and its effect on industrial structure

We have seen previously that it is not simply the shape of the cost curve, but what technological change does to it that is also important. We looked at the Demsetz view of profitability and concentration. Technological change would push down the cost curve of one firm that discovers a new production technique. When the cost curve falls as a result of that technological change, there is a change in the structure of the industry. If it finds a new technology, its costs fall. Its profit-maximising level of output increases. This, in the Demsetz view, gives a more concentrated industrial structure and also a higher level of profitability.

However, it may not be long before other firms are able to emulate the improved cost structure. They will also lower their costs and they will also be able to compete against this existing firm, so the profits of the original firm are eroded away by the effects of competition. Clearly there is room for disagreement over the speed at which such a process occurs. But we consider here what happens when a sufficient time has elapsed for this to happen.

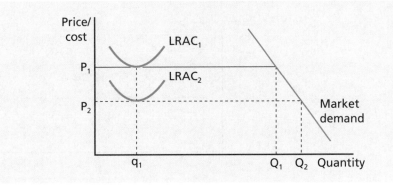

Figure 5.2 Technological change and possible effects on concentration (1)

We now consider the effect on industries and firms when new techno-logy develops and the cost structures of all firms decline. What do we expect will happen over time to an industry and to its level of concentration where that improvement in technology occurs? Let us further assume that the cost curve is a 'U'-shaped curve. Furthermore, suppose that what we have is an industry that is competitive and this new best technology is available to all firms. Thus the price charged by any one existing firm only represents aver-age costs of production. Firms are only making a normal profit. Assume that that is true of all firms in the industry. We can show this in Figure 5.2. The demand curve is the market demand curve. One representative firm is shown with its cost curve, $LRAC_1$. Now consider the price being charged by this firm. Remember it's a competitive industry, so price will reflect long-run average cost. The price is thus given at the bottom of the average cost curve and this firm will produce q_1 output. The market quantity demanded at P_1 is Q_1. So we know how concentrated the industry is. Each firm will produce q_1 output, so if Q_1 is, say, 100 units a month and q_1 is 10 units a month, then there will be 10 firms in the industry. In general the number of firms is given as Q_1/q_1, or Q_1/qmes.

So the degree of concentration in this market is determined by the cost struc-ture. Now suppose technology improves and firms find that as a result cost structures decline. For simplicity we make the assumption that this techno-logy is immediately available to all firms, so that all firms experience the same fall in the cost structure. Whether this increases concentration depends upon the way in which the technological change affects the cost curve.

Technology *could* drive the cost curve down so that minimum efficient scale is at the same level of output as before. If that is true, the level of con-centration will actually decline, even though minimum efficient scale has not altered. We show this in Figure 5.2. Concentration will decline because as prices come down in response to the declining cost structure (remember this is a competitive industry), the quantity demanded in the marketplace will rise so that output will now be higher than it was before. Thus each firm's output,

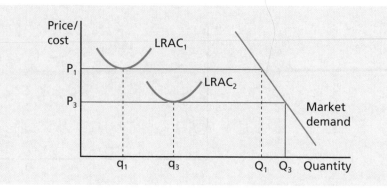

Figure 5.3 Technological change and effects on concentration (2)

as a proportion of the market, has actually been reduced. Output has risen from Q_1 to Q_2 but q_1 stays the same. Q_2/qmes is greater than Q_1/qmes. There will be more firms in the market.

It is distinctly possible, however, that the technological change will not result in the cost structure falling in such a way that minimum efficient scale stays the same. It may well result in MES being at a larger level of output than before. Will that not result in an increase in concentration? Consider Figure 5.3.

This time technological improvement drives the cost curve of each firm down from $LRAC_1$ to $LRAC_2$. The minimum average cost now faced by each firm as a result of improved technology is not q_1 but q_3. Would not that suggest an increase in concentration, as each of the existing firms grows? To stay at the same level of output as before would mean failing to take advantage of all the economies of scale. However, it might still not increase industrial concentration. The lower costs will drive prices down and at this lower price, market quantity demanded will increase from Q_1 to Q_3. To see whether there is now a more concentrated industrial structure we need to look at the relationship between q_1 and Q_1, and compare it with the relationship of q_3 to Q_3. This might indicate that concentration is higher, lower or the same as before the technological change. So, if there is a decline in the cost structure and minimum efficient scale is at a higher level of output, it won't necessarily increase concentration if market quantity demanded increases considerably.

What determines whether market quantity demanded would increase considerably is to be found in the market elasticity of demand. If demand is highly elastic, the lower price will sharply increase the quantity that consumers wish to buy, making it less likely that concentration will increase. So, to summarise, if technology improves, and drives the cost structure down to the right, so that minimum efficient scale is at a higher level of output, it may or may not result in an increase in concentration. Whether it does or not will depend critically upon the elasticity of demand for the product in the industry. Remember that we assumed new technology to be quickly diffused within an industry. The changes that we have been describing may well take many years. They are long-run changes to the structure of industry.

Even allowing for adjustments over time, evidence suggests that industrial structures do not always conform very well to what we have suggested above. We now consider briefly a few other factors that complicate the relationship between industry output and firm size.

BOX 5.1 Economies of scale in housebuilding

MES changes over time. Sometimes it is because technology changes. Sometimes it is because of government policy. Management may be slow to react to changes in the market.

A planned merger between two of the [housebuilding] sector's largest groups has triggered a bout of takeover activity in an industry previously regarded by investors as fragmented and dull.

Consolidation is driven by the trend towards 'brownfield' development and the greater opportunities for economies of scale. But it is being hastened by the passing of a generation of regionally based entrepreneurs who have, until recently, guarded the independence of their family companies.

Britain has more than 25 housebuilders listed on the stock market and an even larger number of medium-sized private companies. Together they build 150,000 homes a year.

The surge in corporate activity began when Bryant and Beazer agreed a merger to create Domus, which would have had a combined valuation of £760m. Last week Taylor Woodrow, a company that started life as a housebuilder in the 1920s but evolved into a general contractor, made a £530m bid for Bryant and Persimmon announced plans to acquire Beazer, currently valued at £513m.

In spite of the buoyancy of the UK housing market, housebuilders have been out of favour with the City for several years. Investors and analysts have memories of the boom and bust years of the 1980s and early 1990s, when the companies financed ambitious land purchases only to find their balance sheets under pressure when recession struck.

Apart from their doubts about the ability of managements, the City's main complaint is that there are just too many small companies.

But if the City was wary, the industry was equally suspicious about institutions' desire for consolidation.

So why the change in attitude? The prospect of losing out as the industry consolidates around it is undoubtedly a factor in the 'me too' bids from Taylor Woodrow and Persimmon.

But the merger activity goes deeper than that. First, there has been a dawning realisation that the industry's conventional wisdom – that there are no benefits in size – no longer applies.

The consensus used to be that housebuilding was a matter of knowing your local market so you could buy the right patch of land and put on it the homes that would match local aspirations. For this reason, the larger housebuilders operated decentralised regions, each building about 500 properties a year.

Heavy materials such as bricks and window frames were also purchased locally, to keep transport costs down.

But government policies aimed at promoting the use of reclaimed 'brownfield' land and revitalising the inner cities have transformed the economics of the industry. Instead of erecting detached, 'executive' homes on farmland on the edge of town, housebuilders need to be able to manage large, often difficult sites including shops, offices and restaurants as well as homes.

The emphasis on city centre sites, many involving apartments rather than single homes, has also changed the industry's financing requirements. Once, a housebuilder would sell the first few homes in a development to finance construction of the later houses. But an apartment complex must be completed in its entirety before the first owners will be willing to move in. More capital is tied up, which requires larger companies with bigger financial resources.

All of this is happening at the same time as a changing of the guard in the industry, as the founders or descendants of the founders of housebuilding companies retire.

The independent streak of these men, who often built their companies from modest beginnings, has held up consolidation of the industry.

With three deals mooted in recent weeks, the era of self-made entrepreneurs may be drawing to a close. A sceptical City is waiting to see whether a consolidated, professionally managed and nationally organised industry will emerge in its place.

Source: Financial Times, 19 January 2001 **FT**

- There may not be a common technology. One company may have a patent right on a particular process. Its MES may be at a larger level of output or its cost structure may be lower, or both.
- A firm may have lower costs through having moved down the learning curve in a way that we described in Chapter 4.
- There may be significant forecasting errors by firms such that investment decisions have been sub-optimal. There may therefore be more firms in the industry than is optimal or each firm may be too large. It has been calculated, for example, that at the beginning of 2001 capacity in world car production was 20% more than the size of the market.

B2B commerce and production costs

One example of the change in costs brought about by technological change is B2B commerce. This is business-to-business transactions that take place via the Internet. Huge cost decreases are made possible, especially in the purchase of inputs. The only software now needed for a firm to run the necessary applications making this possible is a web browser. Large companies may be buying inputs from many thousands of suppliers. The computerisation of purchases and the ability to check the best deal easily makes possible considerable savings. For example, Brookes and Wahhaj (2001) quote, *inter alia*, the case of BT. BT estimates that the average cost of processing a transaction will fall from $80 to $8. Furthermore, the direct savings on the cost of goods and services bought will amount to $1 for every $9 spent. All this moves cost curves downwards substantially. What is as yet unclear is what B2B will do to the industrial structure. Some believe that the removal of barriers to trade and the great improvement in information will make for a world closer to the perfectly competitive model. Others believe that it is large firms whose costs will fall most dramatically so that MES is at a higher level of output. Thus although costs fall, it will move LRAC downwards to the right. As we have seen, this may or may not make for a more competitive structure of industry.

Economies of scope and the industrial structure

We now look at a related, but rather different concept from economies of scale and see how that might also have an effect upon the structure of industry. This idea is known as economies of scope. We have been assuming that each of the firms we have been looking at is a single product producer. In reality most firms produce a range of products. There is evidence that in some industries, the range of products that a firm produces will also enable it to get economies. So we can say that for any given level of output of a product, if the firm engages in producing more products, it is possible that it will find that it will be producing at less cost than other firms who are producing fewer products. The gain in economies is not by producing more output; the gain is by producing more products. Why might we expect such a firm to gain some advantages in its costs? There are a number of possibilities, but there are perhaps two that are of particular importance.

The first one is cost complementarity. Sometimes the cost of one product is directly related to the cost of producing another product. A common example might be where a firm produces some output and there is a by-product of that production process that is itself valuable. So, for example, in oil refining some of the by-products are themselves useful for producing other products such as detergents. Now because the production of one product gives the by-product of a second product that is useful, the marginal cost of producing that second product can be quite low.

Another reason why firms will sometimes gain economies of scope is that once they have set up their capital equipment to produce some output, they can produce a range of products using that same equipment because the range of products requires some resources that are similar. So, for example, many car plants are very large. Once the plant is set up a firm can have cost savings by producing a range of vehicles from that one assembly plant. So by producing a range of products it gets cost savings.

We can express the idea formally in the following formula:

$$S = \frac{C(Q_1) + C(Q_2) - C(Q_1, Q_2)}{C(Q_1, Q_2)}$$

C = costs, Q = output and S is the percentage cost reduction through joint production. Focus first of all upon costs, if products are made separately. CQ_1 is the cost of producing one particular good, good 1. CQ_2 is the cost of producing another, different good, good 2. If we add those two we have the costs of producing the goods separately. But now if they are produced jointly, that would give $C(Q_1, Q_2)$. If there are economies of scope available, CQ_1 plus CQ_2 is greater than $C(Q_1, Q_2)$. Now we can calculate the extent to which we get economies of scope. We take CQ_1 plus CQ_2 minus $C(Q_1, Q_2)$. If we then divide that by the costs of producing the products jointly, we get the percentage cost reduction through joint production.

Of course, it is possible that in some industries there will be no advantages whatever, no economies of scope, but if there are some economies of scope then we would expect firms, *ceteris paribus*, to take advantage of those economies and to become multi-product producers.

Some attempts have been made to produce figures for the extent of scope economies in industry. For example, see Table 5.1. These refer to the percentage increase in average costs if firms in this industry only produce half the number of models that they are at present producing. Take motor vehicles. If a manufacturer producing a range of models decided to produce only half that number of models *but still produce the same level of output of each of the models*, they would find that their average costs would be 8% higher. Notice, though, that not all industries have the advantage of economies of scope. Machine tools have very little, cement, lime and plaster no economies of scope whatsoever.

Table 5.1 Estimates of economies of scope

Activity	E of S*
Motor vehicles	8
Pharmaceuticals	5
Machine tools	1
Cement, lime and plaster	0

* % ↑ in average costs with half the number of models
Adapted from *European Economy* (1988)

Economies of scope in publishing

Researchers have not done major studies into many industries. One industry where this has been tried is in publishing, where the attempt was made to find out to what extent there were economies of scope by producing a larger number of journals rather than just one journal. Remember, in order to be able to do this we must know how much of an advantage there is to producing more journals but with a given size of circulation and a given journal size. We are interested in the effect on firms' costs in changing the number of titles, not the number of one particular journal produced. To increase the number of copies of a given journal creates economies of scale.

The following figures come from the work of Baumol and Braunstein (1977). For this industry an equation was produced which we can examine in order to see what it tells us about the extent of economies of scope. This is information from US non-profit-making publications. The equation was:

$$\log TC = -0.735 + 0.171 Ds + 0.588 \log C$$
$$+ 0.0793 \log P - 0.062 \log J$$

where $\log TC$ is the log of total costs. Ds is a variable to isolate scientific from non-scientific journals. C is the circulation of any individual journal. P is the number of pages in each journal. Now comes the term that we are most interested in. J is the number of journals produced. The negative sign says that when other factors are held constant, total cost will fall as the number of journals published rises.

We can use the above to calculate the extent to which costs fall as a firm produces more titles. We can do that quite simply because we know the value of each term in the equation. Focus on the term $-0.062 \log J$. We can interpret this in the following way. If a firm produced 10 journals rather than just one, we can work out the extent to which it would save, that is, the extent to which it would get economies of scope. $10^{-0.062}$ gives us 0.87. So for any given level of page size etc., if a firm produced 10 different journals its total costs would be only 87% of the costs of the firm that produced only one. We can work out the equivalent figure for any number. Suppose, instead of producing just one journal it produced 30. Then we have $30^{-0.062}$ which gives us

0.81. That is to say, a firm producing 30 journals would have only 81% of the costs of a firm producing just one journal. Check for yourself that a firm producing 50 different journals would have only 78% of the costs of a firm producing just one journal.

So in some industries there are economies of scope to be gained. What effect does that have on the industrial structure? First, we would expect firms to be larger where there are economies of scope to be made. It makes sense for firms to produce a wide range of products. So we would also expect firms to be more diversified. The question of diversification is something we will return to in a later chapter.

We may also find that economies of scope also result in more concentration in industry. Often the economies of scope that are available are available provided that the different models that are produced are fairly closely related. Take motor vehicles as an example. If we find that there are significant economies of scope in being able to produce a large number of different models, one firm will produce a larger proportion of all the cars in the market. So if economies of scope are fairly specific to a narrow range of products, then economies of scope will produce a more concentrated industrial structure.

Economies of scale are quite important for individual firms' cost structures in some industries but we can see also that economies of scope can be significant in influencing the industrial structure as well.

Economies of scope and core competencies

We have already discussed in previous chapters that businesses may gain a competitive advantage via its architecture. This firm-specific architecture is sometimes referred to as a firm's *core competencies*. In some industries they can be closely linked to economies of scope. In industries of rapid technological change a firm may acquire expertise in computer design, data communications and related technologies. It may even produce products in these areas that are not particularly profitable. This may be a rational strategy in that it acquires core competencies that will give it an advantage in products yet to be produced or even thought of. These core competencies can be thought of as a kind of economy of scope in that they relate to the reduced costs of being in a range of products because of the skills the firm has acquired. It is not a measurable economy of scope, however, since some of the products to which we are referring have yet to be produced.

Stochastic factors

We have looked so far at three important determinants of the industrial structure, economies of scale, technological change and economies of scope. We might call them deterministic factors. We now consider a *stochastic* factor, that is, a random chance process.

Some economists have argued that over time we can have increases in concentration that will arise for no reason other than sheer luck. One of the first people to examine this phenomenon was Gibrat. His formulation of the idea is known as Gibrat's Law or the Law of Proportionate Effect. He showed that for any given time period the chance that a firm will grow by a given percentage is independent of its absolute size. One economist who tried to illustrate a form of this process was Scherer (1980). He looked at a period of the US economy when companies were, on average, growing by 6%. But not all companies were growing at that rate. Some were doing very well, some were doing less well. He worked out the standard deviation of growth over that period of time and he found that it came to 16%. Taking those numbers, an average growth rate of 6% but a standard deviation of 16%, he set out to find out what would happen to concentration over time. He started with a very unconcentrated structure and supposed that the variation in firm growth was a matter of random chance.

He began with an assumed industrial structure such that 50 firms each had 2% of the market, so the CR4 is 8%. Suppose that in the next year those firms grow by an average of 6%. Some grow faster, some grow more slowly and the standard deviation of growth rate is 16%. Imagine now that the same thing happens in year 2. Some firms, who were lucky last time, may be lucky again. Some firms who were lucky last time may not be so lucky this time. Suppose we get a computer to attach randomly a growth rate to all these firms averaging 6% with a standard deviation of 16%, what would happen to the industrial structure over time? The computer attaches a growth rate randomly. There is nothing here whereby a firm is growing because of its wisdom, its cleverness, its superior techniques, or its lower costs. Whether it grows a great deal or not is purely chance consideration.

We can see Scherer's results in Table 5.2. In year 1 we start off with a CR4 of 8. Within 20 years the top four firms have now got 19.5% of the market. Why? Because some firms just keep getting lucky. Within 40 years the top four firms have gone to 29.3%, and within 140 years the top four firms have got 41.3% of the market. This is a random chance stochastic growth process.

Scherer repeated the process many times. Every time he did it he found that he got the same pattern. The rate of increase in concentration varied from

Table 5.2 A stochastic growth process model

CR4 at year:	1	20	40	60	80	100	120	140
Run 1	8.0	19.5	29.3	36.3	40.7	44.9	38.8	41.3
Average	8.0	20.4	27.0	33.8	42.1	46.7	52.9	57.4

Adapted from Scherer (1980)

time to time but every time he found the same pattern where concentration increased relatively rapidly and then relatively slowly towards the end. Table 5.2 gives an average of all the runs that he tried. If we average out all the runs that he did, by the time he had got to 140 years, on average the top four firms had finished up with 57.4% of the market.

Now that, of course, is only one particular model. Those results came by using a 6% growth rate and a standard deviation of 16%, taken from the US stock market for a particular period. By varying our assumption we could have produced a different set of results. Let us try another stochastic model with different assumptions.

Imagine this time another very unconcentrated industry. There are a very large number of firms and each of these firms produces £100 worth of output. Now imagine that in the coming period, half of these firms are lucky, and they get to grow by 10%. So half of the firms in the industry now have an output of £110 but the other half of the firms were not lucky. By assumption they did not grow, so they are still only producing £100 worth of output. Suppose the same process takes place in the second year. That is to say, half the firms get to grow by 10% and half do not. Then of the firms that grew by 10% last time, half of them will be lucky again. So half of those firms will now have £121 worth of output but half of the firms that were lucky last time won't be lucky this time, so they will still have £110 worth of output. Focus on those that were unlucky in the first period. Half of them will be lucky this time and they will grow to £110, the other half who were unlucky last time will be unlucky again and they will still be at £100. Notice that we have increases in concentration over time. The largest firms have a greater market share. But notice also that we have more class sizes. Originally every firm was at 100; at the end of the first year we had two class sizes, some at 110, some at 100. At the third year, we've got three class sizes, some at 121, many at 110 and some at 100. Indeed, for every year that passes there is an additional class size and greater concentration.

Many economies in Europe have seen many markets grow rapidly in concentration over a period of time, although the growth in concentration has slowed down in the past 20 years. That is exactly what the Scherer model predicts. We also have an economy where the number of class sizes of firms in an industry tends to vary very considerably. This is what the second stochastic model predicts, not only more concentration but also more size classes. Few economists believe that one can explain the industrial structure of an economy entirely by random stochastic processes. But it is an interesting idea and it may be the case that luck does play its part in determining the structure of industry.

One study that tends to give some support to these ideas was by Davies and Lyons (1982). They found evidence that deterministic factors are the most important in explaining the industrial structure changes until firms reach MES. Thereafter, random stochastic effects are important for explaining firm growth.

We have examined a number of features that contribute to our understanding of the industrial structure. Economies of scale can have a significant and maybe decisive influence on the structure of industry. Economies of scope can affect the concentration of an industry and also the degree of diversification. Technological change is also important. Stochastic factors may also have their part to play in helping to determine the industrial structure. Finally, remember that the architecture of firms can be decisive in explaining why cost structures can vary between firms in the same industry. This can also influence the structure of industry.

The structure of industry and technological change

In the last part of this chapter we return to the question of innovation and technical change. Earlier we considered how such change could induce change in the industrial structure. Now we consider the possibility that the rate of technical change is itself a function of the structure of industry.

In theory the incentive to innovate and drive down costs is greater in competition than in monopoly. To see why we consider Figure 5.4. Again we assume that MC = AC. Before a technological improvement the monopoly output and price will be Q_1 and P_1. Q_1 is where MC = MR but for simplicity MR is not drawn. A competitive structure would give Q_2 as the output since MC = D, and therefore a price of P_2. Suppose now that a firm innovates and reduces costs to MC' = AC'. A monopolist would gain approximately area B. To simplify, we assume that its output will not change, although in Figure 3.5 we showed that it would increase slightly. The competitive firm, however, would gain much more. In terms of the diagram it would be approximately area B + C. This is because it will move from being a competitive firm making a normal profit to being a monopolist with all the monopoly profit that entails. By setting a price just below P_2, no competitive firm would be left in

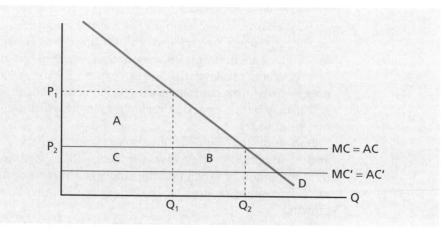

Figure 5.4 The effect of innovation on profit

the industry since for them price will be below their average cost. Of course, the competitive innovator will have to assume that other firms could not replicate its lower cost technology. If it can patent its innovation, this is a reasonable assumption. So in principle, competitive firms have more incentive to innovate.

Now recall what was said in Chapter 2 about the Austrian school. The ideal industrial structure is the one that maximises an economy's growth rate. This is not perfect competition but a monopolistic structure. This argument is most famously made by Schumpeter (1942), a leading exponent of the Austrian view. Only large-scale firms have the ability to invest in risky innovatory research. They have funds available from their greater profits. The argument is further strengthened if there are economies of scale in research activity that makes the balance of risk and reward more favourable. The large firm is probably better able to withstand losses if the investment in the research does not pay off. Furthermore, the pressure to continue to innovate is considerable. Monopoly profits are always under threat. The successful firm is forced to stay ahead of the game. That pressure comes from:

> competition from the new commodity, the new technology, the new source of supply, the new type of organisation . . . competition which strikes not at the margin of the profits and output of existing firms but at their very foundations and lives. (Schumpeter, 1942, p. 84)

In the Austrian view, then, the most likely innovators are the large, monopolistic firms.

The argument that large monopolistic firms innovate because of the resources available from past profits is in itself not convincing. A Chicago school belief is that markets are efficient. This includes capital markets. If this is so, it does not matter that the competitive firm making only normal profit in the long run has no spare funds. It can borrow from the market, for example a venture capitalist. However, the argument for an imperfect capital market, at least with respect to innovation, is strong. If a firm with an idea approaches the venture capitalist for funds it will probably have to reveal its idea and thus risk losing control of it. Refusing to disclose it may well result in the venture capitalist being unwilling to commit to the risk. There is therefore a strong possibility that the funds will not be lent. The innovator is unlikely to reveal the innovation without a commitment to lend. The venture capitalist is unlikely to lend without first knowing the details of the innovation. So even if the incentive to innovation is greater with competitive firms, the ability to do so is greater with larger, monopolistic enterprises.

Recognition of the risk of investment in innovation leads us to another conclusion. Small gradual improvements are more likely to be made by incumbent firms but drastic innovation is more likely to be made by potential entrants. An illustration will make clear why this is so. Suppose a side is three goals down in a Cup Final with five minutes to play. The manager may well risk making substitutes, sending on attackers for defenders. It increases the risk of conceding more goals but losing by one goal is essentially the same as losing by five. A higher risk strategy makes sense. Similarly, a firm with too high a cost structure to compete with an established firm may find that small improvements in its costs may still leave it uncompetitive. A high risk strategy of looking for fundamental cost changes may well be chosen. At least this gives some chance of success.

It is now apparent that there is some case for a system of patent laws and indeed copyright laws also. These essentially grant monopoly rights to the owner of the innovation. Monopoly power is allocatively inefficient. However, without such laws there is less incentive to innovate. The innovation can often be successfully copied, with other firms acting as free-riders on the invention.

There is also a dilemma for policy makers over whether to allow companies to cooperate on research and development work by establishing strategic alliances. We shall examine such alliances in Chapter 8.

Suffice it to say for now that public policy in the area of research activity is fraught with difficulty. The correct choice for the public policy maker is far from clear. This applies to any research and development activity, including, as we shall see, cooperation between firms.

Evidence on the Schumpeter hypothesis

Many attempts have been made to test empirically the ideas of Schumpeter, although he did not attempt to test them himself. The results are not uniform but on balance they do not give strong support to his theories. We give just two pieces of evidence.

Geroski (1994) looked at the period 1945–83 in the UK. He sought to see whether innovative output was related to each of a whole series of variables. These include seller concentration of the industries concerned by CR5, the change in concentration over the period, the degree of competition from imports, the price–cost margin, the ease of entry into the industry and the rate of industry growth. Most of the evidence was not statistically significant but there was a significant inverse relationship between innovative output and seller concentration. So he found no support for the Schumpeter hypothesis.

One industry where research and development activity is very high is that of pharmaceuticals. Alexander *et al.* (1995) researched this sector via 26 international firms between 1987 and 1989. One variable tested was a dummy variable to control for differences in government regulatory control in the USA as opposed to other countries. Two conclusions are worthy of comment. First, they found that in this sector there was a statistically significant positive relationship between research and development output and firm size. Secondly, the dummy variable was also significant, showing that in the USA firms were more productive with respect to innovations owing to a more favourable regulatory climate.

Conclusion

We can explain to a large extent the variations in seller concentration in industry. These include economies of scale, economies of scope, changes in technology, market imperfections and stochastic factors. We have argued in a previous chapter that individual firm architecture can also be important. Technological change, however, is not simply given. It comes from the innovatory effort of firms. There are arguments for saying that competitive firms have more incentive to innovate. The alternative, Schumpeterian hypothesis that large monopolistic firms are the engine for growth is not well supported empirically.

KEY RESULTS

1 Concentration is partly determined by the size of MES in relation to industry output.

2 Technological change may change the degree of concentration through its effect on cost structures.

3 Economies of scope may have an effect on industry concentration.

4 Some economists believe that random stochastic processes play a part in determining the structure of industry.

5 Competitive firms have an incentive to innovate but larger, monopolistic firms may be better placed to do so.

Questions

1* Schumpeter's view was that perfect competition had no claim to being an ideal structure for an economy. Why did he think so? Would you agree?

2* 'The best of all monopoly profits is a quiet life.' Are there other reasons for thinking that monopoly power results in less research and development activity? What does this mean? Would Schumpeter agree? Why or why not?

3* What kinds of industry would most likely exhibit economies of scope? Why might the presence of such economies encourage innovation among firms in that industry?

4 Refer to Box 5.1. Why are house builders merging? To what extent is the process explained by scale economies? What effect will the process have on a) industrial concentration and b) house prices?

5 Refer to Box 5.2. Why might the market for innovation funds be less than perfect? Would the Chicago school accept this view?

* *Help available at http://www.e-econ.co.uk*

BOX 5.2 The role of venture capitalism in innovation
What is the link between innovation and the provision of finance?

In the heat of last year's internet mania, European corporations appeared to be falling over each other to announce some kind of venture or incubation initiative. And no wonder, seeing what it did – temporarily – for the share price.

Now the flood of new funds has slowed or halted and a fairly extensive shake-out is expected as some imprudent investments founder.

So it may come as a surprise to find management consultancy Booz-Allen & Hamilton urging, in the latest issue of Strategy+Business, that 'every' European chief executive should explore ways of developing a corporate venturing initiative. Surely the period when everyone thought they could be a venture capitalist – and, yes, Booz-Allen has an incubator – is over?

Rob Schuyt, a Booz-Allen partner based in Amsterdam, maintains that corporate venturing, if done properly, remains an effective way for companies to refine the innovation and commercialisation process – an area in which European businesses famously lag behind their US counterparts. 'Too many top managers in Europe take the old-fashioned view that research and development is "our knowledge" and would rather leave it on the shelf than commercialise it.'

This view is especially pertinent given the convergence of previously discrete areas – voice and data communications, computing and telephony, mobile telephony and financial services – which demands that businesses can operate outside their normal fields.

The research, which largely bases its conclusions on best practice from the US, identifies three distinct reasons for corporate venturing: access to technology; building on research and development; and driving demand for core products. A number of structures should be considered by corporate venturers, depending on the degree of commitment envisaged. They can, for instance, invite a venture capitalist to run an operation on their behalf – a strategy adopted by Adobe Systems, the software company, and Procter & Gamble, the consumer products group. Causing 'minimum disruption to core operations', this is 'an attractive entry proposition', the researchers found.

Alternatively, companies – Shell, the oil company, for instance – can act as business incubators, using corporate venturing as a tool to promote innovation. This suits companies with considerable research and development resources, as well as those concerned with softer issues such as staff retention.

Building an in-house investment team – as Cisco, the networking technology company, and Intel, the computer chipmaker, have done – represents the biggest commitment. It can make sense when access to new technologies and or strategic defence is the priority.

Getting the structure right is crucial, Booz-Allen finds. 'Successful units steer clear of the commonly used functional heads and have their investment managers report directly to the CEO or to a key business unit head.'

All sorts of tensions are bound to arise, the authors acknowledge, because of the innately different characteristics of large companies and start-ups. Compensation is among the most contentious issues, particularly in Europe.

A really successful corporate venturing operation can in time be a significant contributor to group earnings. But on a quarterly basis, private equity earnings are notoriously volatile. In periods of weak public stock markets, such as now, there is a lot of extra explaining to do to shareholders. As Mr Schuyt says: 'That is why setting up a corporate venturing unit purely for financial reasons is probably extremely dangerous. There have to be more strategic reasons.'

And Booz-Allen's own incubator? Innovate@ was launched last October in alliance with Lehman Brothers, to provide incubation services for clients' spin-outs as well as to help staff germinate their own ideas. It has made about $40m (£27m) of investments – either in cash or in consulting fees saved. But not all since October. 'That was more a case of doing and then announcing,' says Mr Schuyt. 'It was formalising something we had been doing for a while.'

Source: Financial Times, 1 February 2001

6 Merger behaviour

The battle is well and truly on if it wasn't on before and it certainly was.

MURRAY WALKER

One feature of the changing business environment is that of mergers and takeovers. We consider the motives of management engaging in this activity.

OBJECTIVES

After reading this chapter you should be able to:

- Distinguish different kinds of mergers.
- Understand the major motives for horizontal merger activity.
- Understand the Marris model of firm growth.
- Understand the main motives for diversified merger activity.
- Assess the benefits to firms and society of horizontal and diversified mergers.

Introduction

A notable feature of the industrial landscape is the growth of large firms. Firms may grow either internally or externally. Internal growth occurs when firms increase the nation's productive capacity through investment in new capital. External growth takes place when firms take over existing capital stock via the transfer of its ownership. It is external growth that is one of the central features of this and the next two chapters.

Types of mergers

Traditionally economists have distinguished three kinds of merger. The first is called horizontal integration, the second is diversification, and the third is vertical integration. We explain briefly the meaning of these terms.

Horizontal integration

Suppose we have a paper company, A, and another paper company, B. If these two companies that make the same product join together and form a new company, C, we refer to that as a horizontal merger: 'horizontal' because it is the same industry that these two companies are engaged in; 'merger' because the two companies that have come together form a new company. If A takes over the assets of B, so that B disappears and company A still exists but in larger form, we would refer to that as a takeover. In this chapter we shall make little of the distinction between takeovers and mergers since the economic effects are much the same.

Diversification

This occurs where two companies that produce different products come together, for example the paper producer takes over an insurance company. There is a difficult question of definition here. How different do the products have to be? If a crisp manufacturer acquires a biscuit maker, is that diversification because they are different products or horizontal integration because they are both snack-food producers? We shall return to this problem later.

Vertical integration

Vertical integration refers to a situation in which two companies come together, who are not producing the same product but who are at different stages of the same production process. If paper-maker A buys sawmill company C, they are both in the same industry, but they are at different stages of production. This is vertical integration. We call it backwards vertical integration, because the paper maker has taken over a company at the earlier stage in the production process. Firms that are nearer to the raw material production are said to be *upstream*.

Vertical integration can also be forwards, where the company chooses to take over another company that is closer to its market. If paper-maker A has taken over retailer D, this is forwards vertical integration. Firms nearer to the final consumer are said to be *downstream*.

In this chapter we focus on *horizontal* and *diversified* mergers. Vertical relationships are the subject of the next chapter.

Motives for merger activity

Why do companies engage in this kind of activity? The motives we consider first are largely those that explain horizontal integration, but as you will see, some of these explanations are valid for any kind of merger. So what reasons can we offer which are either for horizontal or for any mergers?

Market dominance

One advantage to a firm in merging or taking over another company is clearly to raise its share of the market. The larger the share of the market, the more possibility it has of raising price above cost. We have already seen that a perfectly competitive industry just makes a normal profit, whereas a firm with monopoly power is much more likely to be able to raise the price above marginal cost in the short run and so exploit consumers. A larger market share can also make it more difficult for new firms to enter. To raise entry barriers strengthens a firm's position, enabling it to make greater profits in the long run.

Mergers as a defence mechanism

One of the things which has interested economists for some time is that mergers often take place in waves. Merger activity is always taking place, but sometimes at a relatively low level. Then for some reason there is a spate of activity and mergers take place at a rapidly increased rate. This will often last for a year or two and then will go back to a period where merger activity continues, but at nothing like the previous frenetic rate. One attempted explanation for this phenomenon is that mergers take place during periods of high uncertainty. One of the things that companies hate is lack of knowledge about the future. When they invest they are looking for a return over many years. One thing that makes it difficult to know how successful the investment will be is that they have got to guess how well the product will sell over the coming years. If uncertainty is very high, there is a greater margin for error. So if there is any way in which a company can eliminate that uncertainty it will be keen to take it. Some have suggested that if we look at periods in the last 30 years, where we have had merger waves, they correspond to periods of high uncertainty. Such times might include a change of government, periods when there has been some uncertainty as to the adoption of a single currency, and the possibility of a coming recession. The argument is that mergers take place to reduce the uncertainty in the economic environment. To become bigger and stronger means greater control of markets. One of the problems of testing whether that is true or not, is that it is not easy to get an unambiguous measure of the degree of uncertainty that exists at any one time. It is also difficult to see why a profit-maximising firm would not wish to increase the control of its environment in other periods.

It is, however, relatively easy to explain the phenomenon of merger waves within any one industry. Suppose two firms in a concentrated market merge. They may well reduce output and raise price as a means of exploiting their power. This gives an opportunity for the other firms in the market to increase their profits, either by raising their price or by increasing their output. They may be better able to exploit the opportunity if they also merge. Hence one merger creates others. This, of course, is an explanation of merger waves only within a given industry.

Economies of scale

The third motive, which we have already examined, is economies of scale. Mergers will sometimes take place in order to rationalise production. This may lead to less output and higher prices but it may mean the same level of output but with fewer inputs. It could also mean increased output for proportionately fewer inputs. Alternatively expressed, firms can move down their long-run average cost curve where the enlarged company will have lower unit costs. Sometimes companies do not express their motives in these terms. For example, Angwin and Savill (1997) surveyed some top European executives about their European acquisition strategy. They found that a key benefit of takeover was the speed with which it allowed the build-up of 'critical mass'. So economies of scale constitute a motive for horizontal merger activity. It is this that can make government policy towards mergers so difficult. Sometimes economies of scale motives are mixed with market power considerations.

Sellers' motives

When takeovers occur it is not always the result of aggressive activity by the acquiring company. The smaller company is not always fighting off the predator. That certainly happens, but sometimes it is a friendly takeover, where the larger company institutes an approach to a smaller company to which the smaller company agrees. But often, the original approach comes from the smaller company. The smaller company wants to be taken over. Why should this happen? If it is a very small company it may be that it is a family business and a key family member dies. It then passes into the hands of the next generation who feel uncomfortable about running the business and they simply want to sell out. Sometimes they have to sell out because of death duties and inheritance taxes and simply cannot now afford to keep the business going. But even quite large businesses will often look for somebody else to take them over. If they are in a market where companies are getting larger and larger, they may feel that they are too small to survive, and that a takeover is inevitable. It is only a question of when it is going to happen. Then they may feel that the best approach for them is to come to a company with whom they feel more comfortable and suggest the takeover. This may seem preferable to waiting for a period of time and then find that they are being taken over by a company with which they do not want to be associated. So often it is the smaller company that initiates the original move. One example from recent years has been in the banking sector, where more and more merger activity has taken place. Some of the smaller companies, sometimes ex-building societies, have felt uncomfortable that they are too small and so they seek a larger partner. So there are aggressive takeovers which are against the wishes of the smaller company, but it is far from often the case, and many are initiated by the company that wishes to be taken over.

Taxation considerations

The next motive is a financial one. Sometimes a company finds that the government's tax laws are such that it actually pays them to engage in merger activity. Suppose there is a large company that finds a smaller company operating in a different market. The smaller company has £2 million worth of assets, but it also has liabilities of £1 million so that the net value of the company is £1 million. Actually it might be worth more than £1 million to the large firm. It may be able to use its profits to set the debts or losses against taxation. So by setting off the losses against taxation, the net cost of acquiring the company may actually be one that makes it attractive to purchase. Clearly the potential depends upon the particular nature of the tax laws. The evidence suggests that this is not a very powerful motive generally. For example, Berger and Ofek (1995) found that the tax saving would typically amount to only 0.1% of sales, too small to justify the costs of acquisition.

Stock market buoyancy

The next motive that has been suggested to explain why companies engage in merger activities relates to stock market prices. There is an argument that the more buoyant the stock market, the more likely takeover bids are. One way of acquiring companies is to offer cash. But an alternative way to do it is to offer shares. Some have suggested that the buoyancy of the stock market helps to explain takeover activity in the following way. As share prices rise, it makes it easier for companies to acquire others by share offerings. Of itself this does not make sense. If an acquiring firm's share prices are rising, so are the share prices of the companies that may be taken over. We need some change in the *relative* prices of shares to make this possible. However, sometimes that does happen. For example, around the turn of the century there was a period in the UK where large companies' shares grew, on average, more quickly than those of smaller companies. That does make it possible that it is easier for a large company to acquire a small company. But this is not because stock market prices in general have risen, but because stock market prices of large companies have risen relative to small companies. Even this argument is unsatisfactory by itself, however. Presumably the reason why small companies' shares were falling was that their outlook had become less profitable. In that case they were less worthwhile acquiring. A profit-maximising decision to buy such companies has still not been found. What is required is an imperfect capital market. If the stock market value of a firm is less than the value of its assets, a motive for takeover exists. One interesting example of such a circumstance is a period when technological change is great. This makes the valuation of a company particularly difficult since future profitability is so difficult to gauge. The increased potential for value discrepancy might well enhance takeovers. There is some evidence for this theory from the work of Gort (1969) on mergers in the US economy. So under certain circumstances stock market buoyancy may help to explain takeover activity.

Non-profit-maximising behaviour: the principal–agent problem

Finally, we consider motives for merger that are not driven solely by profit. It may be that sometimes merger activity does not take place as a result of companies trying to increase their profitability. Perhaps companies are not profit maximising. Because they are not profit maximising they may be willing to buy up companies, even though they do not think that it is justified in terms of the enhanced profit that the merger activity will allow. We explore this more later but we introduce this concept now.

It was once the case that businesses were generally small and the owner of the business was also the one who ran the business. The owner's income depended upon the level of profits. Under these circumstances the owner would be a profit maximiser, because income depends upon the profits made. Now very large firms dominate the economy and the owners are not the managers. The owners of large firms are those who have shares in the company. They, however, have no day-to-day control over its activities. The company is managed by a professional group of managers. This is one example of the principal–agent problem. A principal appoints an agent to carry out instructions. But the agent may choose not to follow fully the principal's instructions if by doing so it is not in his/her own interests. In this case the principal is the shareholder and the agent the professional manager. There is a divorce here of ownership from control. It is only one more step now to argue that the managers may find that their best interests are not served by maximising the profits of the company and maximising the value to the shareholder. There is an argument that suggests, for example, that income to a manager is more closely related to the size of the company than it is to the amount of profit that the company makes. If that is true, the pursuit of size may be followed even if it sacrifices profit.

Box 6.1 Does the longevity of companies matter?

Market economists support the 'creative destruction' of businesses. Not everyone is convinced and the doubters believe they have empirical evidence to support their views.

When Blue Circle, the UK cement maker, agreed this month to a takeover by Lafarge of France it waved goodbye to more than 100 years of British industrial history. Blue Circle, founded in 1900 as Associated Portland Cement Manufacturers, was one of only five surviving companies from the FT30, the UK's oldest equity index, set up in 1935.

Cement is a commodity business; price competition is fierce; the industry is consolidating; and Blue Circle was not going to be among the survivors. That is capitalism, goes the conventional wisdom. Blue Circle's takeover is an example of creative destruction. If companies are not strong enough to survive, let their shareholders get the best price for them and invest their capital where it can be more productive. That is how economies thrive, how new companies and technologies emerge and how new jobs are created.

Is that all there is to it? One of the most influential management authors of the 1990s thinks not. Arie de Geus spent 38 years at Royal Dutch/Shell, holding several senior posts, including head of group planning. To Mr de Geus, there is always something tragic about a company's end.

When companies disappear, bonds with employees, suppliers, customers and local communities are broken. The old industrial regions of the UK, France and the US bear the scars of the companies that have closed down. Even if many employees stay with a new owner something is lost.

Mr de Geus thought he knew where the fault lay: with the view that companies were merely generators of profits rather than communities of human beings.

The notion that shareholders should take precedence over everyone else involved in the company is damaging and out of date, Mr de Geus argues. It is a throwback to the time when capital was scarce.

'The move to extreme shareholder power is the remnant of a time when the supply of capital was the critical success factor in a business. Then, the provider of capital was quite rightly given critical power. But we're past that period. Capital is now a commodity. The companies that are coming to the top today have very little asset value. The assets that are provided by capital in a modern company play an ever decreasing role. Giving capital close to total power seems to be totally in contradiction to the times,' he says.

To advocates of shareholder value this might sound like the sort of flabby European thinking that comes from free visits to health spas and six weeks' annual leave – were it not for one thing. Two US academics, James Collins and Jerry Porras, studied 18 highly regarded and long-lasting companies and discovered that they adhered to many of Mr de Geus's principles; moreover, their shares had, over several decades, outperformed the market by huge margins.

Mr Collins and Mr Porras began in 1989 by asking 700 US chief executives to name the companies they most admired. That gave them their list of 18 companies, which they spent five years studying. The youngest companies, Wal-Mart and Sony (the only non-US group on the list), were founded in 1945. The oldest, Citicorp, was founded in 1812. The companies' average founding date was 1897. Others on the list included 3M, American Express, Ford, General Electric, Hewlett-Packard, IBM, Procter & Gamble and Walt Disney.

Mr Collins and Mr Porras discovered longevity was no guarantee of outstanding success. They drew up another list of 18 long-living companies, including Chase Manhattan, Colgate and Columbia, which were less admired by their peers.

They discovered that if on January 1 1926 you had invested $1 in a general stock market fund and reinvested all your dividends, your money would have grown to $415 by December 31 1990. A dollar invested in a fund of the 18 less admired companies would have generated $955. But $1 invested in their most admired companies would have grown to $6,356 – 15 times the performance of the general market.

What makes these admired companies what they are? In their book *Built to Last* Mr Porras and Mr Collins reach a conclusion similar to Mr de Geus's: the most successful companies have a purpose beyond making a profit. They sometimes act in ways that damage their short-term profits because they believe that to do otherwise would be to go against their business philosophies. But by living by strong guiding ethics they generate higher shareholder returns in the long run.

Source: *Financial Times*, 29 January 2001 **FT**

The Marris growth model

Here we develop the principal–agent problem in explaining why mergers may take place that are not part of a strategy of maximising profit. The model we use to illustrate this particular idea is the model of an Oxford economist by the name of Robin Marris (1964). A key part of the Marris model is the concept of the *valuation ratio* of a company.

We can value a company in two different ways. First of all, we can ask the accountants what they think the assets of the company are worth. This valuation is given in the company's accounts. But there is another way of defining the value of a company. We can look at the stock market valuation of it. In other words, we can discover from share prices what those who buy the shares think the company is worth. We know how many shares there are in the company, and we can find at any time the price that people are willing to pay to buy the shares. If we multiply one by the other, we get the valuation of the company in the view of the stock market at the present time. The valuation ratio is given as the stock market valuation of the firm divided by the book value of the assets.

The next step in the Marris argument is to consider the valuation ratio that shareholders want. It will, of course, be as high as possible. They want to maximise the valuation ratio, because the value of the shares of the company determines the worth of their financial assets. A shareholder is not just interested in the value of the shares, but also in the income that will be received in the coming years from the dividends that come from the ownership of the shares. This does not change the argument. What determines the stock market valuation of the company is the expected future value of the income. So the higher the future stream of income expected from the shares, the higher the valuation ratio. Therefore the shareholder wants managers to maximise the valuation ratio of the company.

Is that what the managers of the company want? According to Marris, they do appreciate a high valuation ratio. The higher the valuation ratio, the more they are protected from a takeover. If you are the manager of a company you will fear a takeover. This may lead to rationalisation in production or a different management structure. Your job may no longer be secure. What protects you from a takeover is a high valuation ratio. Suppose the book value of the assets is £1m and the value of your company as quoted on the stock market is £3 million. If someone wants to take over your company, they will to have to compensate the shareholders. They must pay at least £3 million to acquire the company. They will be reluctant to do that if the company's book value is only £1m. So the higher the valuation ratio, the higher the likelihood that the company will be protected from a takeover bid. There is some empirical support for this view. Kuehn (1975) examined in excess of 3500 companies listed on the UK stock market and concluded that a high valuation ratio was a significant deterrent to takeover. So everything we have suggested so far would indicate that the managers' and the shareholders' motives are one and the same. However, Marris says that the valuation ratio is only *part* of what the managers care about. They also want to see the company grow fast. Managers are interested in a rapid growth in the business, and are prepared to trade off a high growth rate against the valuation ratio. So whereas a shareholder is interested in just one thing – a high valuation ratio – the manager is interested in two things, the valuation ratio *and* the growth rate of the firm.

Look at Figure 6.1. The diagram represents the interests, not of the shareholders, but of the managers. The set of indifference curves shows the trade-off between the valuation ratio, v, and the growth rate of the firm, g. The management is prepared to accept a lower valuation ratio, in return for a higher growth rate. So around any one indifference curve, they are indifferent between any of the combinations of v and g represented by the curve. Each curve is convex to the origin. This is because the lower the valuation ratio, the

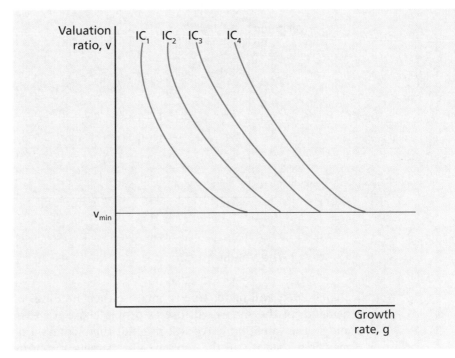

Figure 6.1 Management preferences in the Marris model

more reluctant the manager is to trade off a further increase in the growth rate for a further fall in the valuation ratio. Of course, management would always prefer a higher valuation ratio *and* a higher growth rate where possible. This is shown by the successively higher indifference curves. Management would always prefer to be on a higher indifference curve to a lower one, because the higher indifference curve gives a better combination of both valuation ratio and growth rate. Notice also the line v_{min}. There is a minimum valuation ratio that the management is assumed to be willing to tolerate. If the valuation ratio were to fall below this level, the manager fears that the takeover is more or less inevitable. Hence no increase in the growth rate can compensate for a fall in v below this level.

Next consider the relation between the actual growth rate of a company and the valuation ratio. If a company grows faster, what will happen to the valuation ratio of the company? Suppose we have a company that is not growing at all. That would suggest that there are probably investment opportunities that would be profitable, which would increase the valuation ratio of the company that the company is not taking. So if the company then begins to grow faster, taking on investment opportunities which are profitable, the valuation ratio will tend to rise. But there are only a limited number of investment opportunities that will add to the profitability of the company. To take on ever more investments means that the marginal return of the investment will fall. We can see the effect of this in Figure 6.2.

As the company moves from a low to a higher growth rate and takes on profitable investments, the valuation curve rises because profits will rise.

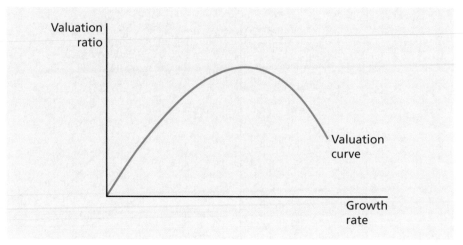

Figure 6.2 The valuation curve

Shareholders will be looking to increase their holdings of this company, the demand for the shares will rise as people chase the expected higher profits and so the valuation curve will rise. But there comes a point where management has used up all the profitable investment opportunities. If they try to grow any faster than this optimum amount, the valuation curve will fall. The higher growth rate will lead to a lower valuation ratio, because these extra projects are simply not profitable.

Now we put those two things together, the management's indifference curves and the valuation curve, and compare management preferences with what shareholders want. We do this in Figure 6.3.

From the valuation curve that we had before, a shareholder wants the company to grow at the rate g_1. At this rate the valuation ratio is maximised, at v_1, and shareholder wealth is maximised. This is *not* what the managers will choose. They will choose to be on the highest possible indifference curve within the constraint imposed by the valuation curve. So the spot on the valuation curve that puts management onto the highest indifference curve is at A, on curve IC_3. They can get onto that by picking g_2 as the growth rate and v_2 as the valuation ratio. Notice what that means. They will go for a higher growth rate than is ideal for a shareholder. They are prepared to trade off some of that valuation ratio in order to push up the growth rate beyond the level that shareholders would choose. So these managers want the company to grow faster than the shareholder optimum.

How does that relate to the question of merger activity? As we have seen, there is internal growth, where the company creates new assets, or external growth, where the firm acquires existing assets. Either of those two ways of growth involves making an investment decision as far as the company is concerned. As far as the nation is concerned they are rather different. In the first case, this is new investment for the economy, in the second case it is simply the transfer of existing assets, but as far as the company is concerned these are simply alternative ways of making investment decisions. Now imagine

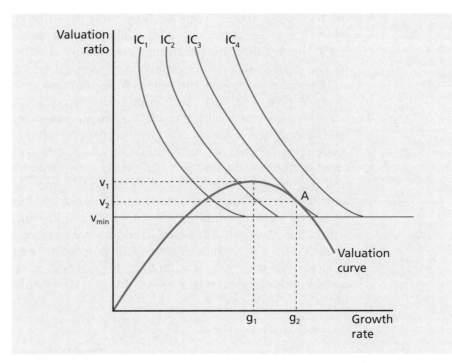

Figure 6.3 Management and shareholder preferences for growth

managers thinking of making a takeover bid. They work out the price that they will have to pay to acquire the assets. They look at the investment decision and come to the conclusion that it is probably not worthwhile in terms of the enhanced profits that are going to result. Therefore it is going to lower the valuation ratio. It is not in the shareholder interest. But each shareholder has little power over the company's management decisions. Management is prepared to make a bid because even though the valuation ratio is now going to be a little lower, they are prepared to trade that off for the higher growth rate that this entails. So there is more likely to be merger activity at the margin, and more likely that companies are going to make decisions about taking over other companies that are not particularly profitable, than the shareholder thinks is optimal. So Marris believes that growth is important to many managers and that there is a divorce of ownership from control, giving a limited amount of power in the hands of the shareholders. If this is so, the result may well be a higher growth rate of companies than is optimal. Some of this suboptimal growth will be via merger activity.

The efficiency of horizontal mergers

We have already seen that the Demsetz view of the world and that of others of the Chicago school is that markets work efficiently. So, if two companies want to merge, the presumption is that this would be privately and socially optimal. If these companies make significant profits as a result of the merger it will simply attract new firms into the industry and those profits over time will be eroded away. If the merger worsens profit performance, other more efficient firms will replace the inefficient merged company. A more traditional view would be to say that where a horizontal merger takes place there is potential benefit for consumers if it results in economies of scale and there are potential disadvantages if the effect is greater monopoly power. Then price is raised above marginal cost. So, mergers may or may not be socially efficient. Some societies like the USA and some European Union countries have a presumption that merger activity of a horizontal kind is probably bad for consumers and it is very difficult for companies to engage in merger activity at the horizontal level if both firms are of a substantial size. In the UK government attitudes are relatively more relaxed and the competition authorities will look at each case on its merits. They will attempt to look at advantages of economies of scale, the disadvantages of increased market power, and then make a decision on each merger individually. We explore government policy further in Chapter 13.

Diversification

So far we have focused on a number of motives for takeovers, which are either horizontal or alternatively could apply to any kind of motive. Now we focus on diversification. Why do companies diversify? Shortly we suggest a number of motives. First though, we think more precisely about what diversification means.

Classifying diversified activity

Diversification activity is commonly divided into three:

- *Product extension diversification*. This refers to diversification into a range of related products. These might be related on the demand side or related in terms of production.
- *Market extension diversification*. This is diversification in the sense that the same products will be sold but in different areas or countries.
- *Conglomerate diversification*. This refers to the diversification by a firm into products that are unrelated to the firm's previous interests.

Although the above distinction can be useful it is still essentially arbitrary. There is no obvious way of determining how related the products have to be to fall into the first category rather than the third. The second category could also be classified as horizontal integration.

Motives for diversification

Economies of scope

At any given level of output, if there are economies of scope available, a firm can produce other products more cheaply than another company which is not diversified. So economies of scope are one motive for diversification.

Notice, though, that generally economies of scope are only available at the plant level. There will be a need to integrate production in some way. So simply acquiring another company and then continuing to operate that company with its plants separately is not likely to create economies of scope. It will require the reorganisation of production in order to gain the economies of scope that may be available. Some estimates of the extent of economies of scope were given in Chapter 5.

Avoiding market dominance

The second motive may at first seem rather strange, but it might be significant in some cases. Diversification is a motive if a firm wants to avoid market dominance. It is true that market dominance enables companies to raise prices above costs. But market dominance will tend to attract the interest of the competition authorities of any particular country. Most countries have competition authorities that will not take much notice of firm growth until it shows signs of dominating particular markets. So if it is interested in growing but also in avoiding the attention of government anti-monopoly bodies, then a way of doing it may well be to grow into other markets sufficiently unrelated as to be regarded as diversifying rather than horizontally integrating.

Diversification from failure

A third motive is the response to failure within the existing market. If a single-line producer finds its market in decline, and the growth prospects in this market are minimal, then one way of solving the problem might be to diversify into other markets. Now if the reason for failure has been poor performance, it is likely that capital markets will refuse to provide funds to make this possible. But if the reason is a secular decline in demand, it may well be quite rational for capital markets to fund a movement into other markets that are growing relatively quickly. So a further motive for diversification would be in order to overcome the problems of decline in the existing market.

Excess capacity and transactions costs

A further motive for diversification is the excess capacity of some resources such as financial management. If there is excess capacity of such a resource, the marginal cost of taking on another firm to manage is small. If the skill of which there is excess capacity is not specific to one industry, then diversification is a rational strategy.

However, the argument as it stands is incomplete. One has to consider why it is better to use the spare resource by a process of diversification rather than simply sell it. In principle, the value of the resource on the open market should not be less than the value of the resource if used within the firm. A possible explanation for retaining the resource can be found in transactions costs. Perhaps the most obvious example is asset specificity. A management team is not just a collection of individuals. They may have skills as a team unique to the firm. Their worth to that firm may be greater than the sum of the parts sold on the open market. If the firm is to diversify one might expect it to do so coherently. That is, it would diversify into a closely related activity. How far would the process go? Montgomery and Wernerfelt (1997) use Tobin's q to give an answer. Tobin's q is the ratio of two numbers. The first is the stock market valuation of the firm, which should be the discounted value of the firm's expected profits. The second is the replacement value of the firm's assets. If the first number exceeds the second, q is greater than one. Then a firm should wish to invest. If q is less than one it should divest assets. If it expands by coherent diversification because q is greater than one, the act of diversification will cause q to fall towards unity as successively more marginal projects are taken on. They find that the evidence seems to support this view. Some support for this view is given in the study of Rondi *et al.* (1996) in their study of diversification in the EU. They reported that the most important reason for diversification was the exploitation of specific assets within the industry.

Spreading risk

There is one more motive that is most commonly quoted as an explanation for diversification. That is diversification to spread risk. If a firm is focused narrowly on just one or two product ranges and something goes wrong in those markets, perhaps a sharp and unexpected decline in demand, there are doubts about its survival. The law of large numbers will work for a company that is diversified into many different markets. One product's decline is less serious. So diversification becomes a motive in management minds for minimising the problem of a decline in any one market. To an economist, this does not make much sense for the shareholder. A shareholder may well be interested in spreading risk. Shareholders do not want to be in a position where they only hold one particular share, knowing that if that company fails, the value of their assets will decline sharply. Do they need, then, that the company spreads itself into a large number of markets in order to protect them from that problem? The answer is no. The shareholders can have their own diversification policy. If they are worried about the concentration of shares in one particular market, they can buy shares in other companies in order to diversify the portfolio and spread risk. So diversification to minimise risk may well have logic in it for the manager of the company. It has no particular logic for the shareholder.

Trends in diversified activity

As we noted earlier, merger activity often comes in waves. During such a wave in the 1960s the fashion was for conglomerate diversification. To a large extent this move was supported by the stock market. Subsequently, evidence began to emerge showing that such activity did not improve company performance. By the 1980s and 1990s there was a move towards the divestment of activities not related to the core of the business. Since conglomerate diversification had tended to worsen company performance, businesses tended to be worth less as a whole than in their component parts. Although diversification still takes place, it tends to be much more in product extension and in market extension rather than in conglomerate activity. Hence diversification strategy is now much more coherent.

The efficiency of diversified mergers

Do mergers of a diversified kind benefit consumers? Clearly some can do so. Where there are economies of scope to be gained then output can be produced using fewer resources at lower costs with all potential benefits to consumers that those lower costs bring. Are there any disadvantages of a diversified company? In most countries, certainly in the UK, the general view tends to be that diversification raises no great issues for consumers. If a company engages in diversification there is no particular problem for consumers because there is no increase in market power in either of the industries. Although the company is bigger, it does not have any more control in either market. Although diversified activity may be shown to be a mistake, that is a judgement for shareholders. Although they may get it wrong, they are less likely to make mistakes than governments. However, there is a case for saying that things are not quite as easy as that, and that diversified companies do present problems for consumer welfare. One illustration of this would be the way in which large diversified companies can deny information. If there is a single-line producer, the company accounts at the end of the year reveal the level of profit made in that line. If there is a highly diversified company making a total profit, how much profit is made in each area of activity? Some of the costs are general overhead management costs. According to the way in which these are allocated to different lines of activity it is possible to show different cost levels and therefore different levels of profitability in each area. If there is an area of activity where barriers to entry are relatively low the company might want to show itself making very little profit in that area by allocating large amounts of overheads to that particular line of activity in order to discourage entry into the market. So by denying information to potential entrants a company can effectively use its diversified nature as a passive entry barrier. Also, the denial of information can be a problem because for markets to work efficiently we want resources to flow where profits are being made. We want companies that are making profits to find it relatively easy to attract new investment. By denying information to shareholders as to which area of

activity makes the most profit there is a danger that resources are not allocated in the most appropriate way.

So new firms may well find it difficult to compete against incumbent firms.
On the other hand, the potential source of new competition is likely to come,
not from new companies, but from existing companies diversifying into other
areas of activity. So diversified organisations may well be of benefit to consumers
as they provide the most powerful source of new competition into a market.

Conclusion

There are different kinds of merger activity, horizontal, diversified and vertical. Some of the motives that cause companies to engage in mergers are specific
to horizontal integration. Some are general to all different kinds of mergers,
and we have seen now that some are specific to diversification. We have yet
to look at the question of vertical integration. Although we have defined it,
we have not tried to think why companies might engage in vertically integrated activity. We shall do that as part of the next chapter.

KEY RESULTS

1 Merger activity can be for reasons of efficiency or market power.

2 The principal–agent problem explains why mergers may not be to the
benefit of shareholders.

3 The Marris growth model can be used to explain some merger activity.

4 Diversified mergers can be conglomerate, or for product extension or
market extension.

Questions

1* In 2001 Lloyds TSB made a takeover bid for Abbey National. The bid was
referred to the Competition Commission, which argued against it. What
factors would you expect the Commission to have taken in assessing the
benefits and costs to consumers of such a takeover?

2* In discussing the benefit or otherwise of mergers, no mention was made
in the chapter of the effect on employment or the balance of payments
account. Why would most economists not rate such matters as important
when assessing the social benefits of a merger?

3* Assess the relative advantages to a large firm of growth by diversification
and growth by horizontal integration.

4 Consider Box 6.1. How convincing are the arguments against the creative
destruction of businesses?

5 Consider Box 6.2. To what extent does the policy of Whitbread demonstrate
recent trends in company growth policy?

* Help available at *http://www.e-econ.co.uk*

Box 6.2 Whitbread policy is to focus on a core business

One company, once a diversifier, now focuses on a strategy of expanding a core business.

David Thomas, chief executive of Whitbread, came over all poetic when explaining his company's decision to sell its 3,000-strong pub estate and focus on its hotels, sports and restaurants chains.

'It is like a butterfly emerging from a chrysalis,' Mr Thomas said of the prospects of Future Whitbread – as he called the remaining business.

Somewhat more prosaically, he explained that the stock market had failed to appreciate the underlying growth potential within the group's leisure businesses, which include Marriott and Travel Inn hotels, Brewers Fayre and Beefeater restaurants, and the David Lloyd sports club chain.

Whitbread's withdrawal from pubs and its recent disposal of brewing – businesses with which it was once most closely identified – vividly highlights the startling changes that are taking place in both these sectors.

The UK beer market, which was once highly fragmented, is now being rapidly consolidated by the likes of Interbrew of Belgium and Scottish & Newcastle.

But the pubs business has also seen sweeping changes, as specialist retail chains and finance houses, such as Punch Taverns and Nomura, enter the market.

'Strategic logic drove this decision,' Mr Thomas said. 'We see great financial returns coming from Future Whitbread, which to date has been hidden within the existing Whitbread.

'Whitbread is now about rest, eat, and play. Whenever anyone does any of these things, we want them to think of Whitbread.'

Mr Thomas argued that 90 per cent of Whitbread's pub estate was unbranded and therefore unlikely to generate good long-term profits growth. The on-trade has also been under immense pressure as the big retailing chains sell an ever-increasing share of beer. But pub estates can still generate serious cash. Where Whitbread sees problems, other investors can still see opportunities.

Brian Stewart, chief executive of Scottish & Newcastle, Britain's biggest brewer which still has a large pub portfolio, has also championed the virtues of pub ownership.

He argues that it all comes down to focus and quality standards. 'At the end of the day, the desire for consumers to visit pubs is the same, the issue for the brewers is how to manage the pubs effectively,' he said.

'Can you tell me a retail business that tries to be everything to every consumer? What you have to do is be specialist and play to your strengths. Basically, it's the same story everywhere, people don't want to be all things to all men – and that is healthy for the industry because it adds impetus,' Mr Stewart said.

Ironically, Whitbread's withdrawal from pubs could help improve the economics of the sector. As investment falls, the returns should surely rise. 'This reduces the amount of capital going into the pub sector and helps improve the long-term fundamentals. You can now see some light at the end of the tunnel,' said Mr Eadie of Deutsche Bank.

Maybe Mr Thomas has inadvertently released some butterflies for other investors too.

Source: *Financial Times*, 20 October 2000

7

Vertical relationships

The Spirella corset factory is closing because the bottom has dropped out of the market.

TV ANNOUNCEMENT

This chapter considers the benefits to business of extending control over the production process. It also considers relationships with other firms even where there is no common ownership.

OBJECTIVES

After reading this chapter you should be able to:

- Appreciate why vertical relationships are different from others.
- Know why firms engage in vertical integration.
- Understand the significance of transactions costs for vertical relationships.
- Understand the benefits and costs to firms and society from resale price maintenance.
- Appreciate the issues raised for efficiency by exclusive dealerships.

Introduction

The essence of the market system is exchange relationships. Those exchanges that we have considered so far have been between producers and consumers. We now focus on vertical relationships. These deal with exchanges between producers. Such relationships are different in several ways.

- *Control over price etc.* A producer (outside of perfect competition) controls the price at which the product is sold to the consumer as well as its quality etc. Producers of cars, for example, sell them through dealerships they may not own. The price at which the car is sold to the consumer and other variables such as after-sales care are to some extent out of the car producer's control.

- *Competition between retailers.* Retailers compete with each other to sell. Consumers do not. As a consumer I look for the best deal. When I buy I neither know nor care what price you paid. As a retailer of cars I care both how much I must pay the producer *and* how much you as a rival producer pay. Your costs matter to me as well as my own because we are in competition with each other.

- *The fewness of intermediate firms.* A firm selling to the final consumer is usually selling to large numbers of customers. A firm selling to other firms is selling to relatively few buyers. The fewness of buyers restricts a seller's market power. Farmers, for example, sell much of their produce to a handful of supermarkets. The fewness of supermarkets gives them some market power over the farmers. Indeed, this was a cause for concern in the Competition Commission Report (2000) into supermarkets that we referred to in Chapter 1.

The unique nature of vertical relationships therefore requires separate treatment. Accordingly, in this chapter we shall first examine the motives for vertical mergers. Later we shall consider some key elements of behaviour between vertically related firms where there is no attempt to bring about a common ownership of resources.

Motives for vertical integration

In the last chapter we considered the benefits to firms of engaging in merger activity. Some of those motives are common to any kind of merger. Here we consider those motives that are fairly specific to vertical integration. The definition of vertical integration was given in the last chapter.

Asymmetry of information

When we look at decisions about buying or selling either as producers or consumers, we tend to make the assumption that all the parties engaged in the process have the same degree of information. When we buy a good we know what that good will do in terms of improving our utility. The producer knows what it will do for him in terms of what it will cost to produce it and how much profit he can make. We both have adequate information. Now of course there are markets where there is not that equality of knowledge. That is, we do not have symmetry of information. For example, when you go to a private doctor, you are at a significant disadvantage. She knows more about healthcare than you do. That is why you have made the visit. This may create a problem for the market. She may decide to recommend an operation that you do not need. What gives rise to this potential problem is asymmetry of information.

Asymmetry of information can be a motive for vertical integration. Suppose that you are buying from an input supplier. Suppose you have information through, say, market research that the demand for your product is going to rise sharply. Suppose the input supplier does not know that. You might find that it is to your advantage to buy the firm, to integrate vertically, because you can buy the firm at a relatively low price. The firm does not know about the expected future profits that you know are coming into the industry. It becomes worthwhile to integrate vertically only because the upstream firm does not know the profits that are going to be made and the price of buying the company is therefore low. Where there is asymmetry of information there may be an advantage in vertical integration.

Raising barriers to the entry of new firms

Vertical integration can sometimes be used to make it more difficult for competition to come into the industry. Suppose there is only one major input supplier of a product and that input supplier is supplying a number of firms, including firm A. Suppose now that firm A makes a takeover bid and buys up the input supplier. It vertically integrates. The advantage it now has is that its competitors will struggle to buy the inputs that they need. The competitors can either find alternative and perhaps higher cost suppliers or they can go to firm A and pay a price which reflects the market power of the monopoly producer. Knowing this to be the situation, newcomers may well be deterred from entering the market.

So the more vertically integrated the industry, the more difficult it is for new firms to come in. Even if there is not the problem of finding alternative suppliers it can still be harder for new firms. The vertically integrated company can be large enough to dominate the market. A new company may feel it cannot afford to come in at a relatively small level of output for reasons we considered in Chapter 5. Sheer size becomes a factor in discouraging new firms from entering the market.

Exclusive dealing can also be used by large firms to raise entry barriers. During 2000 the Competition Commission reported on the sale of impulse ice cream. Birds Eye Walls, the frozen foods division of Unilever, has around two-thirds of the market. It was criticised in the report for insisting that retailers stock only Walls ice creams in the cabinets it lent them. This was regarded as raising entry barriers to other suppliers. They may now reserve only half the space for their own products. To the Chicago school (and indeed to Birds Eye Walls) such a restriction is pointless. Should a firm's lorries be made to carry rival products in order to enhance competition? The government, and indeed other firms such as Nestlé and Mars, took the view that such vertical restraints limit competition to the detriment of consumers.

Technical motives

There may be lower production costs as a result of being vertically integrated. Take an industry, such as the car industry, that uses inputs of steel panels. At the moment the steel firm is a separate company. Suppose that a car firm now vertically integrates with it. It may be possible to reorganise and lower costs by undertaking a series of production processes under one roof. This may well save on heating costs etc. Presumably, the car industry has decided that this particular example is not feasible. Steel production requires specialist production processes so that the costs are lower if the car industry does not vertically integrate.

Internalising external economies existing in the market

External economies and diseconomies may well give reasons as to why we might want to integrate vertically. There is a hotel on a small island. The hotel is only half full even at the peak of the tourist season. The owner comes to the conclusion that it is worth stepping up advertising to fill up the hotel and hence make more profit. Those who are supplying the travel to the hotel, such as a ferry company, will find an increase in demand for their product. The advertising creates an external effect in the demand for ferry travel. If advertising boosts hotel occupancy rates it may be worthwhile vertically integrating, moving upstream to acquire the ferry company.

This particular motive is linked to the question of asymmetry of information that we referred to before. The ferry company is unaware that the hotel's advertising campaign is likely to increase its profits. So internalising external economies is another motive for vertical integration.

Using vertical integration for price discrimination

Price discrimination means selling the same good to different customers at different prices. Examples abound. Airlines charge different prices for the same seat to different passengers. Railway companies do the same. The benefit to the firm is that it can acquire some of the consumer surplus that would otherwise go to those customers who value the product more highly. In order to price-discriminate successfully a firm needs:

- *a degree of monopoly power*. Perfectly competitive firms cannot price-discriminate, as they must sell all their output at a given market price.
- *different elasticities of demand in the different markets*. The higher price is then charged in the market for which demand elasticity is less.
- *barriers between the two markets*. These will prevent arbitrage, the process of buying at the lower price and reselling at the higher price.

Vertical integration can increase or enhance the possibilities of such price discrimination. A company has a patent on a chemical compound used in hand cream and also in an anti-eczema treatment. Assume the compound can be produced at constant marginal cost, MC = AC in Figure 7.1. Demand for the compound, D_e, from the eczema producer is greater and less elastic than demand from the hand-cream producer, D_{hc}. The compound producer wishes to price-discriminate. Its output is Q_{pm} where MC = ΣMR, the horizontal summation of the two MR curves. It would then allocate that output between the two markets such that MR in each market is the same. This means selling Q_e

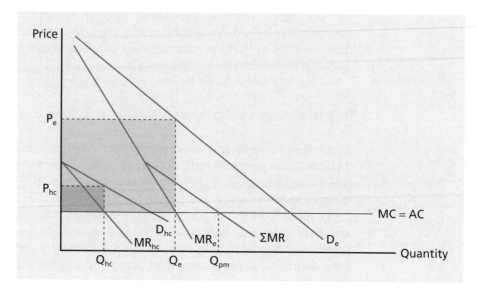

Figure 7.1 Vertical integration and price discrimination

in the eczema market, charging P_e, and Q_{hc} at a price of P_{hc} to the hand-cream manufacturer. However, arbitrage may prevent its doing this. The hand-cream firm may buy more than it needs and resell to the anti-eczema producer. Vertically integrating forward and buying the two manufacturers may enable price discrimination to consumers who will not be able to engage in arbitrage in the way that producers can.

Multinationals, taxation and vertical integration

Multinational corporations, or transnationals, are not companies that simply trade in a number of different countries. They actually own or control productive capacity outside of their own country. Many have a country where they are based but they will also have operations in other parts of the world, often in relatively underdeveloped economies. Here inputs are made and then shipped out to the more developed country where the component parts are put together and sold in the domestic market. That arrangement creates the possibility for the company to increase its profitability by using the different national tax systems. The tax rates in the less developed country may well be low relative to the domestic country. A powerful multinational uses its power to secure favourable tax treatment with a threat to move elsewhere. So taxes on the profits that are made in the developing country may well be lower than taxes on the profits made in the developed country. How much profit is made on operations in the developed country and how much in the developing country? The multinational may well be able to decide.

It can choose to make relatively high profit in the underdeveloped country. It does so by setting a high 'transfer' price, the price it records as the price of the inputs 'sold' to the parent in the developed country. Alternatively it can choose to show profits being high in the developed country by setting a low transfer price. If the taxes on profits are lower in one country than in the other the firm can arrange to show that most of the profits are being produced in the country where the taxes on profits are at their lowest. The multinational is in effect using its power so that governments must compete on their tax rates. It is vertical integration that gives more control over that process. A decision to locate is not only affected by tax policy in less developed economies. Low tax economies within the EU such as Ireland have attracted substantial investment of subsidiaries.

The above is only one instance of vertical integration decisions made as a result of distortions brought about by taxation policy. For example, if sales taxes are imposed only at some stage of a production process, firms will have an incentive to integrate vertically, thus avoiding the tax.

Cutting out the middleman?

To some non-economists the middleman is a useless parasite on society. There are people who make a 'real' contribution to the economy by making output and there are people who contribute to the economy by selling that output to consumers. But in the middle, between the producer and the seller of the product, is a middleman who does nothing except take a profit. He achieves nothing for society, he simply causes the prices of products to be higher. Thus one motive for vertical integration, it is often said, is to control the whole production process from raw materials to final consumer. This eliminates the middleman and avoids the profit mark-up which he is charging. Thus the firm could make more profit *and* sell to the consumer at a lower price. So eliminating the middleman is said to be a reason for vertical integration.

This is a misunderstanding. The middleman is not a parasite, he produces value to society. If he did not do so he would not be there. When a company claims to eliminate the middleman, it simply does the middleman's job. If a firm vertically integrates and undertakes the middleman's function itself it is not doing things more efficiently. It is simply changing the ownership of assets.

Suppose we have an economy of 100 people. Each produces output that he/she wishes to exchange with each of the others. The number of transactions in each period is 4950. Since each of the n people must transact with n − 1 people, 100 multiplied by 99 gives 9900. However, an exchange is between two parties (if A swaps with B, B has swapped with A). So we divide by two to give the number of exchanges. In general, in an n-person economy we have $\frac{n-1}{2}$ exchanges. Here 9900/2 = 4950. Suppose now a middleman agrees to receive goods from anyone in exchange for any other goods required. The total number of exchanges is n − 1. In this case it is 99. In a society with many

Table 7.1 Cutting out the middleman

Firm	Stock market valuation (£)	Task	Rate of return on assets
A	1 million	Makes kitchen units	10%
B	1 million	Sells A's kitchen units to retailer	10%
A+B	2 million	Makes kitchens and sells units to retailer at same price as before	10%

people $\frac{n-1}{2}$ will be far greater than n – 1. Given that there are transactions costs associated with each exchange, the presence of a middleman is efficient in reducing such costs.

Now suppose firm A is making kitchen units and making a 10% profit margin on them. It is selling its product to middleman B, who then sells the kitchen units to a retailer that sells to the public. Suppose the middleman and retailer each makes a 10% profit margin. Suppose further that companies A and B each have £1 million worth of assets. This is summarised in Table 7.1. Is it true to say that if this industry now becomes vertically integrated we can have lower prices, lower costs and more profits?

Suppose we now have an AB company because of vertical integration. We now have a £2m company and all the work is being done making kitchens and selling direct to the public without using a middleman. This company is now twice as big as it was before. It will need to have profits of 10% at each stage in the production process in order to make a return to the shareholder of 10%. The company is twice as big; it needs twice as much total profit in order to have the same rate of return. Unless it is possible to streamline the production process in some way, simply acquiring another company that is making a mark-up on cost is not a way of improving profit performance. One could make the company bigger by buying any assets, whether it is vertically integrated or not. There is no logic in vertically integrating to eliminate the middleman unless it is for one of the other advantages that we have already considered. In and of itself the middleman performs a valuable function to society. If a firm decides to do that function itself, the shareholders will expect that function to be performed in a way that gives a rate of return to the shareholder. Vertical integration to eliminate the middleman makes no economic sense in and of itself.

Birds Eye Walls believes that it can distribute its frozen ice creams more efficiently itself rather than use a middleman. The Competition Commission report mentioned above recommended that the company be made to use middlemen in order not to undermine the distribution system upon which rival firms relied. This was largely rejected by the government, although pressure was placed upon Walls to raise the commission it paid to middlemen, in order to protect the distribution system.

Transactions costs and vertical integration

Further light is thrown on the process of vertical integration by the use of transactions cost analysis. We will illustrate these important ideas of Williamson (1989) by way of an illustration. Suppose there's an industry of six firms which produces a product called an XYZ. Each of the six companies needs an input of an X, a Y and a Z. These inputs are bolted together to make a unit of XYZ output. Now suppose that we are one of these six firms. Shall we buy our inputs from other companies or shall we vertically integrate and make them ourselves? We need to think about what it will cost us if we produce the inputs ourselves and compare that with the cost of buying them in from an outside producer. Focus on the decision regarding the production of X. Further suppose that we are producing 100 XYZs a week, and the market produces 600 XYZs in total each week. This is because there are five other companies each producing 100 XYZs a week as well. Should we produce the Xs ourselves or buy them in from some other organisation? We can think about the costs in terms of Figure 7.2.

The diagram shows a familiar long-run average cost curve, but this is not the average cost curve of producing XYZ, it is just the cost of producing input X. If we make X input ourselves it would cost us c_1 per unit. We are only producing 100 units of output, we do not get the economies of scale available if we were producing a much larger level of output, so our unit costs are going to be relatively high. Suppose now we decided to buy the inputs from some specialist supplier. Assume that other companies follow us in buying from the specialist supplier. What would it cost? The specialist supplier would have the advantages of economies of scale because it would be producing 600 units of X and because the economies of scale are available it can sell it for less. Could it do so for an average cost of c_2? This will not be possible. Although the firm is a specialist input supplier it must set up in the market and this gives

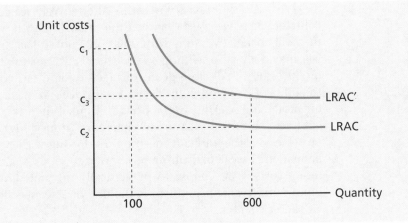

Figure 7.2 Unit costs of input X

that firm some costs that we, the established firm, do not have. Therefore although our costs are on LRAC, the specialist input supplier's costs will be on LRAC', the specialist production of X plus the set-up costs of beginning production.

If all six firms buy from the specialist input supplier it will cost us not c_2, but c_3. You can see from the diagram that it would be better not to integrate vertically because we could buy the inputs more cheaply than we could produce them ourselves even allowing for the set-up costs.

This is only one possibility. The reason for not integrating vertically was because the economies of scale that were available to the firm that became the specialist supplier were large relative to the set-up costs. It would be easy to redraw the diagram and show that if the set-up costs are large and the economies of scale in the production of Xs are relatively small we would be better off if we were a vertically integrated firm and produced the Xs ourselves. So the argument so far is that depending on the relative size of two kinds of production costs we might or we might not want to integrate vertically.

We can take the argument one step further. The cheapest way to get our units of X would not be to buy from a specialist input supplier but for the six firms in the industry to get together and to make an agreement. The agreement would be that one of us would produce all 600 units of X and then supply them to the other companies in the market.

Return to Figure 7.2. We do not need a specialist input supplier with set-up costs and therefore LRAC' is no longer relevant. The relevant curve is LRAC since one of us can expand our output along LRAC to produce 600 units at only c_2. The other five companies would not produce any units of X at all; they would simply buy from us at cost. Indeed it does not matter which of the six companies produces X. Yet this is not an arrangement that companies are usually willing to embrace. What is it that makes us unwilling to agree that the best way to produce X is for one of our competitors to produce them and sell them to us at the cost of production? The difficulty involves transactions costs. How are we to organise a contract with the competitor who is making our X? We can have a short-term contract and agree a price that is fixed for, say, the next six months. Alternatively we could have a long-term contract where we agree that over the next 10 years it will supply us at a price that will change over time with inflation. Look at the short-term contract first. We may well be unwilling to do that. If we go for that option, one firm produces all X, we close down our factory, and our competitor produces all the units of X for six months at a fixed price. We have given up our facilities for producing X. The contract has run out. When it comes to renewing the contract the firm may want to charge us a much higher price. We will find ourselves in the difficult position of having either to agree to be in a permanently weak bargaining position or to set up again and incur the higher set-up costs if we choose to be vertically integrated again and produce the input ourselves. Our problem is the one of asset specificity we considered in an earlier chapter.

Perhaps a long-term contract is the answer, where the firm is committed to supplying us these inputs for, say, the next 10 years. The firm will not be willing to do that over that period of time at a fixed price. It will want to revisit the question of price periodically in the light of changes in technology, changes in prices and so on. So we are going to expect that the price that we pay to buy our X will vary over the next period of years. How do we know that the firm is not cheating us? We could try to police the agreement. However, that is expensive. There will be different transactions costs from those implicit in the short-term contract, but they will still be present and may be substantial.

So the significance of transactions costs is that they make firms reluctant to enter into any arrangement of that kind. Therefore the choice is going to be buying from the specialist supplier or for the firm to produce them itself and be more vertically integrated. What appears to be the least cost method of production may not turn out to be so when transactions costs are considered.

In some circumstances it may be the *quality* of the input that is difficult to police. The transactions costs of policing quality may be so high as to cause the firm to be vertically integrated. Quality assurance procedures will still be required but they may be substantially more easily addressed. Hennessy (1997) found this to be an important issue in the food industry.

Asset specificity has been found to be an important explanation of vertical integration in a number of industries, whether the asset is capital or labour. John and Weitz (1988) examined the specificity of labour in terms of the amount of staff training required to sell a particular product. In general they found that the greater the specificity, the higher the degree of vertical integration. Krickx (1995) examined the large computer companies and found a correlation between the asset specificity of the major components and the desire to integrate vertically.

Timing and vertical integration

There are times when the motive for vertical integration may be stronger than at others. Timing may relate either to the life cycle of the product, or to the economy's trade cycle.

The life cycle of the product

There is an argument that says that the degree of vertical integration in an industry relates to the product life cycle. A typical product life cycle would be described by Figure 7.3.

A new product comes onto the market. Few firms are producing it and consumers are not very familiar with it. Prices may be high, for demand is too low to allow economies of scale. Over the next few years, as consumers get used to the product and see its benefits, they want to buy the product in greater amounts. At some point the market may well expand very rapidly. One recent example might be mobile phones. Only a few years ago, few people

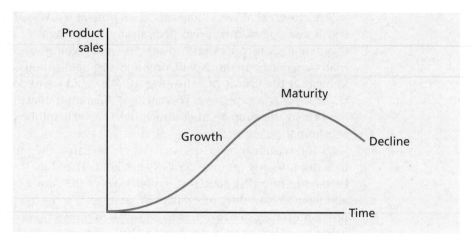

Figure 7.3 A product life cycle

had them, but now the market is maturing, demand has increased hugely and prices have fallen in recent years. There comes a time, however, when the product's life cycle has reached its peak and there comes a time when the product will go into some kind of secular decline, often because some superior kind of new technology has come in to make the old product relatively redundant. So a typical product life cycle will involve small beginnings, growth, rapid growth, maturity and decline. This concept is closely related to the S-curve we considered in Chapter 2, although Figure 2.4 related to an industry rather than to a particular product.

The degree of vertical integration might relate to this product life cycle. We can show this in Figure 7.4. When the product is relatively new the degree of vertical integration, VI, is very high. It is a new product and there are few input suppliers to produce the parts. If a firm is to produce this product it must do so itself. As the product cycle matures and the market expands it becomes worthwhile for new producers of inputs to set up. As we saw earlier, there may well be advantages in buying from specialist input producers if the set-up costs are low relative to the economies of scale that are available. So

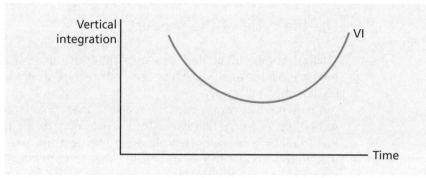

Figure 7.4 Vertical integration and the product life cycle

as the age of the product matures, there will be less vertical integration. Firms will, *ceteris paribus*, buy inputs from specialist suppliers. Now suppose the industry is moving into its decline stage. Input producers are finding that as the market declines, there is less profit and they exit the market. A firm wishing to produce the product a little longer will not be able to buy from the specialist input producers who are leaving the industry. They must vertically integrate. This suggests, then, that there might be a relationship between the degree of vertical integration and the product life cycle.

The trade cycle

There is also an argument that says that the *direction* of vertical integration, if not its extent, is affected by the trade cycle. Suppose the economy is in a boom period. Unemployment is low and the demand for products is high. It

Box 7.1 Upstream and downstream profitability in the car industry

In the motor industry management is moving into downstream activities to protect profitability.

Signs of a slowdown in the global automotive industry have encouraged manufacturers to seek new sources of revenue from downstream activities.

In this difficult trading environment, manufacturers are looking to downstream activities to sustain them through a downturn.

Industry leaders recognise that margins made from selling finance, insurance, parts and even mobile 'infotainment' are much higher than from making and selling cars. There are also considerable savings to be achieved in sales, distribution and marketing.

If carmakers can cut those costs, then it will greatly reduce unit costs per car, and feed through to the bottom line.

A twin-track approach is emerging, therefore, in the auto industry's downstream activities. On the one hand, the manufacturers are exploring new business opportunities in areas such as vehicle financing and incar internet services. Income from such business could supplement their existing sources of profit.

On the other hand, they are seeking big savings in distribution and marketing activities beyond the factory gate.

If the reforms lead to a free-for-all among dealers and new retail entrants, then manufacturers will have to find alternative ways to protect their revenues.

It will also increase the pressure on manufacturers to look for new earnings streams. This is the reason for pilot projects on direct internet sales and the consolidation of dealer activities by some carmakers.

That has alarmed some traditional dealers. But they are still likely to play an important role, if only to deliver the vehicles and offer service functions. Other dealers have realised that they must capture more of the product lifecycle.

Meanwhile, existing downstream operations, particularly in finance and leasing, are likely to become more refined.

All this reflects a structural change in the industry, where a multi-channel approach is emerging in distribution and retailing.

Manufacturers are transforming themselves into service providers, where marketing costs will be much more tightly controlled in future.

In part, this is being forced upon them by changes in the regulatory environment. But it also reflects increasing sophistication on the part of carbuyers, who are much more aware of the choices open to them.

To woo new customers, a broader service is required. Manufacturers are ready to embrace that challenge because these services dubbed 'product-life management' – could be the key to future profits.

Source: Financial Times, 28 February 2001 FT

is not difficult to sell products. However, there may be a problem in finding enough inputs for the production of sufficient output. Other firms also have a high demand for component parts. Thus firms may well, during a boom period, want to vertically integrate backwards in order to guarantee input supplies. Now suppose the economy is in recession. Unemployment is rising, the demand for the product is falling. It is not easy to sell the product. There is no problem in getting the input parts because demand everywhere is low. Thus firms might want to vertically integrate forwards. The logic of this is to guarantee an outlet for selling. A paper producer, for example, might want to buy up some retail stores in order to make sure that their product is promoted. The motive is really about security; either security of input parts or security of market, but the amount of vertical integration in which firms engage may well be affected by the point on the trade cycle.

Empirical evidence on vertical mergers

We shall leave until the next chapter a consideration of the effects on profits of merger activity. Here we consider some research on the relative importance of different motives for vertical integration. We have already seen that two studies, Krickx (1995) and John and Weitz (1998), have considered the transactions cost motives and found evidence to support this view. Here we mention briefly one other study.

The study of Spiller (1985) is of particular interest because he was testing to see whether the transactions cost approach or the more neoclassical approach best explains vertical integration. The Chicago school analysis, as one might expect, focuses on efficiency considerations of economies and government-induced distortions. Spiller examined 29 US vertical mergers and concluded that the transactions cost arguments best explained firm motives.

Recent moves towards increased outsourcing

In recent years many firms have increased the 'outsourcing' of their input requirements. In essence this simply means a movement towards less vertical integration. Given the preceding analysis we can suggest some reasons for this trend.

- In some industries technological improvements have meant more flexible production methods. Assets are less specific than previously. As we have seen, this reduces the need for vertical integration.
- Technological change has also reduced communication costs. The development of trade on the Internet is only one illustration of this. Whereas firms would previously integrate vertically to avoid costly communication problems with suppliers, that need is now reduced.

- The move towards lower international trade barriers has made the use of markets more efficient. This further reduces the need for vertical integration.
- As we shall see in the next chapter, evidence suggests that most merger activity has not succeeded in raising company profitability. As this has been increasingly recognised, there may be a tendency for a market correction. Thus failed vertical integration is replaced by outsourcing.

The social benefits of vertical integration

Do consumers benefit from vertical integration? Some economists have tried to make a distinction between motives that are essentially for security and motives that are essentially about efficiency. If the motive is efficiency, so that the result of vertical integration is to lower unit cost of production, then there is every possibility that consumers will gain from a decision to integrate vertically. But if the motive is security then consumers are much less likely to gain. Often, however, such integration can be for both motives. Suppose the firm is integrating vertically in order to increase productive efficiency. It may also raise capital barriers to entry. The possibility is now that consumers will lose because the firm will increase its profits but the market will not work efficiently. New resources may not be drawn into the industry in response to the profits above the normal which the vertically integrated firm is generating. So in any individual instance it will not always be easy to decide whether the main attraction to the firm is security or economy but in principle we can say that if the motive is primarily security it may well not benefit consumers. If the motive is primarily economies then consumers may well gain.

Vertical restraints

So far we have focused on decisions to integrate vertically. Finally we consider some relationships between *independent* firms at different stages of production in the same industry. In particular, we consider the practices of resale price maintenance and the granting of exclusive territories.

Resale price maintenance

In many markets resale price maintenance (RPM) has been observed. This involves a producer setting the price at which the product must be sold to the consumer. Failure to conform can be punished by refusing to supply goods to the retailer. In markets such as electrical goods, products sell at almost identical prices wherever one chooses to buy. Manufacturers argue that this is the pressure of competition. Since there are many retail outlets it would be easy for customers to go to the lowest price store, forcing other retailers to match the lower price. Others have suggested that manufacturers exert pressure on retailers with respect to price. This is a sensitive issue since such RPM is illegal.

RPM raises two questions. The first is why would manufacturers wish to use this device? The second question is does it make sense for governments to ban the practice? It seems strange at first that the manufacturer might wish to force firms to charge higher prices. A lower price could only increase the volume of sales. The answer can be found in the familiar concept of externalities. An externality occurs when an economic agent undertakes an action that imposes costs or benefits on another agent when that cost or benefit is not traded. An illustration would be a chemicals firm dumping a waste product into a river, damaging a fishing industry that receives no compensation for its dead fish stocks. This is an untraded interdependency. We can now see how RPM relates to this.

Sales of a product depend upon more than price. They depend also upon the sales effort made by the retailer. Suppose now that consumers are price sensitive, as we suggested above. Suppose further that one retailer makes a substantial effort to increase sales through advertising. Another retailer might make no effort but reap the benefits of increased sales through offering a lower price. A customer could be attracted into a retail outlet because of the advertising but subsequently buy from a lower priced retailer. The lower priced retailer is free-riding upon the sales effort of its rival. A way out of this dilemma is to prevent the externality via the imposition of RPM. If a consumer is attracted into a shop via that shop's advertising, she has no incentive to purchase elsewhere.

We are now in a position to answer our second question. Does it make sense for governments to ban RPM? Since there are clear efficiency gains in reducing externalities it may not be in the public interest to do so. However, there are also efficiency losses in RPM. It reduces the possibility of price competition among retailers and may thus give rise to higher prices for consumers.

To the Chicago school, of course, the only reason for enforcing resale price maintenance is the efficiency reason of internalising the externality since there is no problem with monopoly power except that which governments themselves create. Thus we need no laws to prevent RPM. However, one study by Gilligan (1986) suggests otherwise. He analysed the effects on share prices of RPM behaviour and concluded that the principal effect of RPM was to raise share prices of firms. He argued that this share price effect was not through efficiency gains but because markets were distorted and profits were increased.

Exclusive dealerships

A second form of vertical restraint is that of exclusive dealerships. At present, car manufacturers are able to sell through exclusive dealerships. They may refuse to supply cars to be sold outside these dealerships. Again it might seem strange that they should wish to do so. More outlets might lead to a larger volume of cars sold. The justification for such arrangements is again externalities. Advertising by one dealer might provide a benefit to another dealer on which he could free-ride. This affects more than direct advertising. Efforts may be made to entice consumers into the showroom via the provision of more sales staff. The customer makes up her mind in the showroom. But she then purchases the car from a lower priced dealer who has taken a free ride rather than make the sales effort himself to provide such facilities. The car manufacturer may wish to prevent such free-riding via the establishment of RPM but it can also be done through exclusive dealerships. Again this can be seen as an efficiency gain in that it internalises an externality.

Again, though, there may be inefficiencies in such arrangements to remove externalities. For example, some car producers have tried to prevent dealerships in one European country from selling to consumers in another. This can be an attempt to create conditions for a form of price discrimination if the profit maximising price differs in the two countries. The exclusive dealership arrangement is designed partly to prevent arbitrage.

A slightly different form of exclusive dealership is practised by the perfume industry. Companies in this industry will sometimes argue that sales are *lowered* if they have to sell to any supplier. Perfumes may be more difficult to sell unless they have an 'exclusive' image. This essential image cannot be created if the perfume is available at any outlet. Again, there is a mixture of efficiency and market power considerations involved in this form of vertical restraint.

Conclusion

We have now seen in this chapter that there are potential benefits and costs in vertically integrated mergers. However, vertical relationships are important even in markets where there is no attempt to merge operations. Analysing the social costs and benefits of any vertical restraint is fraught with difficulty.

KEY RESULTS

1 Various explanations have been offered as to why firms vertically integrate.

2 Some motives appear to create market power, others to increase efficiency.

3 Transactions costs can also be used to explain vertical integration.

4 Resale price maintenance can increase efficiency by reducing externalities. The reduction in price competition may, however, lead to higher prices for consumers.

5 Exclusive dealerships also raise issues both of efficiency and of market power.

Questions

1* In the text we argued that firms might vertically integrate because of asymmetry of information. Why might this be a matter for concern? Would the Chicago school economist agree?

2* Consider Figure 7.5. The firm knows its demand and cost curves perfectly. What output is produced by the monopolist that is unable to price-discriminate? Suppose the firm can perfectly price-discriminate so that it can charge different prices to each customer. How much output does it now produce? Compare this with the socially efficient output. What assumptions are being made that the transactions cost economist might question?

3* The supply of petrol is an industry that has many features of a vertically integrated industry. The tie between oil companies is an informal one rather than a formal one. In many cases the oil companies do not own the retail sites. Do consumers gain from this arrangement?

4 Consider Box 7.1. Reread the first paragraph. Why is this only happening in a recession? Is such behaviour consistent with the assumption of profit maximisation?

5 Consider Box 7.2. How important do you think 'cultural issues' might be in explaining the success or otherwise of merger activity?

* Help available at **http://www.e-econ.co.uk**

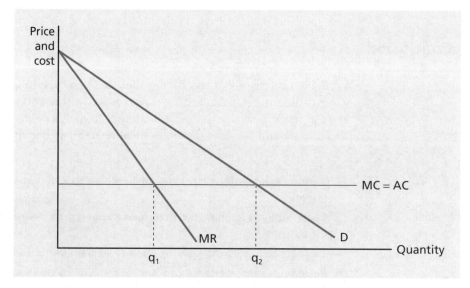

Figure 7.5 Price discrimination and transactions costs

Box 7.2

The new economy is taking shape with the creation of super-companies that have strengths in IT, telecoms and content. But the big issues raised in many old economy mergers have not gone away.

A flurry of mergers and alliances, such as AOL's planned merger with Time Warner and the recently-announced link-up between Vivendi and Seagram, are set to create a generation of super-companies with strengths in three camps: IT, telecoms and content.

The internet provides the perfect vehicle for them to succeed. But will differences in culture and technology prove too much for the pioneers of convergence?

'The problem with the "new economy" is that people have tended to think that old economy problems have gone away,' says Peter Brown, client services director of London-based Pagoda Consulting. 'The old economy problems which haven't gone away are those traditionally experienced in the mergers and acquisitions arena, namely technological integration and cultural incompatibility.'

These two problems will continue to be experienced as companies converge, he says.

Mr Brown argues that a lot of these mergers will not be voluntary. 'Many of the new e-businesses, spawned from a bright technological idea, will be potentially unbalanced, and need to bring in new activities,' he says.

Martyn Roetter, vice president of Arthur D Little's telecoms, IT, media and electronics practice, says the greatest revenue potential for merging companies will lie at the intersection between different segments, where compound applications can be formed – for example, education and entertainment equals edutainment.

'Our research shows that of all the new growth segments, the most lucrative are likely to be those which overlap with entertainment because the largest markets will be driven by customer desire for ease of use and attractive presentation,' he says.

But to take advantage of the opportunities, the problems involved in bringing different businesses together must be overcome.

Technology issues

One challenge could be integrating two or more converging businesses' front-office technology – the IT systems seen by customers or used to interact with them.

'In the old economy, mergers and acquisitions tend to involve vertical integration, conglomerate acquisition (i.e. different businesses) or a merger of the same type of business, where one of the two merging businesses' systems replaces the other. In many cases, therefore, front-office technologies would not need to be integrated as part of the core business proposition,' says Mr Brown.

However, in the new economy, mergers are often about integrating front-office technologies, which is where the business benefits lie (for example, feeding content from Time Warner's publishing systems into AOL's internet service or providing access to AOL over Time Warner's cable networks).

'The fact that different internet technologies tend to be more compatible with each other makes things somewhat easier,' he adds. 'But the technical and operational challenges should still not be underestimated, as technology always accounted for only 25–30 per cent of the problem.'

In fact, integrating behind-the-scenes (or back-office) IT systems could also be a problem. Mr Brown says: 'To take the varnish off, every major corporate coming together results, by definition, in the binning of massive sunk investment in one or other of the parties' back-office IT systems.

'Don't be fooled by the fact that both may have the same enterprise resource planning (ERP) system. There will need to be extensive reworking to gain the kind of competitive advantage they were striving to achieve before the merger.'

Cultural issues

These are the other main problems faced when bringing two or more companies together. Many apparently logical mergers have fallen through late on because of 'cultural differences'.

'Without careful post acquisition planning of organisational and cultural integration by top management, the next six months following a merger are frequently spent with the senior personnel from one organisation trying to gain ascendancy over and then cull their opposite numbers. The failure to deal with these cultural issues effectively in advance is enormously wasteful in financial terms.'

Further levels of cultural complication are added when there is an international element to the merger, as is often the case with deals that have been driven by convergence. National differences have often thwarted successful mergers in the old economy, so why should things be any different in the brave new economy?

▶

Box 7.2 continued

'Will technology wonks and content providers – the latter, by definition, being turned on by their interest in the content, rather than by business issues – be able to talk to each other?' asks Mr Brown.

People power
An additional problem faced by converging companies is how to hold on to staff who can easily get jobs elsewhere. 'The new economy needs a new paradigm for management and motivation which recognises that power is slowly shifting from the employer to the employed,' says Pagoda Consulting.

'These merging organisations are "acquiring" that well-known class of asset – human assets which walk out of the door every evening . . . These individuals need both direction and empowerment in a subtle blend, and woe betide the acquiring organisations that are incapable of providing it.'

It looks as if converged companies are going to need a new breed of super-manager to make them work. These super-managers, today's answer to the renaissance man, will have to span the worlds of content and technology. The cost of paying their salaries will be yet another challenge the converged company must face before it can start profiting from its three strengths.

Source: FTIT, 5 July 2000   **FT**

8

Mergers and strategic alliances

Marriage is like a besieged castle. All those on the outside are trying to get in and all those on the inside are trying to get out.

This chapter focuses on the evidence that many mergers fail. It also considers some alternative strategies for firms seeking to strengthen their market position.

OBJECTIVES

After reading this chapter you should be able to:

- Understand how researchers measure the success or otherwise of mergers.
- Appreciate why much evidence suggests that mergers do not improve company welfare.
- Understand the potential benefits and problems of strategic alliances.
- Know why some industries are characterised by franchises.
- Appreciate the problems of alliances for research and development.

Introduction

The central consideration for the first part of this chapter is whether the evidence suggests that those firms who engage in merger activity gain as a result of it. Our focus here is not so much on the effects for consumers' well-being but on firms' well-being. This is an important question. Merger activity is very considerable and as a result of this activity resources in society get reallocated. It is important to know whether this reallocation is successful in terms of the profitability of firms and industries. It may also have an effect on government policy. How willing should governments be to allow merger activity? The answer may be affected by studies of their profitability. We shall discover in the first part of the chapter that, although results are mixed, in general, mergers do not improve company performance. Thus, in the second part of the chapter we examine alternatives to mergers provided by *strategic alliances*. This term covers a variety of ways in which firms cooperate with one another, such as franchises, networks and joint ventures on research and development. First, though, we focus on research into the success or otherwise of mergers.

Studies on merger performance

Many studies have been conducted into this question. We examine a number from the last 30 or so years. In doing so we shall discover that mergers tend to fail to improve the well-being of companies. However, we shall learn more than that. We choose studies that have used different approaches, over different time periods and in different countries. By doing so we shall be gaining insights into how researchers have approached this topic as well as finding their results.

Meeks' study

The first study we consider is that of Meeks (1977). His book was called *Disappointing Marriage: A study of the gains to mergers*. The very title conveys what his results showed. Meeks argues that in general there is no particular gain to firms of engaging in merger activity. The word 'marriage' is an interesting one. Meeks is drawing a parallel between merger activity and people getting married. A young student is fit, handsome, good looking and concerned to stay that way in order to attract a suitable marriage partner. He is successful and gets married. After a year or two he decides that he does not really need to continue to make all the effort to retain his physique. So he begins to overindulge and gets fat. He is not trying very hard anymore; he does not feel the need now that he is married. The parallel is clear. A company has some limited control over the market. Suppose it now merges with another company, it 'marries'. Suppose the result is now that it dominates the market. It may feel that it does not need to try so hard; it has eliminated the competition via the takeover. The company gets flabby and uncompetitive. It is protected from its problems by the barriers to entry into the market of any new competitor.

Table 8.1 summarises some of Meeks' key results. One problem for a researcher is that it may take some while for the benefits of any merger to work through in terms of improved profitability. In the short term there is a lot to be done in reorganising production and merging different cultures. Perhaps the improved profitability that results from the merger may take a while to appear. So Meeks decided that he would follow the results of a merger for a period of seven years in order to make sure that he had a long enough period of time to pick up any of its advantages. This itself creates a problem. After a period of time the new company itself may get taken over or the company may engage in another merger. This makes it impossible to isolate the effect of the original merger. The company may even cease to exist. Thus it may be impossible to follow the merger through for a period of seven years because other things change. So the number of mergers that he was able to follow through for that period of time was much smaller than the original sample. Hence we have 233 observations for the year of the merger, falling to just 23 for the full seven years.

Table 8.1 Post-merger profitability of firms

Year	E	P	n
y	0.038	0.378	233
y + 1	−0.168	0.582	211
y + 2	−0.503	0.571	191
y + 3	−0.369	0.565	161
y + 4	−0.197	0.681	113
y + 5	−0.567	0.658	73
y + 6	−0.659	0.600	50
y + 7	−0.082	0.609	23

Note: E = profitability relative to the industry average
P = proportion of cases for which E < 0
n = number of cases qualifying for inclusion

Source: Meeks (1977)

The next problem is knowing what would have happened in the absence of the merger. Suppose we find that the result is improved profitability. How can we be sure that the improved profitability would not have taken place in the two companies in the absence of the merger? For example, in a period when the economy is in boom profits of companies are rising anyway. How do we isolate the effects of the merger from other conditions that are affecting the profitability of the companies? Meeks solved this problem in the following way. He looked at profitability compared with the industry average. So by focusing not on profitability itself but profitability as it relates to the average level of profitability of the whole industry one can to some extent isolate the effect of the merger.

E is the profitability relative to the industry average. Note that in every one of the seven years except the year in which the merger takes place, the value is negative. This indicates that the result of the merger is to reduce the profitability of the companies engaged in the merger relative to the industry average.

This is perhaps surprising. The only year in which there is seen to be some small improvement in profitability is the year in which we least expected it, the year in which the merger actually took place. We do not, however, attach much importance to that because although the number was positive it is not statistically significant. P is the proportion of cases for which the value of E is less than zero, This shows the large number of cases where mergers are not successful. Note though, that in a substantial minority of cases profits either stay the same or improve. So after two years, for example, this is true of 46% of the 192 mergers for which results were available.

The Newbould study

The second study is from the work of Newbould (1970), whose approach is to start with the fact that a takeover is an investment decision. As we have seen before, an investment decision can be either a decision to acquire existing assets via a takeover or a decision to invest in new capital. Newbould says that we would expect a profit-maximising company to take the same approach to deciding whether to engage in a takeover bid as it would when it decides whether to invest in new capital. When a company invests in new capital it undertakes an investment analysis. It writes down the cost in year 0, then it looks at the benefits which will accrue from the investment over a period of years, and discounts the benefits accruing in the future years back to a present value. It compares the discounted future revenue stream with the capital cost and on that basis decides whether the investment is profitable. Newbould's approach is then to see whether this is what companies appear to be doing with takeover decisions.

If a company is to take over another it will have to pay a premium to acquire it. Then it must be expecting that as a result of the takeover the company will grow faster. After all, the current share price should reflect the discounted value of the currently anticipated profits. So he estimated the necessary growth rate of the company after the takeover in order to make it a financial success. Table 8.2 summarises the results. He looked at a total of 242 horizontal takeovers over a period of time, and for each of these he estimated the required compound rate of growth necessary to achieve the profitability that would justify making the takeover, assumed to be a 10% rate of return on capital. In 21.9% of cases – 53 of the 242 mergers – it only required a compound rate of growth of the merged companies of under 3.5%. You can see that only 23 cases would require a growth rate of somewhere between 3.5% and 7%. For 22 cases, nearly 10% of the sample, it requires a compound annual growth rate of in excess of 50% in order to justify the price they paid for the firm they acquired. Newbould's conclusion is clear. Most takeovers are being undertaken with no hope of achieving a required growth rate in order to justify the price that was paid for the acquired company in the first place. So although Newbould went about his research in a very different way from Meeks, he came to much the same conclusion. There is little to suggest that takeover activity generally improves the profitability of the companies that engage in it.

Table 8.2 Compound rate of growth required for a 10% rate of return

Compound growth rate (%)	No. of firms	%
Less than 3$\frac{1}{2}$	53	21.9
3$\frac{1}{2}$ –	23	9.5
7 –	17	7.0
10 –	30	12.4
15 –	34	14.1
20 –	63	26.0
50 –	22	9.1
	242	100.0

Source: Newbould (1970)

The Cowling study

The next study is that of Cowling *et al.* (1980). Instead of looking at a very large number of mergers like the other two studies that we have looked at, Cowling *et al.* focused on just nine, but in some depth. They also decided not to use profitability as an indicator of the success of the merger. Profitability has a problem attached to it. It is not clear whether any increased profitability is a result of more market power or the result of lower costs. If the latter, there is potential for improving consumer welfare by being able to get more output for fewer inputs. So the decision was to focus on a unit factor requirement index. This measures the amount of inputs necessary to produce a unit of output. The study covered only the UK.

An improved ratio of output to inputs through mergers could come in two ways. Assets could have been used inefficiently prior to the merger. In other words, there was scope for reducing X-inefficiency. Alternatively, the merger could result in economies in production as a result of moving along the average cost curve. However, the general result seems to be very similar to that found by the previous studies. Typically the results of the mergers showed no general efficiency gain, that is to say, there does not seem to be any general reduction in the volume of inputs necessary to produce a given volume of outputs. However, there were efficiency gains in just a few cases where superior management came to control resources.

The Holl and Pickering study

The next study we examine is by Holl and Pickering (1986). One of the things making this study interesting is that again the approach that is being taken is rather different. They found 50 matched samples of abandoned and consummated UK mergers. The idea was to find a case where a merger was undertaken and then to find a parallel case where a merger was proposed but not consummated. The parallel case was of roughly similar sized firms in much the same industry. Holl and Pickering decided to focus on two measures, profitability and growth. Several conclusions worthy of note were drawn. First, they found that there was no general efficiency gain from mergers. Both bidding and target companies in the abandoned mergers tended to outperform the matched successful bidder. Second, they found that the takeover threat spurs efficiency. Now this is particularly interesting because, just as we have seen with the other studies, there does not appear to be improvement as a result of a merger. Although a merger does not typically cause an improvement in efficiency and profitability, the threat of a takeover does. A firm can be shaken out of complacency because of the possibility of its being taken over. When it realises it is under threat it begins to improve its efficiency, to push up its profitability as a defence against takeover. In other words, merger activity can be valuable to society not because of the effect of a merger itself but because of the *threat* of a takeover, which can help to see that resources are efficiently used.

The Mueller study

A further study, which is worth considering, is the study by Mueller *et al.* (1980). Many studies focus on one country. Perhaps we would get different results if we looked at different countries. Perhaps there are features particular to one economy which are not true of others. So Mueller *et al.* focused on seven countries. There were six in Europe, the UK, Germany, France, the Netherlands, Belgium and Sweden, plus the USA. They used a range of variables as a yardstick for success. We can summarise the results as follows.

● *Growth*. All results on the basis of growth were uniformly negative. Mergers do not lead to increased rates of growth for companies in any of these countries.
● *Share prices*. Returns to shareholders show no long-term gains, although there were short-term gains in some countries for up to three years.
● *Profitability*. In four countries there were small increases in post-tax profits. In the other three the effect on profits was negative.

So the conclusion was that by and large the results of the merger study reinforces the results of some of the studies that we looked at earlier. There are no general benefits to mergers.

The Franks and Harris study

The study of Franks and Harris (1986) is interesting because it encompasses such a large number of observations. They looked at 2000 acquisitions within a 30-year period, although this particular study is concentrated only on the UK. There were large gains to those who held shares in the companies that were being acquired. We should not be surprised at that. Companies that do the acquiring often have to pay a large premium to get control of the company that they are seeking to acquire. But the post-merger performance of the companies who engaged in the merger was interesting. According to Franks and Harris, the typical result was that the post-merger performance of the companies was about equal to the industry average. However, the companies who engaged in the activity tended to be companies which on average had a better than industry average record. So their conclusion was that the result of their engaging in merger and takeover activity was one that reduced their capacity to achieve better performance. So once more the result of the study suggests that there is no typical overall gain as a result of mergers.

The Gregory study

A further study was undertaken by Gregory (1997). The results tend to confirm the earlier studies that we have been looking at. According to Gregory, the reason why takeovers are not successful is the bid premium. This is so substantial that it is not possible to get sufficiently improved performance to justify the bid premium. On average, Gregory claims that those who pay big premiums to acquire companies are paying something like one-third too much. Hence company performance of merged firms is less than satisfactory simply because they paid too much for the assets in the first place.

The JP Morgan study

A rather different study was produced recently by JP Morgan (1998), the merchant bankers (who themselves have now been taken over!). They focused on a relatively small range of activity in this area. They looked at European companies, but they were only interested in mergers, not takeovers, and they were only interested in mergers of companies of roughly equal size. They found that the typical result of these mergers was significantly improved performance. There are reasons why their results are rather different from the results that we have been looking at so far:

- *Mergers of equals.* They are mergers of equals and this suggests that there may be fewer problems in producing one company out of two.
- *Mergers, not takeovers.* Because they are mergers, they do not have to pay a bid premium. They are simply merging the two businesses. So according to JP Morgan there is the potential quite often for gains when the merger means that there is no payment of a substantial bid premium.

The Hitt study

The next study is an American study by Michael Hitt *et al.* (1996). Again we look at this study because it is rather different from any of those we have looked at previously. Hitt has studied merger and innovation activity over a long period. See, for example, his book (1988). He and others have since developed that work. Part of the 1996 paper is interested in the effect of mergers on research and development activity. Is the result of takeover and mergers one that will enhance research and development activity or harm it? Now we are only focusing on one variable here but it is a very important one. They tried to relate merger activity to both the inputs and the outputs of R&D activity. The results were negative. Reduced R&D probably harms society in the long run but tends to impact on firm performance also:

> This research suggests that active involvement in the market for corporate control can be negative to an organisation's health in industries in which innovation is important. (Hitt *et al.*, p. 1113)

Companies who engaged in merger and takeover activity spent less on research and development and did less well in terms of new products and new means of producing products. A number of factors could contribute to an explanation of this. The first is that taking over another company involves substantial costs. Quite often it means that the company making the acquisition is building up a significant amount of debt. It has to service that debt, and may therefore look for ways of economising. A relatively easy target to concentrate on is the R&D activity. A second possibility and perhaps an important one is the link with short-termism. If companies' performance is judged by the shareholders on the basis of shareholder wealth, companies may be forced to focus on the current share price. They keep the share price up by showing that the company is making healthy profits now in the short term. They may do this by cutting back on activities that are costly now but will only produce profits in the longer term. This includes R&D activity. Although the loss in terms of enhanced profits will only occur in the coming years, if its shareholders have a short-term perspective they care about the share price now, so cutting back on R&D activity is going to enhance the short-term share price. So there is a possibility that when a company engages in merger activity, the costs are going to lower the share price. How are they going to get the share price back up? One possibility is to cut back on R&D activity.

There is one more link to consider between mergers and the resultant R&D activity. When a company wishes to engage in R&D activity it has two possibilities. One is do it itself, set up an R&D agency itself and fund it. The alternative and perhaps the easier way is simply to acquire a company that already does it. So instead of setting up a new facility the company simply buys in companies engaged in R&D activity. Hitt *et al.* thought that if a company wanted to increase its R&D activity it might take over a company that engages in it. But having done that it may then look at the company and worry about the costs that are required to sustain it. It might then try to save costs by getting a company that has been very successful in R&D activity to cut back. They conclude:

> it requires a conscious strategic emphasis on innovation and careful selection of target firms for the goals of acquisition and firm innovation to be simultaneously achieved.

So the result of the merger activity is again reduced R&D activity. If the results of Hitt *et al.* are consistent across a large number of countries it would suggest that mergers may harm R&D activity.

The Vita and Sacher study

Vita and Sacher (2001) examined one US merger in great detail. Although it was only a single horizontal merger its results are suggestive. It can be argued that a different view should be taken of merger activity if it is in the non-profit sector. Since a firm's objective function is by definition not profit, the concern about market power leading to high prices is not relevant. The authors examined a merger of two large not-for-profit hospitals in the city of Santa Cruz, California. They found that after the merger prices were still raised. Conceivably, this could be argued to reflect an increase in the quality of the care subsequently provided. However, although the authors do not rule out this possibility entirely, they could find no evidence to suggest that it was the case. Their conclusion was that the price increases 'suggest that mergers involving not-for-profit hospitals are a legitimate focus of antitrust concern'.

BOX 8.1 Merger activity in pharmaceutical drugs

Although many mergers are unsuccessful, some do improve company performance.

Drug company mergers are notoriously disappointing. Once the gloss of cost-savings has worn off, most are found to have destroyed, rather than created, shareholder value.

But one year after its creation, Aventis appears to be bucking the trend.

But what precisely has Aventis been able to achieve that its two component companies could not?

Most telling has been the chance to concentrate its souped-up commercial firepower on a few medicines with real potential.

'We will grow the company by concentrating all our energy and money behind strategic products,' says Mr Landau. 'We have what we never had before: the muscle to turn our products into blockbusters.'

Improved sales performance has been particularly marked in the US, the world's most lucrative drugs market. Before the merger, neither company was big enough to make a dent. But Aventis is making its presence felt.

Although that is heading in the right direction, it is still a far cry from the industry leaders. Aventis has been saddled with an exceptionally long 'tail' of old medicines with annual sales of just a few million dollars each.

As a result, it has among the lowest margins in the business, although again these are improving quarter by quarter. According to Salomon Smith Barney, Aventis had operating margins of 13 per cent in 2000 against a more typical 29 per cent at GlaxoSmithKline of the UK.

If the tail can take care of itself, the job of increasing the size of the head, by supplying a stream of new medicines, falls largely to Frank Douglas, head of research and development. Here too, Aventis is convinced that – also from fairly undistinguished beginnings – it is moving in the right direction.

Mr Douglas has helped to build a more focused, commercially driven R&D organisation. Projects with limited commercial potential have been culled and R&D has been concentrated in three big centres. The company has also set about improving its technology base, ratcheting up the amount spent on outside alliances.

Mr Douglas says he is convinced that productivity is already improving. 'We are definitely getting a bigger bang for our buck.'

Prospects are certainly brighter than they appeared a year ago. But much remains to be done. The job of selling or floating the agrochemicals division has been made harder by a scandal in which genetically modified animal feed leaked into the human food chain.

Aventis nevertheless remains committed to divesting the division by the end of this year.

Something that will take longer is improving profitability. That will only happen slowly as higher-margin medicines begin to occupy a bigger share of the portfolio.

In the meantime, Aventis remains the world's fifth-biggest drugs company by sales, but more like the 15th by market capitalisation.

Management will have to work frantically to close that gap by improving margins and raising the company's reputation among investors.

Source: Financial Times, 2 March 2001 **FT**

A summary of the evidence

Clearly there are some cases where a takeover has been highly successful in enhancing the profitability of the companies that engage in that activity. However, the weight of evidence appears to be that in whatever field, horizontal, diversified or vertically integrated, on average merger activity does not seem to enhance the well-being of the company that engages in that activity. This seems to be true in many countries over a substantial time period. It also seems to be true however 'success' is measured.

It is interesting that in recent years in the area of conglomerate diversification there has been some acknowledgement by companies of these results.

Although much merger activity continues, many companies which had diversified into a huge range of activities are now finding that the way to improve their results is to get rid of many activities which are peripheral to their main business and to focus on a narrow range of activities. So at least in the area of conglomerate diversification it looks as if the results of economists' work is appearing in the behaviour of companies.

Why is it, if all the evidence tends to suggest that mergers are not very successful, that companies continue to engage in this activity? There are a number of possibilities.

- *Management optimism.* Managers are too optimistic about what the merger will achieve. They simply fail to realise that the possibilities that are available by way of economies of scale and enhanced market power are not as great as they anticipated.
- *The time horizon.* A second possibility might be that perhaps managers are very long-termist. Perhaps they are willing to look at the long term so that even though the merger does not enhance profitability for some time, they think it will eventually. Unfortunately, this is unlikely. Some mergers were followed for many years without finding enhanced profitability. Also, as we saw from Hitt's study, this doesn't seem very likely in that it appears that merger activity forces companies to engage in thinking about its short-term rather than its long-term performance.
- *Non-profit-maximising behaviour.* The final possibility is that management is not actually focusing on maximising profits. There are other goals that it has in mind when it engages in merger activity. One such possibility is that although merger activity is not likely to improve the profitability of the companies that engage in it, sheer size has some effect in preventing companies from being taken over. So if managers are not primarily concerned with profitability but primarily concerned with their own welfare they may protect themselves from takeover by engaging in such activity themselves. Other possibile non-profit-maximising motives will be considered later, especially in Chapter 11.

Given the distinct possibility that mergers will not lead to improved company performance, and given that at least some management seeks to maximise profits, there are other strategies that they may pursue to increase profitability. One is to form strategic alliances. These arrangements whereby firms engage in cooperative behaviour do not necessarily involve a transfer of ownership of assets. It is to such alliances that we now turn.

Strategic alliances, franchises and networks

The term 'strategic alliance' covers a wide range of collaborative arrangements between firms. They include, *inter alia*, informal agreements, the licensing of products and joint research activity. They may be national or international in scope. Agreements to restrict price competition, or cartels, are not covered

Figure 8.1 The nature of strategic alliances

here, but we analyse this type of behaviour in the next chapter where we address the issue of pricing. Strategic alliances are hybrid arrangements that lie somewhere between market transactions and hierarchies (see Figure 8.1). At one extreme firms relate to each other entirely on the basis of market relationships. At the other firms are a single entity where the relationship is entirely non-market. Mergers may be seen as moving the relationship from one extreme to the other. Strategic alliances can take a variety of forms along the axis between these extremes. As *The Economist* (1999) observes:

> Mergers, like marriages, can be legally defined and therefore readily counted. Alliances are more like love affairs: they take many forms, may be transient or lasting, and live beyond the easy reach of statisticians. (15 May)

Given what we have seen above, it is not surprising that the benefits and costs to firms of such relationships raise similar issues to those we have covered in the last few chapters. Benefits include

- *Cost sharing.* Investment in new products, for example, can be substantial. It may only be feasible to bring a new product to market if development costs are shared.
- *Pooling of knowledge.* Complex products may require the combined knowledge and expertise of two or more firms.
- *Specialisation.* If the development of new products requires a range of skills, each company can develop work based on its own core competencies.
- *Market power.* Alliances may be able to reduce competition between firms.

On the other hand, there will be potential costs in such alliances. These may include:

- *Clashes in corporate cultures.* It is possible to underestimate the difficulties for firms in working together if they each have different ways of doing things.
- *Problems in the dissemination of knowledge.* Knowledge has some features of a public good about it. Companies may be unwilling to cooperate with others out of a fear that their knowledge is made available to rivals. For example, whilst McDonald's allows franchisees to produce its products on strict conditions that its recipe is followed, The Coca Cola Company will not license anyone to produce its product since it wishes to keep its recipe as a closely guarded secret.

Given the above, it is clear that high-tech industries may well form such alliances. However, there are many other industries also involved in such arrangements. For example, Contractor and Kundu (1998) found a variety of such alliances in the international hotels industry. Harbison and Pekar (1999) estimate that 20,000 alliances in a great variety of industries were formed world-wide between 1996 and 1998.

Since there are potential costs and benefits associated with strategic alliances it is not surprising that some companies find them profitable while others do not. One possible way to address the relative benefits and costs is via transactions costs analysis. Market relationships have clear benefits. They are very flexible and create powerful incentives. On the other hand, as we have seen previously, hierarchies have benefits in economising on transactions costs. A hybrid strategic alliance may provide an optimum trade-off.

The above assumes that there is no government intervention. Sometimes alliances are formed because of government policy. Alliances in the airline industry have soared in recent years partly because there are national barriers to foreign ownership that rule out full-scale mergers. Nevertheless, the Star Alliance looks like a quasi-merger with shared executive lounges and pooled maintenance facilities.

Franchises

One example of a strategic alliance is franchising. This is a contractual arrangement whereby the franchisor provides the franchisee the right to sell a product under a brand name. The contract usually specifies that the franchisor will provide various forms of support such as advertising the brand. The franchisee will undertake to sell the product under certain conditions, meeting particular standards of quality. The franchisee will pay for the services of the franchisor, often a fixed fee plus a royalty equal to a percentage of the profit or revenue that the franchisee receives. The franchisor will have rights to check that the quality obligations of the contract are being fulfilled. One of the best known examples of such a franchising arrangement is McDonald's. Some other fast-food outlets are similarly organised. Although the franchisee is clearly heavily reliant upon the franchisor, both businesses are legally independent enterprises.

Many explanations have been offered as to why a franchisor will enter into such an arrangement rather than produce the good or service itself. We consider two possibilities. First, the franchisor may be risk averse. Some of the uncertainty associated with the sale of the product and the consequent uncertainty over profit levels is borne by the franchisee. A second possibility is that the arrangement may be more efficient. Transactions costs analysis can help to explain this. As we have seen in previous chapters, a part of profit maximisation is the minimisation of costs. Under certain circumstances the local operator can control costs better. For example, the transactions costs of checking the cleanliness of a fast-food outlet would be high for the franchisor, particularly if the outlets were geographically dispersed.

Franchise contracts have two features about them that are worthy of consideration. First, they must be drawn up to minimise the externality problems implicit in such arrangements. The franchisee is trading upon the good name of the franchisor. If the franchisee fails to deliver a high standard of product, all other franchisees are in danger of suffering from the reduced reputation of the franchisor. Hence a typical contract specifies details about the standard of the product that must be delivered.

Secondly, the economic power in establishing the contract lies with the franchisor, who is a monopolist selling franchises into a market where there are many buyers. Hence one would expect the franchisor to extract the monopoly rent and leave the franchisee with a normal profit. Interestingly, this does not seem to be the way that McDonald's operates. The contract price is one that attracts many buyers, a sign that it is set too low. The explanation may well be the way that McDonald's views the externality problem. By setting a relatively low price it has many applicants from which to choose. This enables it to screen applicants so that it is confident that the standards set by the contract are maintained. This minimises the possibility of external effects from poorly performing franchisees. A fuller account of the McDonald's franchise system can be found in Kaufmann and Lafontaine (1994).

It is now easy to see why government attitude to franchised industries is ambivalent. Such an industry raises similar issues to those raised by formally concentrated industries. There are clear issues of monopoly power that may lead to the loss of consumer welfare. However, there are potential benefits, particularly in terms of cost savings. Lower transactions costs means that fewer resources are needed to produce a given level of output.

Networks

Networks refer to the informal, non-exclusive linkages that exist between firms or groups of firms, many of which over time take on the characteristics of more formal relationships. The clothing industry is characterised by such relations. Clothing firms such as Marks & Spencer buy clothes from garment manufacturers. If they are bought in sufficient quantities, they can be produced to specific requirements rather than relying upon standardised production. Again, such an arrangement is somewhere between a purely market relationship and a fully vertically integrated one. Again it may be an optimal one. We have seen that avoiding the problems of asset specificity can mean vertical integration and non-optimal investment levels. The network solution may overcome the problem.

Some networks are international in scope. Although they may have the same potential benefits and costs of national networks there are other considerations. National markets are becoming less relevant in a global economy but gaining access to overseas markets may still be difficult because of government trade policies. International networks may be a way into a foreign market. This benefit may be strengthened if it leads to information exchanges such that companies learn to do things more effectively. However, the cultural problems may also be larger. Jacob (2001) examines alliances between

Western and Chinese businesses. He cites examples of the frustrations felt by management in both cultures. The Chinese felt that Western management was unwilling to learn ways of doing business in China. Western management was often frustrated by Chinese refusal to be flexible and be willing to adapt to change. As a result of such cultural difficulties most joint ventures fail. Nevertheless, the problems are not always insurmountable. P&G and Kodak are just two companies who have made such alliances work over a long period.

Alliances for research and development

Companies frequently form alliances to undertake research and development. We raised this matter briefly in Chapter 5. There are clear benefits from doing so. The EU, for example, makes illegal most forms of cooperation between firms because it may reduce competition. R&D agreements, however, are explicitly excluded from this restriction on firm behaviour. The main potential benefits to society from agreements between firms are:

- Some R&D work will not otherwise take place because the investment needed is too great for any one firm on its own.
- The gains from the investment will be spread between the firms. If one firm does the work on its own it may be able to prevent or slow down other firms and therefore society sharing in the benefits of the research. The fruits of joint ventures are disseminated throughout society.

Nevertheless, if firms cooperate there may be less total R&D activity. The private benefits to a firm of a successful R&D effort may be felt to be too low if the rival firm can also benefit. It may be a social gain if many companies share the fruits of research but a firm may not feel it is a sufficient private gain.

Thus public policy in the area of research activity is fraught with difficulty. The correct choice for the public policy maker is far from clear.

Conclusion

We considered in previous chapters the social costs and benefits of merger activity. We have seen in this chapter that even the private benefits are often, but not always, absent. This appears to be true for different kinds of merger in different countries over a considerable time period. Some businesses seem aware of the problems posed by engaging in mergers. One way of gaining some of the benefits of mergers whilst avoiding some of the costs is through the formation of strategic alliances of various kinds. Under certain conditions these may be the optimum arrangement although they also are not without their problems.

KEY RESULTS

1 Most merger activity does not appear to improve company welfare.

2 This seems to hold for a variety of measures of company performance and across a wide spectrum of industries.

3 The benefits of mergers can sometimes be gained without integration by establishing strategic alliances.

4 The optimum structure of some industries is a franchise system.

5 Cultural problems may limit the benefits of international alliances.

6 Alliances in research and development encourage the diffusion of results but tend to reduce total R&D activity.

Questions

1* Assess the advantages of growth by merger over internal growth.

2* To what extent does short-termism create opportunities for successful takeovers?

3* If firms merge to improve profitability, how could that profitability be measured?

4 Consider Box 8.1. What are the main factors that appear to make this merger a success where so many others have failed? Are there any factors that might make you cautious about pronouncing it an unqualified success?

5 Consider Box 8.2. The number of strategic alliances has increased considerably in recent years. Why do you think that they have become common in the motor manufacturing industry?

* *Help available at* ***http://www.e-econ.co.uk***

BOX 8.2 Mergers and alliances in motor manufacturing

Motor manufacturers are reducing interest in mergers and increasing interest in strategic alliances.

As [car] industry executives return to Detroit this weekend for the US industry's biggest annual get-together, expectations have not been fulfilled. Certainly, there have been significant deals in the past year. But the cascade of takeovers has failed to materialise. Instead, expectations of a takeover wave have given way to a steady flow of less ambitious, piecemeal alliances.

'We are seeing an upswing in limited alliances or collaboration projects. They are proving an attractive alternative to full-blown mergers,' says Professor Garel Rhys, head of automotive studies at the University of Cardiff business school.

'Companies are trying to get the benefits of a merger without actually having to do the deal –

either because one side is too big and overbearing, or because the other side is a financial mess.'

The temptation to opt for alliances has been increased by the uncertain results achieved so far by full-blown mergers.

A second factor favouring partnerships rather than mergers is the easing of revenue pressures on the industry's largest companies.

In the latest deal, General Motors and Honda, the second largest Japanese car manufacturer, unveiled an engine supply arrangement shortly before Christmas. Honda will receive diesel engines from GM's Japanese sister company Isuzu Motors, and in turn will supply GM with advanced low emission engines. This deal followed a far-reaching

▶

BOX 8.2 continued

diesel engine partnership reached last autumn between Ford and PSA, and a strategic alliance in trucks and buses between Volvo and Japan's Mitsubishi Motors.

Since then, Valeo, the French components manufacturer, has teamed up with Zexel of Japan. Ford and GM have unveiled internet joint ventures with Oracle and Commerce One respectively.

Last month, Ford also reached a strategic agreement with IBM. 'We're not looking for acquisitions right now; we're quite satisfied with our brands,' says Jac Nasser, Ford chief executive. 'But we are always talking about co-operation.'

Such alliances are not new to the motor industry – Triumph supplied engines to its fellow UK company Jaguar in the 1940s. But they are more necessary, both for strong companies that want to improve their efficiency, and weak ones that want to survive independently.

The initiative in seeking alliances has often been taken by smaller companies offering specialised services to larger ones. PSA in particular has used alliances to help preserve its independence. 'Our strategy is to implement timely alliances with competitors,' says Jean-Martin Folz, PSA chairman. 'These alliances benefit both partners, while allowing them to retain their independence.'

Would-be predators have been happy to play along with this approach. By joining forces with smaller rivals they can extract technology benefits in areas where both companies are weak. Both Ford and Honda, for example, were late to exploit the trend towards diesel engine technology. Their alliances are part of an effort to combat that weakness, at a fraction of the cost of developing new engines independently.

The search for alliances has also been encouraged by the increasing cost of some new technologies, such as fuel cells. That has led to fuel cell

partnerships between Ford and Daimler-Chrysler, along with Ballard of Canada, and between GM and Toyota. Porsche of Germany has made a lucrative business from seconding its engineers and technical experts to bolster research and development at other companies.

But while alliances tend to be easier to agree than mergers, and carry fewer risks, they can be at least as hard to make work. Volkswagen and Ford have abandoned their $2.6bn Portuguese joint venture that produced 'people carriers' because demand did not fulfil expectations. There are also doubts about Volvo Car's joint manufacturing plant with Mitsubishi in the Netherlands.

Alliances sometimes fail to live up to expectations because companies are reluctant to merge their back office functions. Others are undermined by a clash of corporate culture, or by fears that collaboration could lead to a creeping takeover. Partners to an alliance can also have less incentive to make it work than a merger in which shareholders are directly involved.

'These deals can help in particular geographic regions or product areas, but they cannot deliver the financial benefits of a merger,' says John Lawson, head of automotive research at Salomon Smith Barney in London.

Prof Rhys argues that alliances are often a second best option. 'All they are really doing is buying time. Relationships can be strained, and don't always deliver larger scale at lower cost. For some motor manufacturers, they are simply a way of putting off the inevitable.'

That could mean that companies face a longer-term choice of either letting alliances lapse, or developing them into full mergers. In trucks, Volvo has already shown how an alliance might develop by promising to acquire almost 20 per cent of a new truck and bus subsidiary set up by Mitsubishi.

Source: *Financial Times*, 7 January 2000

9

Pricing for profit maximisation

Get your retaliation in first.

CARAWYN JAMES, rugby coach

Pricing correctly is fundamental to business success. In this chapter we consider pricing strategy in different market structures. We also consider the conditions under which pricing agreements between firms might be successful.

OBJECTIVES

After reading this chapter you should be able to:

- **Understand how prices might be determined by profit-maximising companies in an oligopoly.**
- **Use the theory of games to understand why collusion may occur in the setting of prices.**
- **Appreciate why collusion does not always occur in oligopoly.**
- **Assess the circumstances leading to a breakdown in a collusive agreement.**
- **Understand how the theory of games helps to predict entry-preventing behaviour.**

Introduction

We come now to a new section, pricing activity. How do firms set prices? This is a large topic. Even though we spend three chapters on it we can only introduce the key ideas. There are different views amongst economists as to how firms go about the process of price setting. Essentially, there are three groups of views. The first group says that the driving motive of firms is to maximise profit. This is the underlying assumption of this chapter. There is a second group arguing that firms want to maximise profits, but they do not have sufficient information to be able to do so. They have to find some way of making pricing decisions in the presence of limited information. These ideas form the basis of Chapter 10. The third group of economists denies that the predominant motive of firms' management is to maximise profits. They believe that management has other goals. This view is the subject of Chapter 11. Here we focus on those whose view is that the driving motive of management behaviour is profit maximisation.

We structure this chapter in the following way. We begin by thinking about how prices might get determined if we make the assumption that there is no collusion between firms. There is *non-collusive* behaviour. Firms act independently of one another. Then we consider the possibility that it may pay firms to collude in some way over the choice of price. Finally we introduce some ideas about how firms might set prices when they are conscious of the possibility of drawing new entries into the market. However, keep in mind that all the models in this chapter have the basic assumption that the firm is trying to maximise profits.

Non-collusive price setting

Dominant-firm price leadership

Most of the market structures that we consider in the next few chapters are oligopolistic. This is competition among the few. It means that a market is dominated by a handful of firms. This is typical of most of the industrial scene. We make the assumption that you are familiar with the basic model of perfect competition and the basic monopoly model to both of which we referred in an earlier chapter. In many markets one firm sets the price and other firms in the industry follow that lead. One type of market where this happens is where there exists a *dominant firm*. It is not a true monopolist in that there are a lot of other firms in the market, but they are all relatively small. There is one firm with the power. This firm sets the price and that price will be accepted by all the small firms in the market who will then, in the light of the price set by the dominant firm, decide how much output they will produce. Let us see how the equilibrium price might come about in that kind of market using Figures 9.1 and 9.2.

On the left is the market of all the other fringe firms. Focus first of all on the demand curve. The demand curve is the market demand curve for the product. Also represented is the supply curve of the fringe firms, the sum of their marginal cost curves. Now if the price were to be set at P′, then the fringe firms are willing to supply all the output that the consumers demand at that level. But the lower the price, the less the fringe firms are willing to supply, and the greater is the gap between what the small firms are willing to supply and the quantity demanded by the market. We can use that idea to establish the demand curve of the dominant firm. If the dominant firm sets the price at P′, the small firms in the market will supply all the consumers require and so the amount available for the dominant firm is zero. But if the dominant firm sets a lower price, there appears a gap between what the small firms will supply and what consumers demand. The difference between those two is the amount of demand for the dominant firm. So at the price P*, the gap between

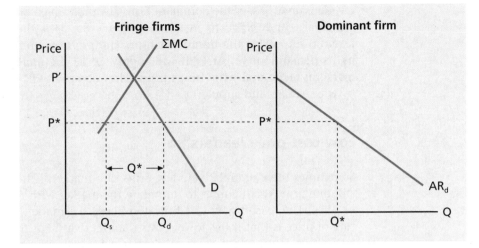

Figure 9.1 A dominant firm model

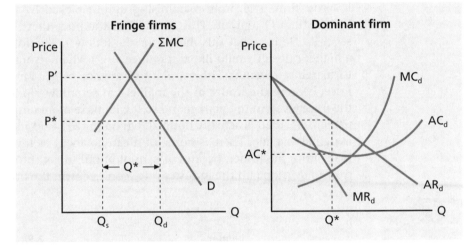

Figure 9.2 Dominant firm equilibrium

Q_s and Q_d is the amount of demand not supplied by the fringe firm. The dominant firm's demand curve at that price would be Q^*, which by construction is $Q_s - Q_d$. So the demand curve for the dominant firm is found by the difference between the market demand curve and that which is supplied by the fringe firms. This gives us the demand curve for the dominant firm. On the right this is shown as AR_d, the average revenue curve.

We can now establish the price set by the dominant firm. Remember the assumption that we look for a profit maximising price and output. Consider Figure 9.2. This is Figure 9.1 redrawn, but in order to find the equilibrium, we have added the marginal cost and the average cost curve of the dominant firm. Also, given that we know the demand curve, AR_d, we know the marginal revenue curve, MR, of the dominant firm. The profit-maximising output is where marginal cost is equal to marginal revenue. So Q* is the profit-maximising level of output for the dominant firm. The profit-maximising price is given by its demand curve. At P* it will supply Q* to the market. The rest of the market is taken up by the fringe firms. They accept the P* price given to them by the market, and supply $Q - Q_s$.

Low-cost price leadership

Sometimes there are relatively few firms in a market. It happens that there is still one firm which comes to dominate the market with regard to the setting of price. The reason why one firm dominates the market in terms of the setting of price is that it has lower costs than its rivals. For the purposes of illustration we assume that there are just two firms in this market and that the product is homogeneous.

In Figure 9.3 we have called the dominant firm the leader, and the other firm is the follower. We can see now why this gives so much power to the low-cost firm. The profit-maximising output picked by the leader is where MC = MR at Q_1 output. This means that the price that the leader wishes to set is P_1. Notice what this means for the follower. The follower would prefer a higher price. It would like to produce at Q_2^* where its marginal cost is equal to marginal revenue. This would give a price of P_2^*. But it cannot set that price, because the leader in the market has set a lower price. It has to accept the price given in the market and so it will make more output at a lower price, namely Q_0^*, than is actually optimal. On output $Q_2^* - Q_0^*$ marginal cost exceeds marginal revenue. There is not a lot it can do about it. It can't fight the dominant firm, the leader, because it cannot afford to get into a price war. If one were to develop and the industry price comes down, the price will come down

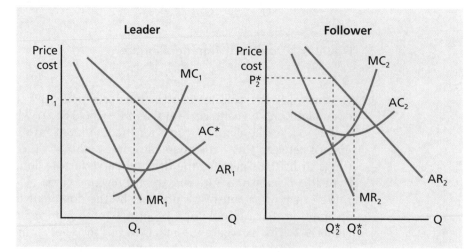

Figure 9.3 Price leadership by a low-cost firm

to a point where the dominant firm can still make profits, but the higher cost producer will be driven out of the market. The upper hand is with the dominant low-cost producer, and so it will accept the price given.

Other forms of price leadership

We have considered perhaps the most common forms of price leadership, dominant firm and low-cost leadership. These are by no means independent possibilities. Firms will dominate markets if they have lower costs than their rivals. However, two other forms are possible. Where no one firm dominates, *barometric-firm* leadership can occur. Maunder (1972) found instances of this in UK markets and Booth *et al.* (1991) found it in North America. The price leadership role is tacitly recognised by tradition or by recognition that one firm has greater information about market conditions. This idea will be developed in Chapter 10. Finally, *collusive-price leadership* can occur. Firms may formally agree on a common price. This possibility is considered later in the chapter.

Collusive pricing behaviour

Motives for collusion: the prisoner's dilemma

The models we have seen so far assume that there is no collusion between firms. That is, we have independent and non-collusive behaviour. But there may be an advantage for firms to get together to agree a price. This can be seen by *games theory*. One way to the idea is via what is called the prisoner's dilemma. If you have not met this before you can follow the argument from Table 9.1.

Think of yourself as having engaged in robbing a bank with your partner. You have been caught with the evidence. But the police have a problem. They

Table 9.1 The prisoner's dilemma

		Rachel	
		Don't confess	*Confess*
Armstrong	*Don't confess*	Armstrong = 1 year Rachel = 1 year	Armstrong = 7 years Rachel = free
	Confess	Armstrong = free Rachel = 7 years	Armstrong = 5 years Rachel = 5 years

can certainly charge you with the crime of receiving stolen property but they don't have enough evidence to convict you of the major charge, robbing the bank. So they take you and your partner, and put you in separate cells. They go to each one in turn and say 'You are going to spend a long time in gaol for robbing this bank. However, confess that you did it and we will be able to get remission of your sentence.' Are you going to confess when you know that your partner is in another cell where the same deal is being put? How are you going to behave? Because you have been taught economics you will ask for pen and paper and construct a matrix of possibilities. Then you come to a conclusion as to whether to confess.

Table 9.1 is the *pay-off matrix*. Assume that you are Armstrong and that your partner in crime is Rachel. You have two possibilities. Don't confess or confess. But you know that your partner Rachel also has two possibilities. She might not confess, or she might confess. So there are actually four possible outcomes. What happens if you don't confess and Rachel doesn't confess either? You each get only one year in gaol because the police don't have enough evidence to convict you of the major charge. Suppose you don't confess but Rachel confesses. She's got a deal that enables her to go free, but you are going to spend a long time in gaol. Her confession convicts you. Suppose now that you confess, but Rachel doesn't confess. You will go free, but Rachel who didn't confess gets seven years. Finally you could both confess. You both get some remission of sentence, but the police make it clear that your confession isn't as valuable as if your partner confesses too, so you spend some longer time in gaol – say five years each.

Given all those possibilities, what are you going to do? It is not entirely certain – it depends upon all kinds of things, but the most likely outcome is this. You will ask yourself, what is the worst that would happen if you don't confess. Also ask yourself what is the worst that could come if you do confess. This is a maximin approach. Minimise the damage on the assumption of the worst scenario for each choice. If you don't confess, the worst you could do is seven years in gaol, on the assumption that Rachel confesses. If you confess, the worst you could get is five years in gaol. On that basis you are highly likely to confess.

You should also think what Rachel is going to do. Using the same strategy she will confess. This makes it even more likely that you will confess. If she is going to confess it certainly makes sense for you to confess also. Notice that you both spend five years in gaol, whereas if you could have got together and agreed not to confess, you could have both done better and finished up with only one year in gaol. If you have a best strategy regardless of the other player's best strategy there exists a *Nash Equilibrium*. So here both players adopt their best strategy and we have a stable outcome even though both players could have done better.

Why do we get this strange result? You had to take your decision in the presence of uncertainty. You did not know what your partner was going to do. If you could agree with your partner a strategy and be sure that your partner would stick to it, you could both do better.

Table 9.2 A profits pay-off matrix (£m)

		Firm 2	
		High price	*Low price*
Firm 1	*High price*	Firm 1: 10 Firm 2: 10	Firm 1: 0 Firm 2: 12
	Low price	Firm 1: 0 Firm 2: 12	Firm 1: 3 Firm 2: 3

Now look at Table 9.2 to see why firms may wish to collude on price. Assume just two firms in the market, a duopoly. Firm one has a decision to make as to whether to set a high price or a low price. It does not know whether the other firm is going to set a high price or a low price. What would make a difference would be if it could eliminate the uncertainty, by knowing what firm two was going to do. If both can agree to set a high price, both gain. Suppose this is not possible. If one chooses a high price, and the other firm goes for a low price, the firm with the high price will lose enormously because consumers will switch out of the high priced product. On a maxi-min basis each chooses the low price and profits are less than they might have been. If they could eliminate the uncertainty they could both do better. How do they eliminate the uncertainty? This is done by collusion, agreeing a price. Such an agreement is called a *cartel*.

The kind of 'game' we have described can be a zero-sum game or a non-zero-sum game. A zero-sum game is one where a gain to one party must be exactly offset by a loss to the other. Market share pay-offs are of this kind. Since the total market share must by definition be 100%, any increase by firm one must be matched by an equivalent decrease for firm two. Table 9.2 represents a non-zero-sum game. Both firms can gain from a higher price.

Conditions for collusive agreements

Despite the attractions of collusive agreements they will not be profitable under all circumstances. There are at least four conditions that determine potential profitability.

- *The legality of the agreement.* In most countries such collusion is illegal and firms can be punished. If the management judges the expected costs of illegal activity to exceed the potential benefits, the cartel is not formed.
- *Fewness of firms in the cartel.* Agreements become more difficult to achieve as the numbers that must sign up increase. There comes a point at which the numbers are too great for the cartel to be effective.

- *The power of fringe firms*. No industry is in a position where there is not some potential competition from competing firms and/or products. We saw something of this in the dominant firm model. The greater the number of firms in the fringe, the more firms there are to undercut the agreed price. However, the larger the number, the less power each firm is likely to have. The power of the fringe is also crucially dependent upon its cost structure. At the limit one could have a perfectly contestable market such that a cartel had no ability to raise price above costs.
- *Transactions costs*. Williamson (1975) sees an agreement to form a cartel as the establishment of a contract. As we have seen in previous chapters, this involves transactions costs. In this context those costs include the specification of contractual terms. As we shall see shortly, agreement must be reached about demand for the product, the joint level of output to be produced, the level of costs of each firm, the future of costs and levels of investment. It also involves the costs of monitoring cheating on the agreement. Finally it requires an effective enforcement of penalties on any cheats. This is clearly difficult and expensive if the cartel is itself illegal. No possibility exists of using courts as a means of sanction.

For all the above reasons there is no certainty that a cartel will be established in an oligopolistic structure. There are clear benefits although they may be outweighed by the costs.

The nature of cartel price agreements

We now consider the nature of any agreement to establish a common price. As we said in the previous section, it will be necessary to consider costs and demand conditions to make the most of the agreement. We illustrate with reference to an agreement between two firms that have different cost structures. Assume that firm one in Figure 9.4 is the higher cost producer. Firm two is in the

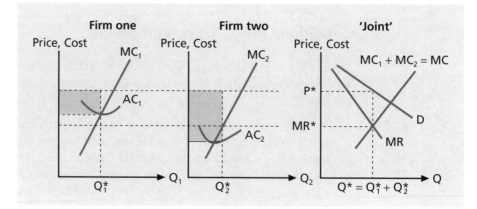

Figure 9.4 A cartel model with two firms

powerful position of having the relatively low cost structure, but it still intends to collude and agree the correct price to maximise the profits of both.

We have two marginal cost curves, one for each firm. If we horizontally sum them, we produce a joint marginal cost curve for the market. We can also sum the two marginal revenue curves. 'Joint' also shows the market demand curve and the joint marginal revenue curve. The profit-maximising output for both is the level of output Q* which represents $Q_1^* + Q_2^*$. The profit-maximising level of output for the cartel is there since $MC_1 + MC_2 = MR$. That means that the cartel price is established at P*. Now you can see from the diagram how much profit each firm makes. Firm two produces Q_2^* output. Then average costs are read from the average cost curve. Average revenue is the price that we set, P*. So output times average revenue is the total revenue, output times average cost is the total cost, and the shaded rectangle shows firm two's profit. Notice that firm one has higher costs and makes less profit, but they have eliminated the rivalry between them by the cartel. How much profit does firm one make? Proceeding as for firm two gives the shaded area for firm one. You can now see Williamson's point. Joint profit maximisation requires the establishment and the sharing of much information. It also requires agreement on total output level and the optimal sharing of that output if joint profit is to be maximised.

Basing point collusion

One form of collusion has been noticed in industries where transport costs form a high part of the price. It is called the basing point system. In Chapter 4, Figure 4.9, we considered a firm with plants located at three different places, A, B and C. In Figure 9.5 we have a similar diagram but this time there are

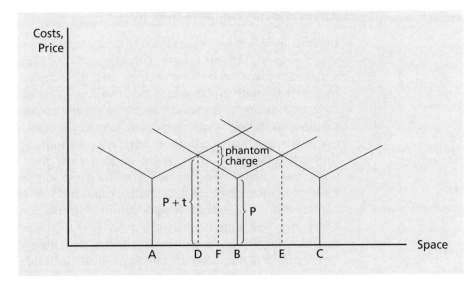

Figure 9.5 A basing point system

three firms, A, B and C, each with one plant. In a competitive industry price reflects marginal cost. Each firm will charge a price that covers production plus transport costs. So, for example, a consumer at B pays a factory gate price p, covering the production cost. A consumer at D pays p + t, the production cost plus the transport cost. Then each firm has an area over which it has a monopoly. It is isolated from competition by transport costs. Firm B has a monopoly extending from D to E. Such a system of pricing is called a free-on-board (FOB) system. A consumer will be quoted at price at the factory gate plus transport cost.

By contrast, a basing point system works by firms establishing an agreed set of prices determined with reference to basing points. These in our example are A and C. So if firm B is asked for a quote from a customer at F it will give it as the production cost plus the transport cost from A, the nearest basing point. Shipment takes place from B so that the customer pays a phantom charge. It pays a transport cost that is never incurred by the producer.

The basing point system, then, is an example of a cartel. A common set of prices is determined. However, this particular form of cartel focuses on prices for transport services as well as for the output of the product itself.

Instability of the Nash Equilibrium and repeated games

On the basis of what we have said so far one might expect a stable outcome in oligopolistic markets. Price levels will be predictable and there will be no incentive to lower price to gain market share. Even in the absence of cartels rivals will simply match price cuts and all firms will lose out. This is inconsistent with the evidence. Some markets are characterised by instability and price wars. How do we explain this? There are a number of important explanations. For *non-collusive* games there are:

- *Different decision rules.* We assumed that all players use a minimax rule. They may not do so. The rule is essentially conservative. Management may adopt a higher risk approach. For example, they may choose a low price if they believe that another player may be unwilling to enter a fight.
- *Different estimates of the pay-off matrix.* We assumed that the pay-off matrix for different decisions was certain and perfectly known. In practice this may not be the case. Managers of some firms may be more optimistic about what they may gain if, say, they choose an aggressive price strategy.
- *Games are repeated.* We assumed that the game was a one off. In practice most games are repeated. If a similar game is to be repeated in the next period, there are further considerations that may make for instability. There may be a time lag between a decision to cut price and reaction by the other firm(s). A short-term gain is made by the price cutter. This may be enhanced if the discount rate applied to the value of future profits is high. It is also possible that a price cut will not be matched at all. See, for example, Rao *et al.* (2000).

For *collusive* games we may still not have price stability for the following reasons:

- *The chances of detection.* If there is an equilibrium reached by collusion, the stability of that equilibrium is in doubt if it is possible for a firm to offer secret discounts and remain undetected. Clearly the more members of the cartel, the more likely any member will feel its chances of remaining undetected. The problem is that once it becomes clear to other firms that someone is cheating they also may lower price and the stability will be gone.
- *Similarity of costs.* What might hold the cartel together would be the kind of situation where there are different cost structures. It may well be that if one firm is a higher cost producer than the other, it will be frightened to get involved in a price war. It feels that it can't win, and so the likelihood is that the cartel will have fewer members willing to cheat. So similarity of costs increases the chance that a cartel will not last very long.

Box 9.1 Collusion in auctions for mobile phone licences?

It has been suggested that collusion has taken place in some auctions for mobile phone licences. Collusion is rarely overt so it is difficult to assess the evidence.

The world's largest concerted transfer of money from the corporate sector to state coffers was never likely to be straightforward. But Europe's auctions of third generation mobile phone licences are turning out to be more of a battle of wills than anyone anticipated.

With auctions in countries including the UK, Germany, the Netherlands and Italy now completed, some governments are more than happy with the sums raised. But in countries where the auctions proved a disappointment – notably Italy and the Netherlands – controversy is growing. Questions are being raised about the methods used by some telecoms companies to minimise their outlay for valuable spectrum.

The ultimate question is whether the companies colluded improperly during the auctions. Some efforts to co-operate with other bidders were legitimate: telecoms companies formed consortia before each auction to bid for licences together. But if the different consortia talked to each other during the auctions, or set out to rig the auctions, they would have acted illegally.

Competition authorities in Italy have already raided the offices of participants in its auction searching for evidence of suspected collusion between competing parties. Dutch government officials have also passed evidence of possible collusion attempts to the local competition authority. Regulators in Austria have warned that any communication between bidders may lead to the suspension of its auction, which began yesterday.

But there are also lingering questions about earlier, more expensive auctions. Concerns about collusion in the German auction first surfaced on its second day, when RegTP, the telecommunications regulator and organiser of the process, ordered a snap investigation into suspected communications between Debitel and Mobilcom, two new entrants.

The decision followed a statement from Gerhard Schmid, chief executive of Mobilcom, to a French newspaper saying his company would welcome customers from rival Debitel should the latter fail to secure a licence. RegTP chose not to exclude the bidders, a measure that would almost certainly have brought the auction to a premature end. It confined itself to issuing a stern warning against future breaches of the rules.

Reports have surfaced elsewhere of signalling between bidders during the auction, where bidders were physically confined for the duration of the auction to prevent direct communication. One operator has privately admitted to altering the last digit of its bid in a semi-serious attempt to signal to other participants that it was willing to accept a smaller licence. If all bidders accepted this, it would have brought the auction to a swift close.

▶

Box 9.1 continued

It was not easy to establish breaches of rules during auctions. RegTP, the German telecommunications regulator, says that inquiring into whether there was signalling between bidders during its auction would have been pointless: 'We knew it would be almost impossible to say whether a coded message had been sent and if it had been received.'

Nor did regulators in some countries have much incentive to act aggressively. In Germany, Italy and the Netherlands – where bidders exceeded the number of licences on offer only by one – any exclusion would have brought the auction to an early end and reduced the proceeds.

But experts on auction procedures argue that any collusion – even if it occurred – was not the biggest problem. They say companies were allowed too much leeway before the auctions to limit competition by forming consortia. Alliances such as that between KPN of the Netherlands, Hutchison Whampoa and DoCoMo of Japan played a big part in reducing competition in the Netherlands and Germany, but were perfectly legitimate. 'While explicit collusion can be a problem, a much bigger concern is tacit, and often legal, coordination among firms,' says Paul Klemperer, the Oxford university academic who helped to design the UK auction.

Alarm about either type of collusion must be seen in the context of the sums the auctions have raised. Telecoms operators who have paid far more than anyone expected before the UK auction might be forgiven for asking what good any co-operation did them.

Source: Financial Times, 3 November 2000 **FT**

Entry deterrence: limit pricing

Now we turn to the possibility that firms will take pricing decisions, not simply with reference to existing rivals, but also with reference to potential rivals. A firm or a cartel will have to bear in mind the possibility that if it sets a high price, it will draw new producers into the market. So we consider the possibility that the price that the existing firm wishes to set is a price that will deter new entrants into the market. For simplicity, assume that we have only one firm in the market. That firm is a monopolist. But although it is a monopolist, it fears that if it sets too high a price, it may well not be a monopolist for very long. How does it make its pricing decision in the light of the possibility of new entries into the market? Look at Figure 9.6.

We call this a limit pricing model, because the price set by the firm is a price which is limited to that which deters a new entrant. If this had been the standard monopoly diagram, we would have drawn not only the demand curve, but also the marginal revenue curve. Then we would show the firm picking the level of output in which marginal cost is equal to marginal revenue, taking its price from the demand curve. The reason this firm doesn't do so is the potential new entrant. If we assume that the firm knows the cost structure of the potential entrant, which is labelled AC_e, then it can price accordingly. It can pick a price that is just below the price which would enable the new entrant to cover its costs of production. So by setting a price at P_L, and therefore producing output of Q_L, it discourages any new entrant from coming into the market.

At first it might seem that what we are saying here is that the firm isn't really profit maximising, because it isn't setting a price where its marginal cost

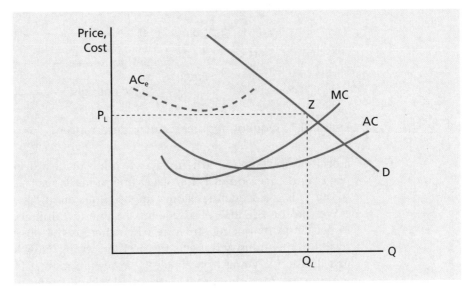

Figure 9.6 Limit pricing

is equal to its marginal revenue. So you might think that this is moving away from the standard idea of a profit-maximising firm. But that is not so. Given that the firm knows that it cannot afford to draw a new producer into the market, its demand curve isn't really D. Its demand curve is really P_LZD. This is because it cannot afford to set a price above P_L and expect to sell as much as implied by D. It will simply draw a new producer into the market.

Given the demand curve, where is its marginal revenue curve? Over the range from 0 to Q_L, if the demand curve is horizontal, the marginal revenue curve is the same as the demand curve. It is like a firm in perfect competition. It can always make one more unit of output, and not drop the price, so the extra revenue it receives is the same as the price. If it chooses to set a lower price than that, then the kink in the demand curve, D, creates a vertical discontinuity in the marginal revenue curve at Q_L. So MC = MR at Q_L output.

Entry deterrence: sequential games

A problem with the above analysis is the assumption that the limit price is always successful. It would be valuable to know what might happen if entry takes place. How would firms now set price, assuming there is no collusion? We can consider some possibilities by extending our analysis of game theory. In the prisoner's dilemma we assume that decisions are being made at the same time so that each person is making decisions as to whether to confess or not, knowing that the other is making the decision at the same time. Subsequently we pointed out that firms are not in such one-shot situations. However, it is also possible to consider that there is more realism in a *sequential game*. Here player one makes a decision and subsequently player two makes

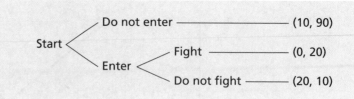

Figure 9.7 Sequential games: entry deterrence

a decision in response. When player two has made a decision in the light of player one's decision, it is for player one to make a subsequent response and so on. This is a sequential game; the decisions are made in sequence.

We can use the idea of a sequential game to think about one firm trying to decide on its pricing structure when there is the possibility of drawing a rival into the industry if it gets the decision wrong. Now let's assume that the first decision is going to be made by a new entrant. It is watching an existing firm making some profit in the market, and trying to decide whether or not it's going to join the market. Once the choice has been made, the incumbent will make the next decision. The key decision will be whether to fight, and try to drive this firm back out of the market with an aggressive pricing policy, or to accommodate the firm and accept that it is now a duopoly market. Let us look at such a sequential game and see what kind of result might take place. In Figure 9.7 we assume that at the start the potential entrant is making the decision. It could either enter or not enter. The numbers refer to profits in £ million following the decision. The first number is that of the player making the decision. If it chooses not to enter it will avoid a fight with the existing firm. So 10 represents the assumed profit for not entering, and 90 represents the profit of the existing firm. It will make a great deal of profit, because it doesn't have a rival. Now let's consider the possibility that the firm decides to enter the market. Now if it decides to enter, it is for the incumbent to decide whether to fight, or refrain from fighting. The kind of numbers that might be realistic would be as follows. If the incumbent firm fights, there is severe price competition, such that profits are low for both the potential entrant and the existing firm. If it does not fight, it may be willing to set a relatively high price in the hope that the new entrant will go along with it. Alternatively it may try to establish a cartel. Then the new entrant does reasonably well. It seems reasonable to assume that the existing firm will do much worse than if there were no entry, but much better than if it fights. So these are the kinds of sequential game figures that we have. Now here is something important to notice. The ideal for the incumbent is that there is no new entry. However, if entry takes place, it is better to accept than to fight. It makes more profit by not fighting than by fighting, even though its strong preference is that there isn't a new entry into the market at all.

Let's consider an alternative possibility now, that the first choice is not with the new entrant, but with the incumbent firm. We might have a situation where the existing firm knows that there is the possibility of a new entry into the market. It might be able to undertake policies to deter the new entrant.

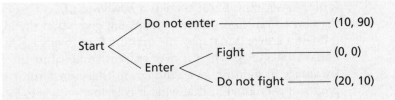

Figure 9.8 Sequential games: entry deterrence with different outcomes

One possibility is limit pricing. Another is to invest in new capacity – even though it doesn't at first sight appear to make commercial sense. Even if the existing firm has sufficient capacity to meet demand, it may well be that it makes sense to create more. Once it has created that excess capacity, it now knows that if a new entrant comes into the market, it is in a very powerful position to fight. Having committed itself to those costs of new capacity, its marginal costs of production are now relatively low. The new entrant still has very high costs to meet in terms of its setting up in the market. Its capital costs are not yet sunk. So the potential entrant is now hesitant to enter the market knowing that the incumbent has put itself into a position where it is in a very powerful position to fight, and can relatively easily drive the new entrant out of business again. What would the sequential game numbers look like if we assume that the first move is made by the existing firm, and that it is one that is related to capacity?

If we assume now that the first move has been made by the existing firm's creation of more capacity, we can now pick up the game in Figure 9.8 at the point where the new entrant is thinking about entering or not entering the market. If it now enters the market, the new entrant is going to watch the existing firm making less profit. This is because it had to spend money on capital that it didn't really need. Suppose the new firm does enter and the existing firm fights, it's in a relatively powerful position to do so. It has this excess capacity. So the profits are better than previously for the incumbent firm, and the new firm will not make any profit. If the existing firm doesn't fight, there are higher profits for the new entry and still some profits, but not very high, for the existing firm.

Now two interesting things follow from that analysis. The first is this. It may well be that the key to understanding price, where there is fear of new entry, is determined by who makes the first move. The first mover has the advantage. If the first mover is the new entrant, it may well be that the existing firm finds it better to accept the new entry rather than fight. But if the incumbent firm can make the first move, then it may be able to increase its capacity to the point where it deters a new entrant ever coming to the market. That is one of the reasons why it's difficult to predict an equilibrium outcome in such situations.

There is a second interesting conclusion from this analysis that concerns what is rational behaviour for the existing firm. As you saw from the first sequential game, it is rational for the incumbent not to fight if a new firm enters the market. It makes more profit by accommodating the firm that has entered, rather than engaging in a price war. So its best outcome is that there is no new entrant, but if there is a new entrant, its best outcome is to accept the new entrant, not to try to fight. But given that the ideal outcome is that it doesn't enter, it may pay the existing firm to engage in an apparently irrational strategy. So when a new entrant comes into the market, there is an advantage in fighting, even though in the short term it is costly in terms of profits. It is rational in that what it is trying to do is to establish a reputation. The reputation is that it cannot be relied upon to act rationally and accept any new entry into a market! So fighting may appear to be irrational, but in another sense it's a rational policy to establish that it may be irrational.

We could draw a parallel in warfare. Suppose you have a nation which has conventional weapons. It is thinking about going against a nation which has a nuclear weapon. It may be rational not to use the nuclear weapon, because everybody gets blown apart in a nuclear war. But if the nation that has the nuclear weapon can establish itself as an irrational player in the game, it may well deter the other nation from fighting the conventional war. So what constitutes rationality in these kinds of games is not clear. Similarly, what constitutes profit-maximising behaviour is not clear. You can look at a large firm, which is engaging in a price war, and say that this is not rational. However, it *is* a rational choice. It has decided to sacrifice short-term profit for a potential long-term gain.

Conclusion

Let us summarise. We started by saying that the way in which firms make pricing decisions will depend upon whether they are profit maximisers. All we have done so far is to consider some models that assume this to be so. We have examined price behaviour if there is no collusion. We have thought through the conditions required for successful collusion over common price using some games theory. Finally we have thought about how firms might take pricing decisions, conscious of the fact that there may be new entries. All those models have had this basic assumption, that the driving goal is to maximise profits. In the next chapters, we will consider the possibility either that firms cannot profit maximise because they do not have the kind of information that we have assumed here, or that management wishes to follow other goals.

KEY RESULTS

1 Price leadership models help to understand pricing when there is a dominant firm.

2 A Nash Equilibrium may be found in oligopolistic markets.

3 Uncertainty can be reduced by price collusion but agreements can be difficult to establish and liable to break down.

4 Limit pricing can be used to deter entry.

5 Sequential games analysis helps to explain the advantages of being a first mover where there are barriers to entry.

Questions

1* An economics lecturer writes a book that is then published. The author receives 10% of the published price for each copy sold. The author argues for a lower price than the publisher. They both share the same views about costs and demand conditions. Show that the author's desire for a lower price is not vanity. Using a transactions cost argument, show that the problem would not be resolved even if the author was paid a share of *profit*.

2* 'Bundling' means selling goods as a package. Hotels offer 'bed and breakfast'. Is this beneficial to firms? To customers?

3* Look at Figure 9.5. How might the conclusions about a basing point system be modified if there were economies in transport such that transport costs are less than proportional to distance?

4 Consider Box 9.1. How would you decide whether collusion to bid for mobile phone licences was more likely in one country than another?

5 Consider Box 9.2. How does the analysis differ if a first mover is entering a new market rather than entering an already established market?

* *Help available at http://www.e-econ.co.uk*

Box 9.2 First mover advantage and the dotcoms.

In some instances the advantage is *not* always with the first mover.

First movers do not always have the advantage. Amazon.com, the online retailer, has announced that growth is disappointing; it is sacking 15 per cent of its workforce. If even the arch exponent of the online land grab is struggling, that suggests a harsh lesson for the dozens of start-ups that rushed into their markets: the dotcom experiment has been a massive exercise in first-mover disadvantage.

Pioneering entrepreneurs often prove a concept can work, only to see large companies come into the market after them to pick up the profits. E-commerce is a middle-distance race in which stamina and patience count; it is not a sprint in which being first to market is everything.

First-mover advantage was the rallying cry of the dotcom light brigade as it charged into apparently new markets. Companies, it was thought, had to move as fast as possible to make their products ubiquitous and their market position unassailable.

The challenge is different: to get to the right market at the right time. That does not always mean being first. Business history is littered with companies that conquered markets by coming in second. Take the history of the computed tomography (CT) scanner as an example.

EMI, the British music company, pioneered the scanner, widely regarded as the greatest advance in radiology since the X-ray (its inventor, Geoffrey Hounsfield, won the Nobel prize in medicine for his work). But while EMI had hugely valuable technology, it lacked manufacturing capability for medical equipment and had no knowledge of the largest market, the US, where it was better known for its association with the Beatles.

Moreover, the CT scanner was easy to imitate. The first competing products were on the market only three years after EMI had launched. Instead of teaming up with partners that could provide manufacturing and marketing clout, EMI tried to go it alone. It soon lost its lead to a highly capable competitor, the US company General Electric. By the early 1980s EMI was forced to quit a market it had created.

There is no reason why e-commerce should differ from other business sectors. First movers can win – but only if four conditions are met:

● First, the market they serve has to be ripe for rapid development. Initially, start-ups are helped by serving marginal markets that are so small

Box 9.2 continued

they are overlooked by larger incumbents. But for a first mover to drive home its advantage, the market has to grow rapidly. That allows a new entrant to translate a slim advantage in a small market into a big lead in a large market.

The trouble with many e-commerce markets is that they have remained small and immature, chiefly because consumer habits have taken longer to change than optimists expected.

- Second, being first is not enough. The first mover has to erect barriers to entry – in the form of distinctive technology that is hard to copy. It must learn from the market and brand itself to establish its position. These barriers have to be so daunting that followers will be deterred.

In most cases, the technology behind e-commerce companies was generic and not distinctive. Most companies bought their systems off the shelf.

As a result, few of the dotcoms managed to generate what first movers need to command a market: increasing returns.

Successful first movers have created increasing returns in which initial success has led to more success. There are online businesses that are attractive because they were first and took advantage of that by locking in their customers.

Despite Amazon's problems, it has carved out a strong position in bookselling.

But true increasing returns with 'lock–in' are rare and become much more difficult to capture once everyone understands the game. EBay generated increasing returns but the first seller of pet food did not.

- Third, a first mover that goes it alone has to have all the skills to exploit a market.
- Fourth, it helps if first movers do not face capable competitors. Unfortunately for many dotcoms that is precisely what they did face. The dotcoms were the innovators that proved the market opportunity, which incumbents then exploited.

Incumbents could do this because of what happened to barriers to entry. Barriers to entry into traditional businesses are falling: it is cheaper to set up an online and telephone bank than a traditional bank with expensive high street outlets.

But barriers to entry into the e-retailing business are even lower. The swarm of entrants to these nascent markets awash with money from venture capitalists demanding high growth and quick returns meant that the dotcoms undercut one another, often giving away content and services in the hope of rapid growth.

Source: Financial Times, 1 February 2001 **FT**

10 Profit maximisation with inadequate information

Wall Street is very good at forecasting. It has predicted six of the last three recessions.

PAUL SAMUELSON

Pricing decisions must sometimes be made when limited information is available to management. How can firms set prices when they are unsure what customers are willing to pay?

OBJECTIVES

After reading this chapter you should be able to:

- Understand how prices are determined in a mark-up model.
- Be aware of how estimates of company demand elasticity can be made.
- Appreciate differences in predictions of the mark-up model from models assuming perfect information.
- Know what determines the size of the mark-up.
- Reconcile mark-up pricing with profit-maximising models.

Introduction

In the previous chapter we began to look at pricing and we concentrated on models which assume that the firm wishes to maximise profits. Given this assumption of profit maximisation, it was simply a question of looking at different kinds of market structure, different possibilities about the size of entry barriers and different assumptions about rivals' reactions. We could then work out how firms and industries would behave.

What we shall do in this and the next chapter is to consider some alternative possibilities. There are two areas of thought to look at. The first is that firms do indeed want to maximise profits, but they may not be able to do so. The other area of thought is that of some economists who want to question whether the driving goal behind firms' behaviour is profit maximisation at all. This will be the basis of Chapter 11.

In this chapter we concentrate on the possibility that firms wish to maximise profits, but for various reasons may not be able to do so.

The cost-plus pricing model

If we think about the models that we considered in the last chapter, they generally involved looking at the firm's cost of production, particularly the marginal cost curve. They also involved examining the demand curve from which the firm is able to work out the marginal revenue function. This information enables the selection of a profit-maximising output. Given that level of output, the demand curve gave to us the appropriate profit-maximising price. The cost-plus pricing model, or mark-up model, questions whether this information is available to firms. Some economists feel that it is reasonable to say that a firm has got a very good idea about its costs structure. It knows how much it will cost the firm to engage in producing an extra unit of output and how much it costs on average to produce. However, it has much less idea about the position of the demand curve. The firm knows one spot on the demand curve. It knows its current selling price and the quantity it is selling at that price. This is one spot on the demand curve. But it cannot know every spot on the demand curve.

It does not know, for example, if the firm raises the price, how many fewer units it will sell. It does not know the elasticity of demand for the product. The firm simply doesn't know what it would be able to sell at different price levels. Thus it takes its costs of production, adds on some mark-up and thereby establishes its price. The output it sells is a kind of residual. It is whatever it can sell at the level of price that it has chosen.

This view about how firms go about making pricing decisions has various names. It is called the full-cost pricing model, the cost-plus pricing model, or the mark-up model, reflecting the essence of the idea that the firm thinks about its costs of production, adds on a mark-up and arrives at the price as mark-up over those costs.

There is impressive empirical support for such an approach. We mention two studies. Shipley and Bourdon (1990) surveyed pricing practices among industrial distributors in the highly competitive engineering and paper markets. Over 54% of these firms said they used 'full cost plus mark-up' as a means of determining price. This represented 50% exactly in engineering and 57.4% in paper distribution. Similar results were found by Hall *et al.* (1996). This Bank of England survey used the Bank's contacts, which means that the sample was not fully representative. In particular, since established companies are larger than new ones and contacts take a while to establish, the average size of the surveyed firms is larger than a truly representative sample. They also found about half using cost-plus pricing. There was evidence that the practice is more widespread in smaller firms: 58% of small companies recognised cost-based pricing as important, compared with 45% of medium-sized companies and 44% of large companies.

In the rest of this chapter we shall consider four things.

● First, we think through the extent to which firms can acquire information about demand conditions. How much knowledge do they really have about the demand curve?

- Second, we consider the implications for markets if cost-plus pricing is used.
- Third, we focus on the extent of the mark-up on costs that they choose.
- Finally, we consider whether the price and output that they choose is close to the price and output decision that would follow from conventional profit-maximising strategies.

Demand estimation

Does the firm know about the place and elasticity of its demand curve, as we suggested in the last chapter, or is it the case that the firm knows only one spot on the demand curve? In practice there are ways of establishing such information. However, as we shall see, none of them provides perfect information and none of them is costless.

The first way would be to experiment by changing price and seeing what happens to quantity demanded. The firm could raise price by, say, 20% and observe the extent to which quantity demanded falls. It could then lower price and observe the extent to which the quantity demanded increases. So it can try to establish the demand curve via a pattern of trial and error. This has two problems. First, it may be very expensive for the firm to do it. They may spend a period with a higher price and discover that demand has fallen very considerably as a result. When they lower their price again, they have lost their market and can't get it back. Markets may not be flexible. Once a contract has been established with another firm, the situation may not be reversible. So it may be very expensive for the firm to engage in that kind of experimentation. The other problem is that we draw the demand curve with a *ceteris paribus* assumption. We are assuming here that nothing else changes other than the price of the product. Suppose that it raises its price for, say, six months and then observes that during that period demand is now 20% less. It cannot hold constant all the other things that affect demand: incomes, the price of substitutes and so on. So the change in the quantity demanded may not simply be because of the change in price. It may be any of a host of other factors which have shifted a whole demand curve. So it is not a very realistic way for the firm to try to establish what its demand curve is and it may be very costly.

A variant on the above is to use a test market. It may be possible to select a small part of a market where a firm can vary price and observe the effect on demand. Table 10.1 gives an illustration of this approach. In 1993, *The Times* newspaper considered lowering price from 45p per copy to 30p in order to increase market share. It experimented by offering its newspaper at the lower price for one month only in the area of North Kent. The table shows the effects there on sales of *The Times* and the effects on its major competitors. Some estimate of the elasticity of demand can now be obtained.

$$PED = \frac{\% \, \Delta \, QD}{\% \, \Delta \, \text{price}} = \frac{+14.7\%}{-33\%} = -0.45$$

Table 10.1 *The Times* sales in Kent County area, per day, August 1993

Title		Net sale	Difference
The Times	Base week	11,565	–
	Week 4	13,266	14.7%
Independent	Base week	9,133	–
	Week 4	8,885	–2.7%
Guardian	Base week	9,009	–
	Week 4	8,474	–5.9%
Telegraph	Base week	44,196	–
	Week 4	44,116	–0.2%
Total	Base week	73,902	–
	Week 4	74,741	1.1%

Source: Industry estimates

Assuming this sample period and area to be representative and assuming that the *ceteris paribus* assumption holds, then for every 1% fall in the price of *The Times* one might expect a 0.45% increase in the quantity sold.

Similar calculations can be made for the cross-elasticity of demand for competitors' newspapers with respect to the price of *The Times*. For example, we can see the effect on the *Independent* whose price remained unchanged, using the formula

$$\text{X PED} = \frac{\% \, \Delta \, \text{QD } Independent}{\% \, \Delta \, \text{price of } The \; Times} = \frac{-2.7\%}{-33\%} = 0.08$$

Thus, for every 1% fall in the price of *The Times*, the *Independent*, on average, loses 0.08% of its sales, *ceteris paribus*.

By using a short period this minimises the possibility of other factors changing. For example, no other newspaper altered its price during that time. However, the information obtained in such an experiment is still limited. Is the test market typical of the whole? Perhaps more seriously, this is an estimate of the short-run effect. In the longer term, matching price cuts by competitors are possible so that the long-run effects might well be different.

Another approach is to use surveys. A representative sample of people are asked what would be their demand at different prices. Firms sometimes use such an approach to test the market before launching a new product. The problems of such an approach are well known. It is difficult to avoid a biased sample unless it is very large. People may behave differently from the way they think they will behave. Interviewers can easily mislead by the way that they ask questions. Again, then, it is possible to obtain information, but it is far from perfect and not costless.

A final way that firms will estimate demand is regression analysis. This involves establishing the relationships between variables. One variable, the dependent variable is regressed upon, or systematically related to, independent variables that are believed to have some influence. So the demand for the firm's product may be related to the price it charges, the level of its advertising, the price of its competitors' products, and average incomes. By looking at data from the past, estimates are made of these relationships. This enables firms to know the effect upon quantity demanded if it varies its price. That is, it establishes the nature of its demand curve and the value of the own-price elasticity of demand. It also enables it to know the effect of other things that shift the demand curve. Some of these variables will be outside of its control, such as price charged by competitors. Others it can control, such as the volume of its advertising.

We illustrate with two examples. Estimates have been made of the demand for cigarettes using such techniques. A summary of these studies is given by Cameron (1998). They include studies from a number of countries. All suggest that demand is price inelastic. Typically the short-run elasticity is between −0.2 and −0.6. So, for example, a 10% price rise would cause a fall in quantity demanded of between 2 and 6%. A rise in price would increase industry revenue. The long-run price elasticity is usually between −0.5 and −0.8. This implies that in the longer term more people give up smoking in response to price rises although demand is still price inelastic.

A second illustration comes from the USA with respect to the demand for milk. This time we concentrate upon the estimates of shifts in the demand curve from advertising. They assume that there is a need to advertise because people forget, and at a constant rate. They estimate the long-run demand elasticity with respect to advertising as 0.0028. They also estimate the cost of advertising. This enables them to establish an optimal volume of milk advertising. They estimate that this is about 55% of the historical level.

Regression analysis, then, provides valuable information. However, a number of things should be noted that limits its value. It is based upon past relationships. The arrival, for example, of a new product onto the market will change the relationships, possibly greatly. The work on cigarette demand was done before the arrival of nicotine arm patches which may make it easier to break the habit. The estimates are at the industry level, not at the firm level. In the case of cigarettes, the reason for the inelastic nature of demand is the absence of close substitutes. The demand for one brand of cigarettes will have a quite different elasticity because rival brands provide close substitutes. Of course, estimates can be made for individual brands using the same regression techniques. However, the information will be expensive to acquire and still subject to error.

Regression analysis, then, is a mechanism by which you can get at least a reasonable idea of the demand curve for the product. The problem is that it is not perfect and there are costs involved in acquiring that information. So some information can become available to a firm, but the information is limited and only available at a price.

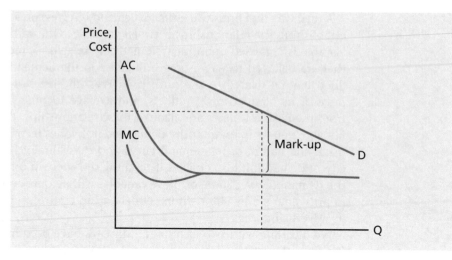

Figure 10.1 Mark-up pricing

Implications of cost-plus pricing

Having established the case for saying that firm information is limited with respect to the demand curve, we now see how the firm goes about making its decisions with regard to price. We also see what this implies when compared with an assumption that knowledge is perfect.

Consider Figure 10.1 showing the firm's demand curve and the cost structure. Now for simplicity we assume that unit costs fall, or reach some minimum and then stay constant. This means that at some point the marginal cost curve, which is below average cost at first, eventually becomes equal to average costs. Remember that MC = AC, where AC is at its minimum. So at some point MC = AC. In some models it is assumed that marginal cost = average cost. In other models MC = average variable cost, but the same principle applies. If a mark-up is on variable costs, it will have to be sufficiently high to cover fixed costs. If the mark-up is on all costs of production, a full-cost pricing model, then any mark-up represents some kind of average profit level. The assumption of constant MC is useful. If this were not so, the size of the mark-up could not be independent of output. Whether this is a realistic assumption is open to question. In the survey by Hall *et al.* (1996) this theory received more recognition by respondents than any other. However, in a survey in the USA by Blinder (1991) this theory received little support from respondents. Here we make the assumption of constant MC.

So the firm knows its level of costs. We show the demand curve, but the firm's problem is that it doesn't know what the demand curve is. So it simply takes its unit costs and adds on some mark-up for profit. This determines price. It will sell whatever it can at that price. Because of the position of the demand curve it will find one spot on it. This is the level of output that it will sell.

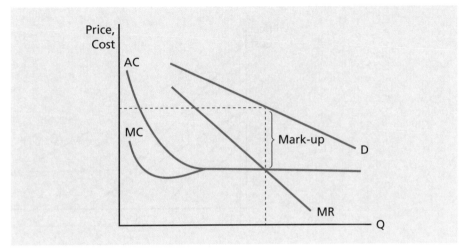

Figure 10.2 Mark-up pricing and profit maximisation

On the basis of the argument so far, we could ask whether this is the profit-maximising level of output. Is that going to be the level of output that the firm would have chosen anyway, had it had all the information that it required? The answer is, possibly, but possibly not because it is guessing. Only if it guesses correctly about the nature of the elasticity of demand will it not matter that information was imperfect. In Figure 10.2 the firm has guessed perfectly. We show the demand curve that the firm doesn't know and the associated marginal revenue curve. At the optimum level of output the price and output are the same. But that is a coincidence. This may well not happen. And before we develop that idea a bit further, we could just ask the question: 'Is that view always going to give us the same kind of results that we would get if we had a more conventional view of a profit-maximising output?' And the answer is that in this form that we have looked at so far, it may well not. Although the two ways of establishing price/output may give the same result, there are differences between what we would predict a firm will do if it makes its pricing decisions using a mark-up on cost. We summarise some of the differences by reference to Table 10.2.

Table 10.2 Profit maximisation and full-cost pricing predictions

Model	Set price or output	Rise in demand	Fall in demand
Profit maximisation with perfect information	Output	Raise price and output	Cut price and output
Full-cost pricing model	Price	Raise output	Cut output; possibly raise price

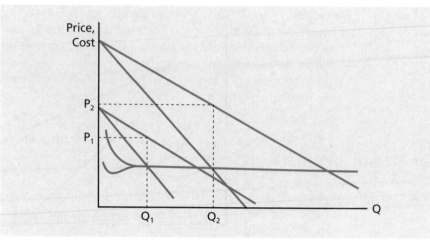

Figure 10.3 Demand increases and profit maximisation

We make three observations, summarised in Table 10.2.

- A firm can choose price or output, but given the constraint of the demand curve, not both. A profit maximiser with perfect information chooses an output and the price is the residual which comes from the output decision that it has chosen, MC = MR. With the cost pricing model, the firm focuses on the price and the output is the residual.
- We think about what would happen to a firm that finds a rise in demand when it is profit maximising with perfect information. If demand increases, marginal revenue increases. Assuming no change in costs, output rises and price rises also. You can see this in Figure 10.3 When demand shifts, the profit-maximising price and output moves from Q_1/P_1 to Q_2/P_2. But suppose the firm is operating on a full-cost pricing principle and now there is a rise in demand. We have assumed that output is one that means that costs are constant at whatever level of output. Then as it raises output in order to meet the increase in demand, because costs per unit don't rise, and because price is cost plus a mark-up, it will raise output, but it will not raise prices.
- Finally think what would happen if there is a fall in demand with a standard profit maximising monopolist's price and output decision. The fall in demand reduces marginal revenue. Hence the firm's profit maximising decision is to cut price and output. The full mark-up model says that if there is a fall in demand, it will certainly cut output. It may not cut price. It may well leave price unchanged. Indeed, it may even raise price, if it is determined to keep the same mark-up. As it reduces output, unit costs may rise. This may mean that it wishes to raise, rather than lower price in response to a fall in demand.

There is one more observation to make, not referred to in Table 10.2. We saw in the last chapter that a consideration about price changes is the possible reaction of rival firms. This problem is much reduced in an industry that is known to use a mark-up on costs as its pricing decision. When costs rise, it will in most cases be a rise which all firms in the industry are experiencing. It may be an increase in material costs or increased wage rates as a result of union bargaining. Under these circumstances each firm can raise its price, knowing that other firms will probably do the same.

The size of the mark-up

What determines the size of the mark-up? Partly we could say it is a question of guessing where a marginal cost equals marginal revenue. This is a price that reflects demand elasticity, which itself in part reflects the degree of competition. However, other possibilities suggest themselves. We shall consider several but we focus mainly upon the threat of new competition. We might see it as a mark-up to forestall new entries, in which case it is a limit price. Again this requires estimation. It must guess what will be a price such that new firms do not enter the market.

We can explore that idea a little more by using a particular model by Bain (1956). He said that essentially there are three key barriers to the entry of new firms into a market that are most important. They are product differentiation, economies of scale and absolute cost barriers.

Product differentiation is a barrier to entry. If there is a particular brand of, say, soup that is differentiated in the mind of a consumer, then a new firm entering the market has a disadvantage that it cannot produce just that particular product. The particular brand of soup has built up in the consumer's mind a brand loyalty. Emphasising that this soup is different in taste to all others makes it harder for the new firm to enter the market. So product differentiation is a barrier to the entry of new firms. Advertising reinforces that product differentiation. We consider advertising more fully in Chapter 12. So Bain's first barrier to entry is product differentiation.

The second barrier to entry according to Bain is economies of scale. We have already seen that economies of scale enable firms to be protected from the entry of new firms because it is relatively difficult for firms to start small and to grow. By starting small they are usually at a significant cost disadvantage with the larger firms. So economies of scale are a barrier to entry of new firms.

The third barrier to entry which is very important is that of absolute cost barriers. Absolute cost barriers are those barriers that mean the new entrant into the market will have a higher cost structure than that of the existing firm. It is important to see that this is a different idea from economies of scale. If there is an industry with a falling long-run average cost curve, the larger firm has an advantage over the smaller firm. However, if a new firm *were* to enter at a large level of output it could gain the same economies of scale as the larger firm. But where there are absolute cost barriers the new firm coming into the market has a higher cost structure than the existing firm. At whatever level of output it chooses to enter the market its costs will be higher than the incumbent firm. There are a number of reasons for this. One possibility again is advertising; the existing firm has built up a huge amount of brand loyalty in the mind of the consumer. How will a new firm entering the market overcome that and persuade consumers to try its product? One way of doing it is to engage in advertising. It may well need large amounts of advertising in order to get itself established in the mind of the consumer, larger volumes of advertising than the existing firm needs. So whatever level it chooses to enter the market its costs are going to be higher than the costs of the existing firms.

Let us look at Bain's model now and see what that means about the behaviour of the existing firm. We will do so in three stages. We will assume first of all that the only barrier that exists when a new firm comes into the market is product differentiation. Then we see what would happen if there were product differentiation *and* economies of scale. Then we shall show what would happen if there were product differentiation, economies of scale *and* absolute cost barriers. First let us begin to build up this model by assuming that the only barrier between the incumbent and the new company is product differentiation. As we do so, keep in mind that the firm will not have all the information it would like. It is taking decisions that are a best approximation to what we show on the diagrams.

Consider Figure 10.4. The demand curve D represents the demand curve of the incumbent. The horizontal line represents the average cost curve of the incumbent and also the average cost curve of the potential entrant. Because, by assumption, there are no economies of scale, the average cost curve for both firms is constant. How high a price will the existing firm charge for its product? The firm reflects upon the danger of attracting a new entrant. So this is a kind of limit pricing model. The higher up the demand curve it moves,

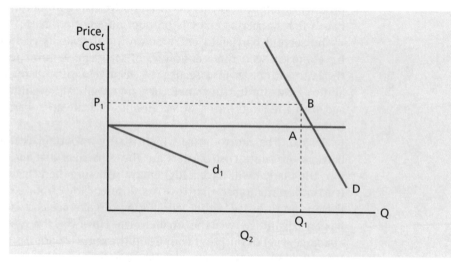

Figure 10.4 Mark-up pricing and product differentiation

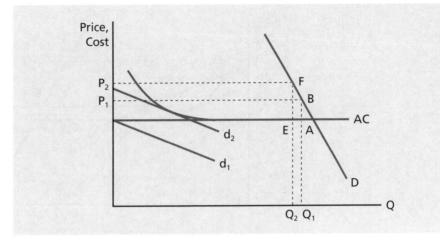

Figure 10.5 Mark-up pricing with product differentiation and economies of scale

and the higher price it sets, the more willing consumers will be to transfer from the incumbent firm to the potential entrant. As we move up the demand curve of the incumbent firm and set a higher price, the demand curve of the potential entrant will move further to the right. The incumbent does not want the new entrant's demand curve to move far enough to the right to bring it above the average cost curve. This would cause it to enter because it can make profits above normal. So the incumbent estimates that the highest price that it can charge without dragging the potential entrant's demand curve above the average cost curve is P_1. So it sets a price of P_1 and will sell at Q_1. The mark-up is AB.

We have assumed so far that the only difference between the incumbent firm and the potential entrant is product differentiation.

Now, let us see how price gets established and the mark-up is determined if there are both product differentiation and economies of scale. We can revisit the diagram but in Figure 10.5 we have redrawn the average cost curve to show a market with economies of scale. What difference does this make to the incumbent? The incumbent can afford the potential entrant's demand curve to move further to the right now. Thus it will raise price to a higher level, P_2, even though the potential entrant's demand curve shifts up to d_2. The mark-up is now EF. This is still satisfactory for the incumbent. The new entrant will not come into the market, as its demand curve is still not above its average cost curve. But the effect of the economies of scale is to raise barriers to entry and to enable the incumbent to charge a price further above costs than it could before.

That is what happens if there are two entry barriers existing in the market. Finally, we will consider the possibilities if all three barriers exist at the same time. The third one is an absolute cost barrier so that the potential entrant has a higher cost structure than that of the incumbent firm. So let us look

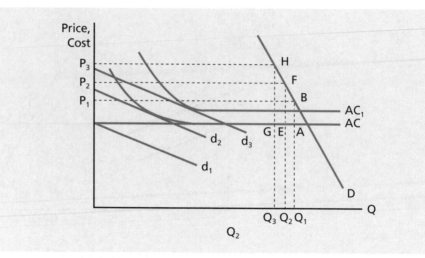

Figure 10.6 Mark-up pricing with product differentiation, economies of scale and absolute cost barriers

Box 10.1 Profit margins in the electrical goods market

Price uniformity in the market for electrical goods can be explained in a variety of ways, including the use of mark-ups to determine prices.

Meagre profit margins will make it virtually impossible for electrical retailers to slash the prices of washing machines and televisions, despite the Government's decision to outlaw price fixing, according to a report published today.

Verdict, the retail consultants, belittles the Consumer Association's predictions of a 25 per cent reduction in the price of electrical goods in September, when suppliers are no longer allowed to tell retailers the prices at which they must sell products.

Margaret Beckett, the Trade and Industry Secretary, helped fuel hopes of reductions of up to pounds 100 on some electrical goods when she ruled last week that restrictive practices in the market had been denying consumers lower prices.

Verdict's report questions the use of the Department and Trade Industry's 'sledgehammer' in the market. 'Yes, there is price uniformity but the report demonstrates that this is a function of a highly competitive environment rather than the operation of a cartel,' said Verdict analyst Richard Hyman.

According to the retail consultancy group it would be impossible for every retailer to negotiate with every manfacturer on every product. 'Some mechanism will need to remain in place in order to communicate product-pricing architecture. Verdict does not believe, therefore, that the DTI's action will make any difference to prices in the shops,' the report concludes.

For prices to fall dramatically a discount retailer would need to step in with aggressively cut prices and then achieve huge sales to survive, Mr Hyman said.

But a discounter is unlikely to be attracted to the market, given the low profit margins on which retailers are operating, he added.

Verdict calculates Dixon Store Group's share of the market at 20 per cent, three times greater than Comet's and higher than the total of the 10 other leading specialists. DSG, which includes the Dixons, Currys and PC World chains, is also the fastest-growing and most profitable of its competitors in the sector.

But according to Mr Hyman, even DSG, with its profitability and a commanding position in the electrical market, would have difficulty cutting prices further.

Source: Guardian, 26 May 1998

again at the diagram and see what happens when all three of those barriers to entry exist at the same time.

In Figure 10.6 we have redrawn the diagram but now AC only represents the average cost curve of the incumbent firm. The potential entrant's cost curve is higher at AC_1, because it has costs associated with coming into the market which the existing firm does not have. You can see the effect of this as the incumbent can now raise price even further above costs of production, shifting price up to P_3. This will draw the potential entrant's demand curve to the right at d_3, but d_3 is still not above AC_1 so the potential entrant still does not enter the market. The mark-up is now GH.

In general, the greater the barriers that exist, the more difficult it is for new firms to enter the market, and the higher is the mark-up on costs that will be used by the incumbent firm.

The mark-up, networks and path dependence

Under certain circumstances the mark-up on costs may be less than implied by the above analysis. One example of this can be found in markets with positive network externalities. The utility from wearing a kind of perfume may be reduced if there is an increase in the number of other wearers. There are negative externalities from an increase in its use by others since it seems less exclusive. The utility derived from using a pen is independent of its use by others. The utility derived from owning a mobile depends in part on the number of others with a mobile or some other phone. Mobiles are an example of a positive network externality since the utility derived increases with an increase in the number of other users.

In markets with positive network externalities there are multiple demand levels, depending upon consumer expectations about the number of others who buy. That is, demand depends upon the expected network size. In such markets a critical mass may be reached where there are sufficient users that it is believed that many others will purchase. This seems to have been the case with mobile phones. Under such circumstances a firm with some monopoly power may set a low mark-up on price in order to move more quickly to the point where a critical mass is established. Even where such externalities do not exist, low prices to reach a critical mass may be optimal if there are significant scale economies for firms. Providers of television services provide digital recording equipment at low mark-ups for this purpose.

Similar arguments apply to path dependency. Sometimes there are competing technologies for a given market. At some stage one is adopted as the market standard. It was widely believed that Betamax was a superior technology to VHS for VCRs. How was VHS adopted? In the early stages of competition relatively few people adopted VHS and the industry became locked into it. The path taken depended upon a few apparently insignificant purchasing decisions. In such markets very low mark-ups on costs may be optimal as a firm fights to establish the critical mass that will establish it as the industry standard.

The mark-up on costs, then, will vary for a wide variety of reasons, but the basic argument remains. Incomplete information requires a firm to add a mark-up to costs as a means of establishing its price/output decision.

Full-cost pricing and profit maximisation: a reconciliation

So far we have looked at the basic idea of a cost-plus model and seen how the firm makes its decisions. There is at least one reason for thinking that it is unrealistic. Many firms say that they use a cost-plus approach to pricing. However, many of them say that the mark-up they choose depends upon demand conditions. See, *inter alia*, Eichner (1987) and Hall *et al.* (1996). So, it is not just a question of finding our costs of production and adding on some mark-up. The size of the mark-up is affected by demand. If either the demand curve shifts or the elasticity of demand changes, the size of the mark-up will alter. Now if this so, it raises the possibility that the firm feels that it has a reasonable amount of information about the elasticity of demand. Furthermore, it is choosing a price and output decision that is close to the price output decision of a profit-maximising producer with full knowledge. If the cost-plus way of determining prices is done with knowledge of demand elasticity, then the result will be the same.

We can see the idea using a little basic mathematics. You should know that

$$MR = P\left(1 + \frac{1}{\varepsilon}\right) \tag{1}$$

where MR = marginal revenue,
   P = price
   ε = elasticity of demand

Now if a firm is profit maximising it will set marginal costs equal to marginal revenue. So given (1), if we simply replace marginal revenue with marginal cost, which would be the profit maximising decision, we would have

$$MC = P\left(1 + \frac{1}{\varepsilon}\right) \tag{2}$$

where MC = marginal cost

rearranging gives

$$P = MC\left(\frac{\varepsilon}{\varepsilon + 1}\right) \tag{3}$$

Now we have by assumption that marginal cost and average cost are the same at the levels of output that the firm is using, so we can therefore say that

$$P = AC\left(\frac{\varepsilon}{\varepsilon + 1}\right) \tag{4}$$

where AC = average cost

rearranging gives

$$P = AC + \left(\frac{-1}{\varepsilon + 1}\right)AC \qquad (5)$$

This is useful because we can now use it in the following way. If we know the elasticity of demand we can work out the appropriate mark-up on costs to give us profit maximisation.

Suppose, for example, the elasticity of demand is –3, then we can simply substitute that into our formula:

$$P = AC + \left(\frac{-1}{\varepsilon + 1}\right)AC$$

If $\varepsilon = -3$, then

$$P = AC + \left(\frac{-1}{-3 + 1}\right)AC$$

$$P = AC + \frac{1}{2}AC$$

$$\therefore \text{ mark-up on AC} = 50\%$$

If, then, we do know the elasticity of demand, and if this firm is a profit maximiser, it can choose its optimum price/output. If it sets its price output decision by finding where marginal cost equals marginal revenue it will get the same answer as if it uses a cost-plus model and chooses its best mark-up.

If that is true, we can see the relationship between the elasticity of demand and the size of the mark-up. A few other examples are given in Table 10.3. You can check these out for yourself and work out any others. The point to notice is that as the value of the elasticity changes, so the size of the mark-up changes accordingly. At first it might seem odd that a value of elasticity of –1 gives you an infinite mark-up on costs; you might care to think about that. It is one of the questions at the end of the chapter.

Table 10.3 Relationship between demand elasticity and mark-up

Value of elasticity	Mark-up (%)
–1	∞
–2	100
–3	50
–4	33.3
–5	25
–6	20
–7	16.7
–8	14.3
–9	12.5
–10	11.1

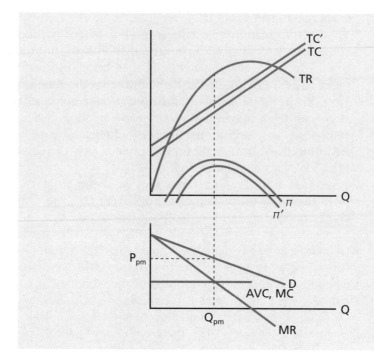

Figure 10.7 Mark-up pricing with search costs

Mark-ups and the cost of information

Previously we pointed out that knowledge of demand elasticity is only available at a cost. Is it worth acquiring that information? Are the costs that are incurred justified in terms of being able to find the right level of mark-up to maximise profit? We follow Douglas (1984), whose mark-up is on AVC.

Consider Figure 10.7. Here we have a firm in which we assume for simplicity a constantly rising total cost curve, TC. The total revenue curve rises, TR, reaches a maximum and falls again, which is the equivalent on the lower diagram of saying that we have a declining demand curve, D, and a constantly falling marginal revenue curve, MR, such that where total revenue is maximised, marginal revenue is zero.

What we have also drawn is a profits curve, π. The profits curve is simply the difference between revenue and cost at each possible level of output. So if the firm had all the information available to it, then the profit maximising decision would be to produce where marginal cost is equal to marginal revenue. This is the profit-maximising level of output, where the gap between total revenue and total costs is at its greatest. Alternatively expressed, it is where the level of output is that which corresponds to the top of the total profits curve. However, suppose that the firm only knows that information via engaging in some kind of research. Then the costs of the research, which can be seen as a fixed cost, will raise the total cost curve from TC to TC'. We shifted it parallel to show that these are fixed costs. The firm will pay the same costs for this information at whatever level of output it chooses to produce. The consequence of paying for this information is to shift the profits curve down to π'. The firm will make less profit than before because it has higher costs in order to establish where the demand curve is.

So is it worth acquiring that information? There's a case for saying that it is not worth it. If the firm is reasonably good at guessing or estimating the elasticity of demand, it may be able to do better, make higher profits, even if it cannot quite find the level of output which corresponds with maximum profit. We can see that in Figure 10.8.

Suppose this time the firm, not knowing what the demand curve is, picks the profit-maximising level of output Q_{pm} and charges the price P_{pm}. It chose the best mark-up on costs. If it could do that, it would be better not to acquire the search costs. Its profits would then be higher. Profits would be at the top of the original profits curve because it didn't engage in the research. It would have been better not to have paid the costs of discovering where the demand curve is. But the problem is that it does not know that Q_{pm} represents the right mark-up. But providing it gets somewhere in the range from Q_2 to Q_1, with whatever range of mark-up that implies, the amount of profit it will make is greater than if it had engaged in the search costs and finished up on π'. If it cannot guess that accurately it would have been better to pay the search costs.

So a firm that guesses, but guesses reasonably well, what its demand curve is, and how elastic that demand curve is, will actually be profit maximising rather than the firm that has got the perfect information but has had to pay in order to acquire it. If this is how firms go about making pricing decisions, we come to an interesting conclusion. The mark-up firm, which goes about making its price output decisions in that way, is actually a profit maximiser. We have recognised that one can only profit maximise if one is willing to engage in sufficient costs to acquire adequate information. There is no difference then between the profit maximiser looking for the point at which MC = MR, and the full-cost pricing kind of behaviour. Both of them, we can say, are profit maximisers.

Conclusion

There is some solid empirical support for the view that firms do not attempt to select an output where MC = MR. They have less than perfect information and so choose to add on a mark-up to costs as a way of determining price. Demand conditions, fear of new entries and the nature of the product all play a part in determining the size of mark-up. It can be argued that, since information is only available at a price, firms will buy the optimum volume of information about demand conditions. Thus the cost-plus method of price determination may well give the same answer as the conventional profit maximisation approach.

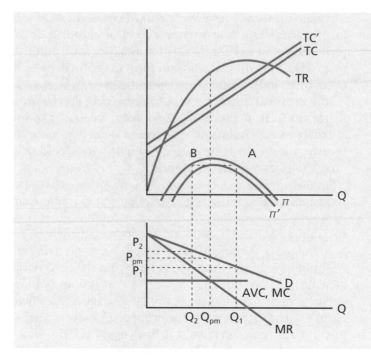

Figure 10.8 Mark-up pricing with search costs

KEY RESULTS

1 In the mark-up model firms choose price by taking costs and adding a mark-up for profit.

2 Demand can be estimated, albeit imperfectly, by questionnaires, test markets and regression analysis.

3 Changes in price will be different from models assuming project information when demand and cost conditions change.

4 The size of the mark-up will depend upon product differentiation, economies of scale and absolute cost barriers.

5 It can be argued that since information can be acquired at a price, cost-plus pricing does not differ from profit-maximising behaviour.

Questions

1* Explain the logic of saying that the optimum mark-up on costs is infinite when demand elasticity is unitary.

2* Hall *et al.* (1996) asked firms the following question: 'What action do you take when a boom in demand occurs and this demand cannot be met from stocks?' Easily the most common response was to increase overtime.

Relatively few said they would increase price. Can this response be explained a) by standard profit-maximising behaviour? b) by mark-up pricing behaviour? Which theory do you think is more consistent with this evidence?

3* *The Times* and *The Sun* are both owned by the same company. At around the time that *The Times'* price was cut from 45p to 30p *The Sun*'s price was cut from 25p to 20p. Why might the outcome of *The Sun*'s price cut be different from that of *The Times*?

4 Consider Box 10.1. An explanation for a common price level of white goods could be illegal behaviour on the part of manufacturers, fierce competition in the industry or an informal recognition among firms that there is a standard mark-up on costs. How would you decide in any individual case which is more likely?

5 Consider Box 10.2. Is the higher mark-up on branded products justifiable from the point of view of consumer welfare?

* *Help available at* ***http://www.e-econ.co.uk***

BOX 10.2 Mark-ups and product differentiation

The mark-up on costs can be increased if the product is differentiated – even if the product differentiation is created by advertising.

Are brands an appalling rip-off, enriching their corporate owners by exploiting people's insecurities and desires? Or are they worth every penny of the price premium they command because of the pleasure they bring?

It is an old question that has been given new life by the continuing battle in Europe between Levi Strauss, the US clothing company, and Tesco, the supermarket chain that sells Levi's jeans at discount prices.

On the one hand, you have Tesco positioning itself as a consumer champion by obtaining Levi's jeans on the grey market and selling them for much less than authorised stores.

On the other, you have Levi fighting to stop this activity out of a belief that its brand is devalued when its jeans appear in a supermarket alongside shelves full of soap powder, tea bags and pickled gherkins.

Take Levi's. In the US, the jeans are seen as a fairly workaday product, and they are widely sold at a competitive price through a variety of channels. Yesterday, Macy's in New York was selling Levi's 501s for $36.99 (£26), JCPenney's online store was selling them for $34.99, and the Canal Jean Company in downtown Manhattan was selling them for $30.

But in Britain, Levi's jeans have been positioned almost as a designer fashion item, and sell for much higher prices through carefully chosen outlets such as boutiques, in-store concessions and Levi's stores.

Prices for a pair of 501s range from £45 to £49.99 – roughly double the typical price in a US department store.

The difference in price is the power of branding laid bare. Britons and Americans end up with exactly the same pair of jeans, but Britons pay more simply because they have been persuaded by skilful advertising and restrictive distribution to credit the Levi's brand with more cachet than Americans do.

At least that has been the position until now. But Tesco, which is obtaining its supplies from an unnamed source outside the official UK distribution network, is breaking the pattern by selling 501s for just £25, much the same level as in the US.

In fact, Levi's is a relatively weak example of modern branding in action. To the extent that it stands for a single product – a pair of jeans – it is more like those old-fashioned trademarks that served as a guarantee of quality and reliability than today's most successful brands, which set out to operate at an emotional level.

▶

BOX 10.2 continued

In the early days of the consumer society, it could be argued, trademarks benefited society by helping people identify products they could trust. But slowly, consumer protection legislation chipped away at that role: then competition diminished it further by flooding the market with ever-better products at ever-lower prices.

Today, competition is such that we have reached something approaching product parity: a situation in which quality and reliability are the price of market entry and nearly all products at a given price-point in any category do much the same job. So companies that want to maintain a price premium need other ways to differentiate their products, and have latched on to emotional branding as a means to that end.

Yet brand owners could come under pressure to modify their behaviour. This is happening already in the drug industry, where global pharmaceutical companies are facing an unprecedented wave of

criticism over the prices they charge for their branded products. Last week, the manufacturers dropped a patent infringement lawsuit against the South African government after being widely portrayed as profiteering at the expense of the sick.

Clearly, there is a difference between life-saving drugs and blue denim jeans. But the Levi's case against Tesco is in danger of provoking a brand backlash, too. Consumers are growing better informed. Many Britons have travelled to the US, have seen how little Levi's cost there and want to know what entitles the manufacturer to charge so much for the same product in the UK.

This presents brand owners with a dilemma. The whole purpose of brands is to enable them to maintain their profit margins. But when profit-making is perceived as profiteering, the brand owners run the risk of being demonised and seeing years of patient brandbuilding destroyed.

Source: Financial Times, 25 April 2001   **FT**

11 Non-profit-maximising pricing behaviour

I lose money on every suit I sell, but I make it up on the volume.

GARMENT TRADE SAYING

Economists often use models in which it is assumed that firms wish to maximise profits. In this chapter we consider that this assumption may not be valid.

OBJECTIVES

After reading this chapter you should be able to:

- Understand why some economists reject profit maximisation as the management goal.
- Understand the sales revenue maximisation model and its implications for advertising.
- Outline Williamson's managerial utility model.
- Appreciate behavioural theories of the firm.
- Understand the Galbraithian view of corporate survival.
- Assess the empirical evidence for non-profit-maximising models of management behaviour.

Introduction

Chapters 9 and 10 explored how prices are determined within industries and firms. A key assumption was that the goal of business is profit maximisation. In this chapter we continue to focus on pricing. However, here we consider some models where the assumption is that the firm is not trying to profit max-imise. Different economists have different ideas as to exactly what it is that firms are trying to achieve. But one thing that is common to them all is a belief in the principal–agent problem as it relates to management behaviour. This idea is one that we have already met. As the owner of the firm, the share-holder, you are the principal. You wish management, your agent, to maximise profits. The agent may not maximise your utility, but their own. What goals might they be? In an earlier chapter we looked at the Marris model, where the assumption was that management was interested in maximising growth rather than profitability. We now explore a number of other possibilities for management.

Sales revenue maximisation

The first model we consider is known as the sales revenue maximisation hypothesis. It is associated with an economist by the name of Baumol (1959, 1961). Baumol's view is that management welfare is maximised if it pursues not profit maximisation, but sales revenue maximisation. For the agent, the manager, income is more closely linked to the size of the firm's turnover than it is to the size of the firm's profits. What will this mean for the way in which the manager behaves? We can look at it diagrammatically in Figure 11.1.

The theory relates to firms with some degree of monopoly power. So the diagram shows a firm with a standard total revenue curve. As output increases, revenue rises, but more and more slowly, and then eventually reaches a maximum and declines. It also shows a short-run cost curve. There are some fixed costs and costs rise as output rises owing to diminishing returns. The difference between revenue and cost is profit, shown by the profits curve. So at Q_1

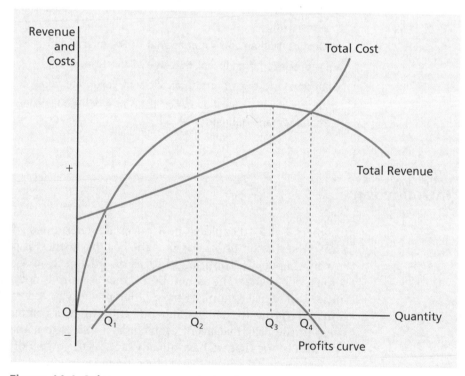

Figure 11.1 Sales revenue maximisation

output, revenue = costs, profits are zero. But if the firm moves beyond that level of output, revenue exceeds costs and positive profits are made. Profits are maximised at Q_2 where the gap between revenue and costs is at its greatest. Beyond that, profits are reduced until at Q_4 output, revenue is the same as cost. There are zero profits. Beyond Q_4, profits become negative.

The shareholders, the owners of the company, wish to maximise profits. They wish for Q_2 output. But the management wishes to make Q_3 output because if they move beyond the profit-maximising level of output Q_2, although profits begin to fall, revenue carries on rising. So Q_3 is the optimum level of output for the managers. The divorce of ownership from control means that the managers attempt to produce more output than shareholders wish.

If management wants more output it will require a lower price. Consider Figure 11.2. We do not have a demand curve here, but we can work out the demand curve, the average revenue curve, by simply taking a line from the horizontal axis to any particular point on the total revenue curve. Revenue divided by output gives average revenue. The sales revenue maximiser wishes a higher level of output at Q_3 in order to make more revenue. However, total revenue at Q_3 divided by the output OQ_3 gives a less steep ray. That is to say, average revenue will be lower. The firm is operating at a higher level of output, further down its demand curve with a lower price.

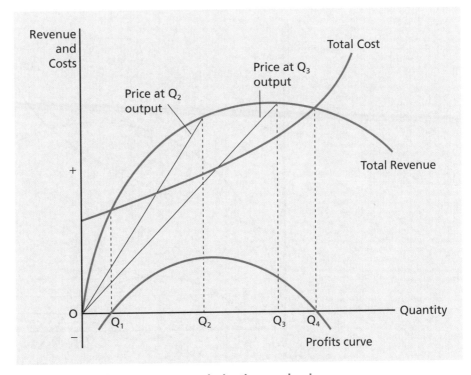

Figure 11.2 Sales revenue maximisation and price

The profit constraint

Is there anything to constrain the behaviour of the management that would prevent it from producing at the top of the total revenue curve and fulfilling its goal entirely? Managers cannot be indifferent to profit. As with the Marris model, if profit is reduced to an unacceptable level, the shareholders will sell their shares. This will cause the share price to fall, and as the share price falls and the valuation ratio of the company declines, the firm will be ripe for a takeover bid. Managers may then find themselves jobless. So there is a minimum level of profit that must be made. This is the profit constraint.

Note that the profit constraint will not be that which maximises profits, because the shareholders do not have perfect information. They only have an idea that there is a certain level of profit below which they will sell the shares. Now given that the manager has to hit the profit constraint, is that profit constraint effective? Can the profit constraint be ignored? Look at Figure 11.3.

If the profit constraint is at PC_1, the manager regards it as an irrelevance as Q_3 maximises total revenue and still gives adequate profit. If, however, the amount of profit that the manager needs to make is more than PC_2, the profit constraint is effective. Although the management would like to get to Q_3 it

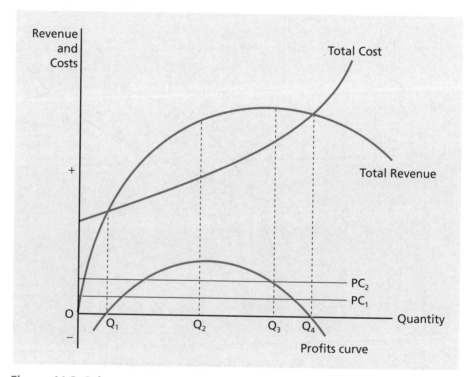

Figure 11.3 Sales revenue maximisation and the profit constraint

must restrict its ambitions and pick a smaller level of output and a higher price, closer to the one which the shareholder wishes to have. On the basis of what we have seen so far, either situation would be possible. But we can develop the argument further.

Sales revenue maximisation and advertising

Baumol argues that the profit constraint is always effective because of the role of advertising. Suppose the profit constraint were to be ineffective. Management would increase its volume of advertising. A profit-maximising firm will engage in some advertising activity. If the returns to advertising are sufficient to justify the cost, it is worth doing. But there are diminishing returns to advertising and there comes a point where it no longer makes sense to advertise further. At some point the cost of additional advertising is greater than the expected benefit.

This is not a concern to the sales revenue maximiser. If advertising causes the demand curve to shift to the right and therefore the total revenue curve to rise over a larger volume of output, even if it adds more to costs than it does to revenue, it will be acceptable. Any advertising that increases sales revenue at all is worthwhile. Management will simply advertise more than the profit maximiser. The effect of course will be to reduce profits, but management will continue with the policy until the profit constraint becomes effective.

We can see in Figure 11.4 what happens as advertising is increased. The quantity sold rises, because advertising is effective. The volume of advertising A_1 enables the sale of Q_1. Successive bouts of advertising, A_2, A_3 etc., leads to more

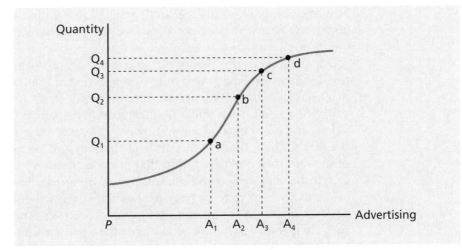

Figure 11.4 Hitting the profit constraint: advertising

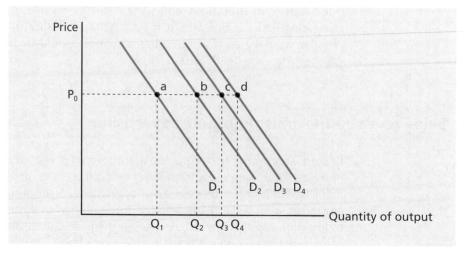

Figure 11.5 Diminishing returns to advertising

sales. But there are diminishing returns to advertising, so it becomes harder to increase the quantities sold. By around A_4 and beyond, the effect of advertising in terms of its effect on the quantities sold is minimal.

In Figure 11.5 we show this. At first, more advertising causes a significant shift in demand, but each successive bout of advertising shifts the demand curve by a smaller and smaller amount. Eventually the cost of marginal advertising expenditures is greater than the expected return. The profit maximiser picks the optimum volume of advertising for profit maximisation. The sales revenue maximiser does not, advertising more than that, until the profit constraint constrains activity.

You may have wondered when you have seen so much advertising, perhaps on television, for some product, whether such advertising volumes can make economic sense. We shall argue in Chapter 12 that it may well do so. An alternative view is that it does not do so for the profit maximiser. It reflects the policy of sales revenue maximisation.

One criticism of this theory is that it is a short-run model. It can be argued that the management goal is long-run profit maximisation. If this is the case managers may be willing to sacrifice short-term profit in order to maximise market share. Short-run sales revenue maximisation amounts to the same thing as long-run profit maximisation. However, one piece of evidence that supports the Baumol hypothesis is the study of Conyon and Gregg (1994). In a study of top directors' pay they found that pay was positively correlated with sales growth but not at all with current accounting profit. They also found some evidence to support what we saw about takeover activity in Chapter 8. Top pay was higher in companies that grew by takeover. The growth in sales of such companies was significantly higher than the returns to shareholders. This is a further explanation of merger activity. It boosts directors' pay even if it fails to enhance shareholder value.

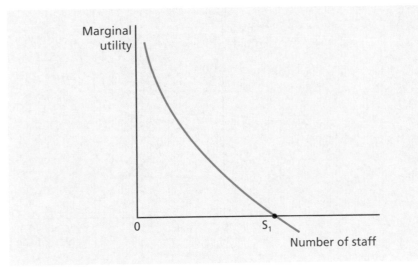

Figure 11.6 Managerial utility and staffing

Managerial utility maximisation

An alternative view of managerial behaviour is that of Oliver Williamson (1964). In the Williamson view managerial utility is a function of status and power. Thus there are three things about which management is concerned. The first is staffing. In the Williamson view, management gets utility out of having staff to control. Status is enhanced by such control. However, as Figure 11.6 shows, as management takes on extra staff, the marginal utility declines. As a manager takes on more and more staff, there are problems in controlling them. So although there is more utility from having more staff, the marginal utility declines as the problem of control increases. There comes a point where the marginal utility of staff becomes zero. If the number of staff is greater than S_1 it becomes negative.

The second thing that enhances status and power is a large budget about which discretionary decisions can be made. A manager is typically given a budget. The larger the budget, the more important the manager feels, the more control he/she is able to exercise and enjoy. Perhaps the most important of these discretionary decisions for senior management is with regard to investment, decorating the walls of the office with a Goya painting etc.

However, what we saw about the marginal utility of staffing will apply equally to discretionary investment. As the size of the budget increases, marginal utility declines. With extra budgets comes extra responsibility. There comes a point where now it is so large that there is no utility at all out of an extra bit of discretionary investment. The disutility of added responsibility is greater than the utility of enhanced status. This is at B_1 in Figure 11.7.

The third thing that enhances management utility is staff perks. Utility comes not just from salary, but the size of the car, foreign travel, and the

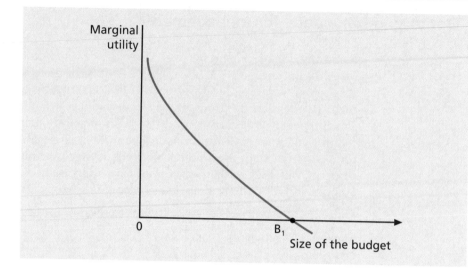

Figure 11.7 Managerial utility and discretionary investment

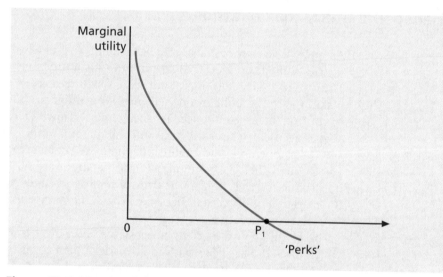

Figure 11.8 Managerial utility and 'perks'

hospitality box at sporting events. What we have said about staffing and budgets applies equally to perks. As the volume of perks increases, the manager is happier and gets positive utility. But the marginal utility is declining, to the point where at S_1 in Figure 11.8, marginal utility is zero. The volume of perks is now so great that the manager fears that if he/she has any more there will be closer scrutiny, either from more senior management or from shareholders.

Optimising behaviour for management

So how will management behave? They cannot simply consume each of these three things until MU = 0 because for each one of these elements some profit is required. Some profit is also needed to keep shareholders happy. Management is interested in profitability, not because of what it does to maximise shareholder utility, but for what it does in enabling management to follow its own goals. So it wishes to maximise utility, where utility is a function of the volume of staff, the amount of discretionary investment and the volume of perks, but they wish to maximise this utility subject to some minimum amount of profit which keeps the shareholders happy. That is

$$U = F\ (S, I_d, P)$$

Maximise U subject to π min where U = managerial utility; S = staff; I_d = discretionary investment; P = perks; π = profit; π min = minimum profit to keep shareholders happy.

How then does management behave in order to maximise its utility? We can look at it in two different ways. The first is to use the concept of marginal utility. Consumers will allocate their expenditure such that the marginal utility divided by the price of each good is the same. That same principle applies here. Management 'consumes' staffing, discretionary investment and perks, such that

$$\frac{MU_s}{\text{\pounds}_s} = \frac{MU_{I_d}}{\text{\pounds}_{I_d}} = \frac{MU_P}{\text{\pounds}_P}$$

There is an alternative way of looking at this that will bring into sharper focus the fact that management is not maximising the well-being of shareholders. Let's focus on one particular item of management interest, staffing. Consider Figure 11.9. If management starts off with no staff at all, and then gradually increases the number of staff, profit will rise. The marginal employee contributes something to the profitability of the firm. But if it goes on adding staff, the utility, in terms of the output and contribution to profit that the marginal person makes, will fall. There comes a point where an extra member of staff will contribute nothing to the organisation's profitability. We can see that from the curve labelled S in Figure 11.9.

S_m represents the profit-maximising number of staff, what is required by the shareholders. But now think about what is in the interests of managers. They enjoy having more staff. However, although they have the enjoyment of more staff, the more staff they go for, the less profit they make, and the less they are able to invest in discretionary investment and enjoy perks. There is a trade-off between staffing and profitability. So we have a set of indifference curves as between staffing and profitability, where for any one indifference curve, management is indifferent as to which point it wants to be. However, the further from the origin, the higher the level of utility, because there is more staffing *and* more profit.

What maximises management's utility? Provided they take on S_u staff, and make P_u profit, they can get onto this high indifference curve, IC_3. So the best

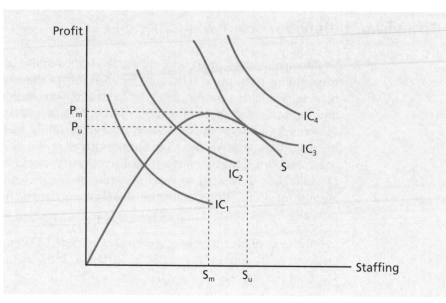

Figure 11.9 Staffing and profitability

combination of staff and profit, for management, is S_uP_u. Notice what that means. It means more staff and lower profit than that which is required by the share-holder whose interest is in the maximisation of profit.

What is true about staff will apply to perks and to discretionary investment. Look at discretionary investment. As a firm takes on more investment, so the profitability rises. But there comes a point where it has taken on all the profitable investment opportunities. Beyond that, any marginal investment is simply going to result in a decline in profitability. The investment is not worthwhile. There is an optimal volume of investment as far as the shareholder is concerned. For managers, given that they are prepared to trade off profits for more dis-cretionary investment, they find that the highest indifference curve they can get on is with a larger volume of investment. So they choose a larger volume of investment and a lower level of profit than is optimal for the shareholder.

Now what we have said about discretionary investment would apply equally to perks. There is a divergence between what is optimal for the shareholder and what is optimal for the manager. In each case what management chooses is greater than the shareholder optimum.

One consideration that supports the Williamson view occurs during a reces-sion, when management often says 'we have got to become more efficient, and lay off staff'. If they are laying off staff because demand is falling, that makes sense from a profit maximisation point of view. But sometimes the motive appears to be otherwise. Management has decided that, given the trading difficulties, it must become more cost efficient, 'leaner and meaner'. But if management is profit maximising, they are already cost efficient. That they are seeking only now to become cost efficient suggests that when market conditions were good, they felt in a position to pursue goals other than profit maximisation.

Behavioural theories

In Chapters 9 and 10 we assumed that profit maximisation was the goal of firms. In this chapter we have examined models where something else is to be maximised. We look now at some views that suggest that maximisation of anything is not the aim of business. Herbert Simon (1959) and subsequently Cyert and March (1963) began to focus on the internal organisation of firms. There are groups of people who band together to form particular interest groups. Some might be concerned, for example, about working practices, others with keeping shareholders happy and others concerned to minimise damage to the environment. The firm is an organisation of conflicting interest groups. Somehow there must be found a way to reduce the conflicts which exist between groups. One way to do this is to have targets. Management can set goals that can be agreed upon by different interest groups who will compromise. This might, for example, lead to an aim for a 10% reduction in costs, or a 10% return on capital, or to reduce environmental emissions by 15%. So there is a series of goals which management sets, partly as an attempt to reduce conflict between various groupings of people, and aims to meet those goals. Not only is it not maximising profit, but it is not maximising anything at all. This is known as satisficing, attempting to achieve a satisfactory performance in a number of different areas.

Periodically the firm's performance is reviewed. If it did not meet its targets, perhaps the targets were set too high and they are reduced for next year. Possibly alternatives can be proposed. If targets were met, they may be revised upwards or the firm may decide to do nothing. Whatever the outcome of the review process, it is satisficing, not maximising. Following Doyle (1994), we can use Figure 11.10 and say that there is a tolerance zone within which the firm wants to be. There are many different management goals. These include the speed of growth of the firm, environmental concerns, the extent to which employees are motivated and so on. Suppose the firm is currently in the inner circle. This would be regarded as unacceptable because it is not achieving sufficiently well to keep the various groups happy. The goals must be revised upwards, represented by a move outwards from the centre. But the outer circle also represents a disequilibrium zone. The firm may be doing very well in one area, say keeping the shareholders happy by increasing shareholder value, but as a result it might be doing it by placing such burdens on employees as to discourage them. The achievement of too much of one goal may begin to reduce the well-being of other groups and become less acceptable. The firm is trying to be within the comfort zone. This is where it is keeping all different conflicting groups reasonably content. It may be that the tolerance zone is a fairly wide area. But it may be that it's a fairly narrow area and so management will constantly struggle. In this view of firm behaviour, if we focus on the way in which an organisation operates, conflicting groupings within that organisation will see to it that we simply cannot focus on one goal such as profit, and expect it to be maximised.

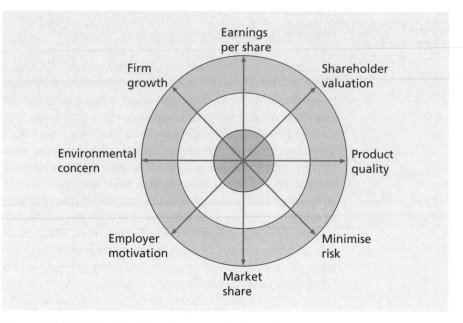

Figure 11.10 Behaviourist theory and tolerance zones
Source: Doyle (1994)

There is an alternative way, however, of looking at what is going on. It would be possible to argue that what firms are actually doing is in one sense to maximise profit. How do we maximise profit? By keeping happy the various groups who are making a contribution towards profit. It is necessary to resolve conflict in order to achieve profit maximisation. So not everybody thinks that the behaviourist view of the world is so different from the view of the world that says what we are interested in doing is to maximise profit.

Galbraith and firm survival

One more view that we consider briefly is that associated with the famous American economist J.K. Galbraith (1967, 1973, 1980). Galbraith's view is certainly that firms pursue goals other than to maximise profitability. Indeed, they serve the community poorly.

> [The modern large corporation] loses its legitimacy as an entrepreneurial and capitalist institution. It becomes instead an instrument of its own organization. . . . Having independent power and being the creation of its own organization, the modern corporation not surprisingly, serves the purposes of its own management. These purposes are frequently different from those of the public, or substantial parts of it, and the latter are less than pleased. Specifically, the corporate bureaucracy, like all organizations, seeks its own expansion. (Galbraith, 1980, pp. 75–7)

What he argues is that the groups that take the decisions within large corporations are those that he calls the technocrats, the scientists, the engineers and so on. Their prime concern is the minimsation of risk. They want job security and so they want to perpetuate the continuation of the organisation. They do so by firm growth. This means constantly looking around for new ideas that will enable them to produce new products which consumers will buy. The problem is that consumers find that more and more of the things they are offered have little use. When income is at a very low level, marginal utility of income is extremely high. They can now afford food and not go hungry. But there comes a point, already reached in the western world, where income reaches such a high level that they will not increase consumption. How can firms persuade consumers to buy things that are of no great value to them? The answer is to advertise. In those models where the assumption was profit maximisation, the demand curve reflected consumers' wants. It reflected their utility. Galbraith is saying that firms do not take the demand curve as given. They manipulate the demand curve via advertising. People are being persuaded to buy things that are quite useless to them to guarantee firm survival. Advertising is not to maximise profit. Firms are seeking to minimise risk, and the way in which they do it is to manage the environment in which they operate and that includes the management of consumer preference.

We have now considered a number of different models of firm behaviour. All these different views vary in terms of what it is that management is seeking to do. But what is common to all the models in this chapter is that managers do not attempt to maximise shareholder well-being. This is because of the divorce of ownership from control.

Some strands of evidence

In this last section of the chapter we look at some strands of evidence which might help us to see which of these conflicting views that we have been considering are closer to reality. Unfortunately we cannot reach any certainty. Evidence sometimes conflicts. We also cannot easily measure *motives*.

The first area of evidence relates to the nature of shareholding. A key to understanding the non-profit-maximising view of the world is that there exists a divorce of ownership from control. The individual shareholders do not have the power to influence what management is doing. Is that realistic? Figure 11.11 represents the distribution of shareholding between different groups in the UK. Only 16.5% is held by individuals. Other groups, insurance companies, investment and unit trusts, pension funds and so on hold by far the largest number of shares. If we compare this with 30 years ago, individuals' holdings would have represented over 50%. One can argue that whereas 30 years ago individuals were the dominant force in shareholding, it is now mainly in the hands of professional managers. Thus companies are under much greater pressure to profit maximise than they were 30 years ago. Individuals have less information than professionals. They also have less power. Individuals

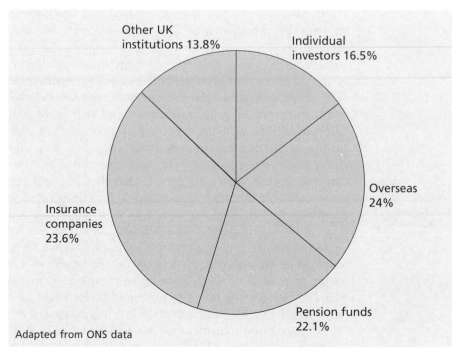

Adapted from ONS data

Figure 11.11 Shareholding in Britain

who are unhappy with company performance can do very little except turn up and complain at the annual shareholders' meeting. Now the shares of a large company may well be owned quite substantially by a small number of unit trusts or other grouping. Professional managers look more closely at what the company is doing and selling large blocks of shares is a more potent threat to underperforming companies. So we could argue that the movement towards fewer individuals holding shares in their own name makes it much more difficult these days for companies to pursue a non-profit-maximising policy.

BOX 11.1 Is business behaviour constrained by shareholders?

Many argue that the extent to which companies profit maximise is determined by the pressures of institutional investors.

How do shareholders actually affect the running of UK businesses? And what do the directors of the UK's 100 biggest companies really think of the institutional investors who own their assets?

The answers, in a no-holds barred survey carried out by the FT, make salutary reading for those who see the Anglo-Saxon model of share ownership as the brave new world order.

Under this vision, well-informed shareholders take an active role in improving company performance; they keep executives on their toes

by asking awkward questions about strategy; they punish mistakes by disinvesting; and they reward good performance by bidding up the share price, making it easier or cheaper for companies to raise more money.

The reality, as seen through the eyes of the company directors involved, is a little more prosaic. While there is widespread evidence that fund managers are demanding more interviews, the usefulness of meetings is often questioned by finance directors called to them. Many of the

74 finance directors interviewed for the survey resented the time spent educating fund managers who are moved on before gaining adequate knowledge.

Several directors were also irked by fund managers who ask for more and more attention. 'When they want a meeting they want it now, which is very frustrating when you are trying to run a business,' said one.

Some of the comments will leave their unidentified speakers open to charges of thinking like corporate dinosaurs. 'Some (institutional investors) believe that they own the business,' said one director. 'But they are traders in financial instruments.' That comment ignores the most basic tenet of the Anglo-Saxon view of capitalism: shareholders do own the business.

A more common criticism of shareholders is that they rarely add anything that the companies perceive to be of value. Almost half of those surveyed felt that their main shareholders 'rarely or never' offered any useful comments about their business.

A surprising number of directors expressed the view that shareholders were too docile a breed in general. 'We often wonder why institutional investors tolerate inadequate performance in other companies,' said one director. 'They could often be tougher. We sometimes wish shareholders would be tougher.'

It is often said that the increasing globalisation of investment habits makes for a tougher environment for companies. But one notable feature of the survey was the dominance of a handful of UK fund management companies. . . . When asked to single out companies for praise or criticism, more directors mentioned Mercury, the Prudential and Schroder – the three largest UK managers – than any other. They were particularly praised for their understanding of the business.

The concentration of ownership could also help explain one of the most surprising results of the survey: company directors disagree with the widely held view among corporate governance groups and government officials that shareholders are short-termist. Almost all directors felt their biggest shareholders were in it for the long term. This provides an important corrective to the view that the City damages companies by forcing them to abandon long-term projects for the sake of quick returns. . . .

The behaviour of UK investors contrasts sharply with that of their rivals across the Atlantic.

'US investors are more concerned to understand the business and want to meet people who run the individual divisions,' said one finance director. 'They are less satisfied with the odd chat with the chief executive and finance director.'

US managers – notably Capital International and Fidelity, which have both roughly doubled their UK equity exposure in the past five years – won plaudits for working harder on meetings and employing more in-house analysts.

In spite of the problems, the relationship between the UK's largest companies and their principal shareholders does appear to have improved. Factors may include increased political and public interest in corporate governance or greater competition.

Some 68 per cent of companies said they were happy with their relationship, while 23 per cent said they were very happy and 9 per cent said they were satisfied.

Desultory questioning of executives, for example over strawberries in the corporate hospitality tent at Wimbledon, does appear to have been replaced with far greater analysis, often to the discomfort of the companies concerned. 'They are more professional and better researched than five years ago,' admitted one director.

Source: Financial Times, 27 April 1998   **FT**

A second strand of evidence would be to ask companies what their goals are. Various researchers have tried questionnaires on senior management. Table 11.1 comes from the Hornby (1995) study of large Scottish firms. Less than 30% said that their goal is the maximisation of profits. Many said they didn't have a single objective. Two things are worthy of note. That nearly one-third claim to have multiple goals lends some support to the behavioural view. The other is this. Many of the other things with which management claimed to be concerned, increasing shareholder value for example, come close

Table 11.1 Declared objectives of leading Scottish firms

Objectives	Number	Per cent
No single objective	23	29.9
Maximising profits	22	29.9
Maximising sales revenue	1	1.3
Increasing shareholder value	11	14.3
Target rate of return on capital employed	7	9.1
Other	13	16.9
Total	77	100.0

Source: Hornby (1995)

Table 11.2 Senior management responses to statements

	1	2	3	4	5
Environmental procedures should always be followed, even if profits are reduced	1	14	20	53	12
There is only one rule for business behaviour – make as much money as you can	37	40	11	9	2
Products which use scarce resources should be banned	7	31	30	23	9

Source: Burke, Maddock and Rose (1993)

to a goal of profit. One might say that some of these goals are effectively profit maximisation.

Another questionnaire study was conducted by Burke, Maddock and Rose (1993) and is shown in Table 11.2. This was asking questions on a wider range of topics than Hornby. We just pick out two or three questions and their answers to consider.

Responses 1–5 correspond to the strength of agreement or disagreement with a particular statement, so that 1 represents strong agreement, 5 strong disagreement. Consider the first question in this survey: 'Environmental procedures should always be followed even if profits are reduced.' Now what would you expect people to say if what they were interested in was profit maximisation and nothing else? Well then, they should have said that they are quite happy to ignore environmental procedures, but 65% of those asked agreed that environmental procedures should be followed even if it reduces profits. Now look at the second question: 'There is only one rule for business behaviour. Make as much money as you can.' Here 77% either strongly disagree or disagree that the unique goal of business should be to maximise profits.

There is a problem with these surveys, in that you may find that the people who are setting the questions are asking something different from what the managers think is being asked. You can see that very clearly from the third

Table 11.3 Profit questionnaires: international comparison

	UK	US	Japan
Good short-term profits are the company objective	87%	80%	27%

Source: Doyle (1994)

question: 'Products which use scarce resources should be banned.' What should management be saying in response to that? It is not possible to produce a product without using scarce resources. So if one agrees, one is saying that no company should ever produce anything. Yet one-third of all respondents agreed with that statement. It is also possible that management does not wish to represent its true views even when it understands the question clearly.

We consider one more questionnaire. Is it true to say that management in all countries is the same in terms of answers that are given to the importance of profitability? One study by Doyle (1994) comes to the conclusion that there may well be substantial differences, so we have to be very careful in making generalisations about economies with different perspectives.

Table 11.3 focuses on declared attitudes of management from companies in the UK, the USA and Japan. The respondents were asked whether they agreed that good short-term profits are a company objective. Notice that 87% of UK managers said yes. A similar response was given in the USA but in Japan only 27% regarded short-term profits as a primary goal.

Remember that it is necessary to treat questionnaires with a considerable amount of caution, but it is interesting that in these and other surveys large numbers of managers deny that the only goal that they are interested in following is profit maximisation.

One straightforward and interesting piece of evidence on company behaviour is the correlation between growth rates and profitability. Look at the largest companies, say in Europe. Look at the leading ones as measured by the speed at which they are growing. Then look at the leading companies in terms of the profitability of the company, perhaps measured by rate of return on capital. For whatever period we examine they are not well correlated at all. So it does suggest that there may be some companies which are following a growth path, willing to do that even if it means reducing the amount of profits that they make. You will remember that this is exactly what Marris said would be the case. This absence of a link between growth of companies and profitability of companies has persisted for some considerable period of time.

We now look at studies examining the behaviour of manager-controlled and owner-controlled firms. We look to see whether owner-controlled or manager-controlled companies make more profits. Some companies are clearly manager controlled. They are owned by shareholders and the shareholders have no real control over what management is doing. Management takes the decisions on how much output to produce and on what price to charge. But other companies are owner controlled in the sense that a small number of people own a large proportion of the shares. It may be that you have a company which is quoted on the stock market, but a large number of shares are in the hands of the family, which retained many of the shares at the time that they were first quoted. Now there is a problem here. How many shares need to be in the hands of how few people to constitute owner-controlled firms? Most studies reckon that if one family owns maybe as little as 15 or 20% of the shares, that is effectively an owner-controlled firm. In many institutions, many shareholders will not take the trouble to vote, so if a family owns that size block of shares, they have effective control over the company.

If we accept this argument, there are large numbers of owner-controlled companies as well as manager-controlled companies in the economy. We could then ask the question: 'Is it true that owner-controlled companies make more profits than manager-controlled firms?' If that is the case it would suggest that the reason is that the management is pursuing goals other than profit maximisation.

We focus on two studies to see what the evidence suggests. This first study comes from the USA. Bothwell (1980) looked at profit margins in owner-controlled and manager-controlled firms. He adjusted profit margins both for risk and for the size of barriers to entry. One would expect, all other things being equal, that more risky ventures would require a higher amount of profit. One would also expect companies where there are larger barriers to entry to make higher profits. Having adjusted for that, he found that there was a difference between the two groups with regard to the amount of profit that they make. Bothwell came to the conclusion that the owner-controlled firms have significantly higher profit margins than manager-controlled firms. The divorce of ownership and control is important.

Now we look at another study, this time for British firms. This is from the work of Radice (1971).

Radice's study of British firms in textiles and engineering found that owner-controlled firms do have significantly higher profit margins *and* significantly higher rates of growth than manager-controlled firms. Now this is quite an important conclusion, for the following reason. When we looked at the Bothwell study we found that owner-controlled firms had significantly higher profit margins. However, we could argue that the reason why that was true was that the manager-controlled firms were more interested in other things such as growth, sacrificing profits to achieve it. But here in the Radice study, we find that the owner-controlled firms have not only significantly higher profit margins, but higher rates of growth as well.

Now that's important because it suggests that owner-controlled firms are more efficient than manager-controlled firms, that they grow faster, and achieve higher profits than those that are manager controlled.

Finally, we consider the link between executive pay and profitability, and between executive pay and the size of the company. You remember that some key ideas of those like Baumol were that executive pay is not closely linked to profits. So management doesn't have an interest in maximising profits, because their own pay isn't affected by it. In the Baumol view of the world, for example, the argument is that pay is much more closely linked to the revenue that the firm earns. There have been a number of studies conducted, which have examined the most important determinants of executive pay.

It is generally agreed that there is a link between the size of the firm and the amount of executive pay. So all other things being equal, management has an interest in the firm growing. However, the link between executive pay and profitability is much weaker. We quoted earlier the work of Conyon and Gregg (1994). Others have found similar results. See, for example, Storey, Watson and Wynarczyk (1995). But there is an argument for saying that over time, the link between executive pay and profitability will become stronger. Thirty years ago management was paid a salary. At least for senior management, these days it is much more common to be offered a salary plus some enhancement through things like share options and so on. So a growing part of senior management's pay is linked to the performance of the company in terms of profitability. One can see that as an attempt to reduce the principal–agent problem. By offering share options etc. the attempt is made to see that the agent's and the principal's goals are now much the same. However, currently the evidence is that the link between company profitability and executive compensation is weak.

Conclusion

All these different strands of evidence do not enable us to argue conclusively which model is most realistic of those we have examined. However, it is clear that, over time, those who analyse business pricing behaviour solely in terms of profitability have come under increasing pressure from those who have sought to question this assumption. Nevertheless, the marginalist profit-maximising view is alive and well. The most important element of the argument of those who argue for profit maximisation still remains. What we are interested in is not so much description but prediction. We construct models that will enable us to predict behaviour. The claim of the marginalist is that many of the non-profit-maximising models do not have the power to predict, in the way that the profit-maximising models can. So for all of the interest in non-profit-maximising models, there are still many economists like the Chicago school and others. If you want to predict business behaviour, there is no better assumption than that which assumes that firms seek to maximise profit. The debate looks set to continue for some time.

KEY RESULTS

1 The Baumol model argues that management seeks to maximise sales revenue subject to an effective profit constraint.

2 Williamson argues that the managerial utility function is based upon staffing, perks and discretionary investment.

3 Behavioural theories focus on the internal organisation of firms and emphasise trade-offs between competing managerial interest groups.

4 Galbraith's view of corporate behaviour is based on the view that 'technocrats' seek survival above all else.

5 A large body of evidence has not succeeded in resolving differences between economists over managerial motives.

Questions

1* Conyon and Gregg (1994) found that directors' pay grew by 10% in real terms between 1985 and 1990. The equivalent figure for their employees was 2.6%. Does this support the view that executive pay is unreasonable? How could the link between pay and performance be brought more closely into line?

2* Is the sales revenue maximisation view inconsistent with the profit maximisation hypothesis? In particular, consider the short/long-term perspective. Also consider the predictions of the kinked demand theory of pricing.

3* Galbraith has argued that firms manipulate consumers into buying goods they do not want. Can this view be sustained?

4 Consider Box 11.1. How far does this support the view that institutional shareholders will be more effective in controlling company behaviour in the interests of the shareholders?

5 Consider Box 11.2. To what extent does the behaviour of companies described here raise questions about the profit maximising assumptions of some pricing models?

* Help available at *http://www.e-econ.co.uk*

Box 11.2 Why companies pursue good works

Businesses spend part of their profits on 'social responsibility'. Is this evidence of a reflection of profit maximisation as an overriding goal?

Nokia's Make a Connection campaign, launched this year, is about to make its presence felt in some UK schools. The Finnish telecommunications company has entered a global partnership with the International Youth Foundation, to provide teaching packages to children with learning difficulties, and to offer volunteers from its own workforce.

The campaign is operating in South Africa, China, Mexico, Brazil, and Germany, as well as in the UK. It is tailored to local needs, with social exclusion and education the predominant themes.

Projects range from internet-related newspaper schemes among aspiring young journalists in China to mentoring programmes in east Germany.

Nokia plans to spend £7.5m on the campaign during the next three years and says it should help up to 1m children and young people. The campaign will not feature the Nokia brand or free mobile phones the company insists. But it raises questions about whether behind it lies a subtle ploy to use good works to strengthen its market position among the younger generation.

Mr Stoneham puts a different business case for Nokia's campaign: 'We hope people will see this as a sincere community issue. Sustainable global success demands respect for our stakeholders – our staff, current and potential, want to see good citizenship and our investors and customers want us to behave ethically,' he says.

The US still leads the way in philanthropy, with foundations holding more than $330bn (£224bn) in assets and contributing more than $20bn annually to educational, humanitarian and cultural organisations.

Traditionally, Europe has lagged behind the US. This is partly because the state has tended to play a more central role and partly because the act of giving has never been regarded as conferring high status.

This may be changing, however, as the European Commission encourages business to form social partnerships and the UK government implements tax changes to increase donations.

The notion of corporate citizenship has developed during the past decade in both the

US and Europe as more companies address social accountability, social auditing, social investment, corporate governance and business ethics.

A survey conducted towards the end of last year by Environics International, the Toronoto-based consultancy group, in co-operation with the Prince of Wales Business Leaders Forum, highlighted the fact that business is no longer only about personal aggrandisement or simply making profits.

It found that six out of 10 consumers form impressions of a company based on broader responsibilities such as labour practices, business ethics, responsibility to society at large and environmental effects.

Doug Miller, managing director of Environics, says companies are being forced to market themselves differently in response to changing attitudes and a new 'aspirational agenda': 'We are living in a period of great expectations, with people expecting to improve the quality of their lives and believing they can get it all.'

He says businesses have to be seen to be responding to the agenda set by aid agencies after 'black eyes' over issues such as child labour and environmental disasters.

'I visit 75 boardrooms a year and I can tell you, the members of the board are living in fear of getting their corporate reputations blown away in two months on the internet,' he says.

While Nokia has encountered no negative publicity from its socially responsible efforts, the same cannot be said for Shell, a company that has received more than one 'black eye' from the media. Last October Anita Roddick, founder of the Body Shop, attacked Shell's ethical advertising campaign. Ms Roddick publicly denounced the 'vast gap' between the company's humane image and the reality of human rights violations in Nigeria.

For Shell, still smarting from the adverse publicity of the 1995 Brent Spar fiasco, the effect of this further blow was to make the company even more determined to project a caring image. In a guide sponsored by the company, Tim Hollins, head of group social investment, wrote: 'The challenge for the 21st Century Company is to bring all the developments in corporate citizenship together . . . into a coherent framework of practice that makes good business sense as well as benefiting society.'

In fairness, Shell had committed itself in its Business Principles to sustainable development well before Ms Roddick's outburst. It had reorganised and changed reporting processes in 1997 so that environmental and social achievements sat alongside financial data in the annual report.

The group has chosen to continue its high-profile campaign and to risk attacks by organised pressure groups. Last month, it circulated the latest information about the activities of the Shell Foundation, a UK-registered charity established in June with the aim of 'supporting efforts worldwide to advance the goal of sustainable development'.

Yet for aid agencies such as the World Development Movement, much more has to be done before hardened campaigners can be convinced that enlightened self-interest is delivering results in a way that truly benefits society.

Barry Coates, director of WDM, feels too many companies fall outside the new ethical agenda and stand to take advantage of unregulated markets.

'If corporate social responsibility is to prove sustainable in the long term, governments must meet their responsibilities and regulate to provide an ethical framework,' he says.

But a study last year of 78 FTSE 350 companies and non-quoted companies of equivalent size, conducted by Arthur Andersen and the London Business School, showed that one in five companies with a code of ethical conduct had not issued the code to all its staff and nearly half had failed to make the code publicly available on request.

Source: Financial Times, 19 December 2000   FT

12 Advertising behaviour

Advertising is like winking at a girl in the dark. You know what you are doing, but nobody else does.

EDGAR WATSON HOWE

How much of a firm's budget should be used for advertising? In this chapter we consider the key relationship between advertising and firm success.

OBJECTIVES

After reading this chapter you should be able to:

- Understand the debate about advertising as information or persuasion.
- Distinguish search, experience and credence goods and know their significance in advertising.
- See why advertising can be seen as a function of market structure.
- See why market structure can be a function of advertising.
- Understand the problems of the relationship between advertising and welfare.

Introduction

In recent chapters we focused on pricing decisions and saw that these decisions cannot always be separated from firm behaviour with respect to advertising. In this chapter we turn the spotlight on advertising, although again we shall see that we cannot understand some aspects of advertising behaviour apart from pricing policy.

Marketing is clearly crucial for the success of many firms. This activity covers research into consumer attitudes to the market and to the firm's product, and also the promotion of the product to potential consumers. Advertising, since it focuses on the second of these two activities, is only one part of marketing behaviour. In this chapter we shall not be concerned with the mechanics of how firms set their advertising budgets. We concentrate on determinants of the level of advertising activity in industry.

Advertising as persuasion, information and signalling

When firms advertise, why might people buy more of their goods? Some have argued that advertising is solely for the purpose of persuasion. Perhaps the most famous supporter of this view is Galbraith (1958, 1967). Consumers' preferences are manipulated such that they buy goods that give little utility. Instead of consumer sovereignty, in which producers respond to the preferences of consumers, there is producer sovereignty in which producers determine what consumers' wants are. They then produce the goods that they as producers wish to provide. In this way advertising is a waste of society's resources.

An alternative view is that of economists such as Telser (1964) for whom advertising is a source of information. Markets work best if consumers are informed and can thus make optimal choices. An important source of such information is advertising. Firms advertise only the optimal amount. If they were to advertise more, their costs would be higher than necessary. New firms would enter the market with an optimal volume of advertising and because they are more efficient, capture the market, or force existing firms to a more optimal advertising strategy.

It is probable that there is an element of information and persuasion in much advertising, although it is impossible ultimately to resolve the argument empirically. One attempt to do so was made by Resnick and Stern (1977). They regarded adverts as informative if they provided specific pieces of information or 'cues' on such things as price, performance, availability, guarantees and safety. In their definition only one such cue was necessary to qualify an advert as informative. However, as they acknowledge themselves, their results are determined by that assumption. Only around 1% of adverts were informative if they provided at least three cues.

Advertising can also be seen as a signalling device. Many adverts provide no informational cues but make little direct attempt to persuade either. The message seems to be largely confined to an implied statement that large amounts of money are being spent upon advertising the product. The company is in effect saying that the product is so good and sells so well that it can afford this expenditure. But is it a *credible* signal? One can argue that it is. Firms with poor quality products may persuade consumers to buy once. Firms who really have high quality products will make repeat sales and so have more to gain from advertising. Advertising is not just a signalling device. It is a credible one.

The advertising/sales ratio

How do we explain the variation in the volume of advertising that is undertaken by industries? It is noticeable that there are huge variations in the amount of advertising that companies in different industries use. Watch commercial television for an hour or so and the same products appear over and over again. One of the reasons for this is that some industries are bigger than others. We expect there to be more advertising in larger industries, but even if we allow for that we still find enormous variations. The way we allow for it is as follows. The question we ask is not why advertising varies between industries but why the *advertising/sales ratio* varies between industries.

We establish the volume of advertising within an industry. Then we establish the total value of sales in the industry. The ratio of one to the other gives us the advertising/sales ratio. So, for example, if an industry with £100m sales has an advertising budget of £10m the ratio is 1:10 and the number is therefore 0.1. This means that of all the income received by the industry's firms, 10% of it is spent upon advertising. If another industry with £200m sales has an advertising budget of £2m, the volume of advertising is much greater than in the first industry but the advertising/sales ratio is the same for both. However, we find huge variations in this ratio between industries.

In this chapter we shall focus on why that appears to be the case. One possibility that we will look at is that we may be able to explain it by the nature of the product. Perhaps some products are more susceptible to being used by advertisers than other products. The other possibility that we will consider is whether we can explain the variations not in terms of the nature of the product but in terms of the nature of the industrial structure in which the advertising takes place.

Advertising and the nature of goods

Our first task is to explain the variations in advertising/sales (A/S) ratios of different industries in terms of the nature of the product itself. One attempt to do so was by Nelson (1974). He suggested, first of all, that we divide up products into two groups. Some he called *search* goods and some he called *experience* goods. A search good is one which, when you go to buy it, you know without experiencing it at home whether this good is going to do what you want. On the other hand, an experience good is one that you do not know, *even having bought it*, whether it will meet your wants. This will only happen when you have taken it home and experienced it.

Let us illustrate with a hat. A lady wants a new hat. She goes to the shops and tries some on. She knows before she has bought a hat whether she believes that she looks good in it. That is a search good.

Now suppose that you decide that you would like to go and buy a can of beer at a supermarket. You do not yet know what that beer is going to taste like. The purpose of buying it is to enjoy the taste, but until you have bought it, taken it home, opened it and experienced the taste, you do not know whether it is going to achieve what you wanted it for. This is an example of an experience good. Nelson argues that the amount of advertising that you would expect will vary between the two groups of products.

Table 12.1 gives some examples of what he found for both types of good. Nelson looked at the advertising/sales ratio for these and other goods. For all the search goods it averaged 1.4. For the experience goods the average comes

Table 12.1 Search and experience goods

Search goods	A/S	Experience goods (non-durable)	A/S
Hats	2.1	Beer	6.9
Jewellery	2.2	Cigars	2.3
Carpets	2.1	Perfume	14.7
Average of all	1.4	Average of all	4.1

Adapted from Nelson (1974)

Table 12.2 Durable and non-durable experience goods

Search goods	A/S	Experience goods (non-durable)	A/S	Experience goods (durable)	A/S
Hats	2.1	Beer	6.9	Books	2.7
Jewellery	2.2	Cigars	2.3	Tyres	1.4
Carpets	2.1	Perfume	14.7	Paints	1.5
Average of all	1.4	Average of all	4.1	Average of all	2.2
				Average of all experience:	3.4

Adapted from Nelson (1974)

out at 3.4. In other words, Nelson found that experience goods are much more heavily advertised than search goods.

Why should that be the case? When you decide to buy a good there are many sources of information that you can use and one source of information is advertising. How sensitive are you to advertising? How much are you affected by the advertisers? Nelson's argument is that you are much more likely to be willing to be wooed by the advertisers if the goods are experience goods. You do not know whether this good is going to achieve for you what you want it to achieve. The advertiser provides some information and says it will, for example, taste superb. So you are willing to give it a try. But suppose the advertiser advertises that hat and says that this will make you beautiful. When you try it on you know very well that it does not do so even before you purchase. Thus you are less likely to be affected by the advertiser's blandishments if it is advertising a search good than if it is advertising an experience good.

Now take the argument one step further. Nelson divided all of his experience goods into one of two sub-categories: durable and non-durable goods. The durable goods are things that last, like cameras, TV sets, washing machines, and the non-durable goods are those that you buy and consume immediately, including beer, ice cream and cigars. Nelson found that there were substantial differences between durable and non-durable goods in terms of the advertising/sales ratio. We can use Table 12.2 to see what he found.

Again the search goods are as before, but this time we have divided the experience goods into non-durable goods and durable goods. Notice that the experience goods that are durable have a lower advertising/sales ratio on average than the experience goods that are non-durable.

Why is this the case? The argument can be understood by remembering that Nelson regards advertising as a source of information. If you are thinking of buying a camera you will probably seek out a number of different sources of information. You will look at some advertising, find out what the price of the camera is, and how good the advertiser claims it to be. There are magazines available that you can look at. But you will probably also talk to friends who have this camera to find out how impressed they are with the results they have got. So there are a number of sources of information that you could go to. Now we can consider how likely you are to take notice of that advertising. You are very reluctant to listen to the advertiser's claim if it is a large expensive item that you are only going to buy on a few occasions in your life. So when it comes to the choice of a £300 camera you think very carefully about it. You are not very likely to listen to the claims of the advertiser. You cannot afford to make a wrong choice.

On the other hand, suppose you are looking at a row of cans of soup and you remember that, when you were watching the football last night, one particular can of soup was advertised. It's cheap – does it really matter if you get it wrong? You have only used a very small amount of money for the information that the soup was tasteless. You are much more willing to listen to the advertising of that non-durable good than you are to the advertiser of the durable good. So we would expect non-durable goods to be less heavily advertised. Nelson's results appear to bear that out.

The decision, though, whether to allocate a good into a particular category is a little arbitrary. Take the case of the hat. We said that it is a search good because the lady can see whether it will achieve what she wants it to achieve without making a purchase. The perfume goes into the experience good category because it will take some while before she knows what effect it will have on others. But is the difference so clear? She knows what the perfume smells like in the shop, so to that extent it is a search good. She does not know whether the hat will bring pleasure to others until she has bought and worn it. To that extent it is like an experience good. Is it so clear that there is this hard and fast distinction in categorising search goods and experience goods?

Is it so clear that goods are either durable or non-durable? Or is there a range of possibilities? How durable is durable? There is always a chance that we could choose to put a good into one or other category not on the basis of whether it fits best in that category but on the basis that is going to give us the results we are looking for. Nevertheless, it is an important idea.

Darby and Karni (1973) have suggested that there is another kind of good and that is what are termed *credence goods*. These are goods which, even when you have bought them, taken them home, and tried them out, you are still not very sure whether they achieved what you wanted them to achieve. Suppose you took your car to the garage, and the mechanic repaired it. Did he really do a good job? Did he simply clean a little dirt from the spark plugs or did he replace the spark plugs? Even when you have taken it home, unless you possess some mechanical competence, you are unaware whether that service has done for it what you really wanted.

Notwithstanding such qualifications to the argument, we are able to offer a partial explanation of how heavily certain goods are advertised, not by looking at the nature of the industry but by looking at the nature of the product itself.

BOX 12.1   Advertising in the fashion industry

We tend to assume that advertising is efficiently targeted. Is it always so?

US clothing retailers, in their focus on tailoring to the fashions of the day, are missing out on a more important trend.

Department stores and clothing chains are failing to attract shoppers over 50, just as America's baby boom population is ensuring that this segment of the market is growing faster than ever.

A member of the boomer generation – born between 1946 and 1964 – turns 50 every 7 seconds, swelling the ranks of 50–59 year olds by 24 per cent in the past five years.

They should be a key target for any retailer, since boomers spend 30 per cent more than the average household, according to research by retail analysts at PaineWebber. The over 50s now account for 55 per cent of US disposable income.

Yet clothing is one corner of retailing struggling to attract these prosperous consumers, and there are few signs that the sector has found a way to address the problem.

Candace Corlette, a principal of WSL Strategic Retail, a New York consultancy, says the only shops that are not seeing a fall-off in customers over 50 are drug stores, which are doing a thriving trade in vitamins and 'lifestyle' drugs.

'[Apparel] retailers have focused on youth in the misconception that older people don't buy clothes,' she says. In fact, according to Walter Levy, managing director for retail trends and positioning at industry consultancy Kurt Salmon Associates, 'the real money is up where these older consumers are'.

Customers over 50 have not stopped visiting clothing stores, but many find nothing they want when they go shopping and are put off by aggressively 'fashion-forward' merchandise and fits that do not suit older figures.

The problem is most visible at department stores, and becoming more acute as the boomer generation ages. The proportion of consumers shopping in department stores has fallen from 85 per cent to 72 per cent since 1996. Chains such as JC Penney, Federated's Bloomingdales stores and Nordstrom were once a clear destination for older shoppers, but they are now 'out of synch with their constituency,' Mr Levy believes.

Not only have department stores alienated traditional shoppers by seeking to appeal to trendier consumers, Ms Corlette says, but their offerings no longer stand out from the selection offered by the average shopping mall. Older shoppers 'would rather avoid the mall altogether', she adds.

A few chains have shown that targeting an older shopper can be successful: Talbots, the women's wear store, and Eddie Bauer are both credited with serving 50-plus customers well.

But the ranks of the boomers are swelling, and analysts say that consumers who no longer have mortgages or college fees may be less affected by any economic slowdown.

So the pressure on retailers to cater for older customers seems likely to increase.

Source: Financial Times, 18 October 2000   **FT**

Advertising as a function of market structure

Now we turn to advertising and market structure. Can we explain advertising levels or the advertising/sales ratio partly in terms of the nature of the industry within which the good is being sold? Does it make a difference whether the industry is monopolistic competition, or oligopoly, or monopoly? Does the structure help to determine the volume of advertising? There are two separate questions here. First, does the structure of an industry influence the volume of advertising? Second, does the volume of advertising affect the structure of an industry? There is a potential two-way causal relationship here. One direction of causality is that the nature of the industry leads to a particular A/S ratio. The other causal relationship is that the volume of advertising leads to a particular industrial structure. There are strong arguments for saying that there is a two-way causal relationship whereby industry affects advertising and advertising affects the structure of industry. We will look at each of these ideas in turn. First we show that the structure of an industry can have an effect on the advertising/sales ratio.

Product differentiation

The first possible link here is that the structure of the industry will affect the volume of advertising because of the nature of product differentiation. Think back to a perfectly competitive industry. Here there are a large number of firms producing an identical product. No advertising takes place. The reason for the absence of advertising is that in a perfectly competitive industry an individual firm cannot distinguish its product from all other products. It is part of the nature of perfect competition where all firms produce the identical product. So if a farmer advertises his carrots it makes no sense because he will be unable to distinguish his carrots from other farmers' carrots. So in perfect competition the identical product means no advertising. In any other structure advertising is possible. Even with highly elastic demand curves for an individual producer's product advertising may occur. Producers may together jointly fund advertising campaigns for homogeneous products. This may be without or more likely with government support. Milk and other dairy products are advertised in this way. As we move to more complex industrial structures, monopolistic competition, oligopoly and monopoly, we find that the degree of product differentiation in those industries is greater. Because the product differentiation is greater, the potential for advertising is higher. In the car industry one firm's car is not the same as another firm's car. Hence because a more concentrated industry tends to mean a more differentiated product, as we move towards a more concentrated industry we will tend to find that there is a higher advertising to sales ratio.

The price–cost margin

There is a second explanation of the link from the nature of the industry to the advertising to sales ratio. As an industry moves towards a more concentrated structure, *ceteris paribus*, the price–cost margin increases. We have seen that the price–cost margin is the extent to which the price of the product exceeds marginal cost at the firm's chosen output level. In perfect competition there is no price–cost margin because a firm produces where marginal cost is equal to average revenue. However, outside of perfect competition the demand curve is not perfectly elastic. As we move towards a more concentrated structure we would expect demand to become more inelastic and thus the gap between price and marginal cost to increase.

We have seen in an earlier chapter that as a firm advertises more, the effectiveness of that advertising is likely to be reducing at the margin. However, for any given volume of advertising and for any given effect in terms of shifting the demand curve, the benefit to the firm in terms of increased profitability is greater where the price–cost margin is greater. That leads us to the following conclusion. Because a more concentrated structure means that the price–cost margin is going to be greater, all other things being equal the volume of advertising will also tend to be higher.

So again we have a link from the structure of an industry to the volume of advertising. We have two explanations now. One is in the differentiated nature of the product and one is in the price–cost margin.

Oligopolistic interdependence: game theory revisited

We also have a third possible connection between the structure of industry and the advertising/sales ratio. This relates to oligopolistic interdependence. That is to say, we can help to explain the advertising/sales ratio by looking at the way in which firms in an oligopolistic structure, where there is just a handful of firms, are likely to behave. There is a strong case for saying that advertising here tends to be high because firms are obliged to advertise simply because if they do not they are going to lose sales to their rivals.

Take the demand for petrol. We may find that as the industry engages in large volumes of advertising there is very little effect on the industry demand curve for petrol. However, although advertising is unlikely to affect the demand curve for the industry very much, it is likely to have a significant effect on individual companies' demand curve. So each company is afraid to reduce its advertising, because if it does so it will lose sales to its competitors. We can pick that idea up by going back to the game theory we met in an earlier chapter in the context of pricing. Let us imagine that there are two firms in a market, A and B, and see from Table 12.3 what the effect of advertising might be.

Table 12.3 Pay-off matrix for advertising game

		B's strategy	
		Don't advertise	Advertise
A's strategy	Don't advertise	A's profit = €50,000 B's profit = €50,000	A's loss = €25,000 B's profit = €75,000
	Advertise	A's profit = €75,000 B's loss = €25,000	A's profit = €10,000 B's profit = €10,000

Company A can decide to vary its advertising budget. There is of course a range of possibilities in terms of the volume that they spend on advertising. However, for purposes of simplicity I am assuming that they will only go for two options, either to advertise or not to advertise. Company B also has an option to advertise or not advertise. So we have a familiar matrix of four possible outcomes. Suppose company A does not advertise and company B does not advertise either, the profits will be very healthy. The reasons for assuming that profits will be very healthy are that if neither company advertises they save themselves the advertising costs and that advertising has very little effect on the industry demand curve. They will sell roughly the same amount as before and have lower costs.

But now let us suppose that A does not advertise and B does advertise. As a result of the advertising B finds its demand curve rising sharply, more than enough to cover the additional costs, and therefore it is making more profit. The extra sales are not from a shift in the industry demand curve but from a switch of demand from firm A. A's demand curve falls rapidly, therefore it cannot cover its costs and makes a loss. So this is the outcome even though the advertising has very little effect on the industry demand curve.

Similarly, if the advertising is done by A but not by B, then A is making large profits and B is making a loss. Suppose both companies advertise. The industry demand curve does not shift very much so they have extra costs and a very small shift in the industry demand curve. Their own demand curves are little changed and so profits are much lower for both companies than if neither advertise.

Assuming that both firms have the information contained in the matrix, what is the outcome going to be? You can see that even though it pays both companies not to advertise, the likelihood is that both companies *will* advertise. Each company will consider the options and ask what is the worst it could do if it were to advertise and what is the worst it could do if it did not advertise. If each company does that, they will each come to the conclusion that the best they can do, or the least worst, is to advertise.

Now go back and look at that in the table. If company A doesn't advertise it could end up with a €25,000 loss. If it does advertise the worst that it could do is a €10,000 profit. Company B would find exactly the same thing. So on that basis A decides that it should advertise, B feels that it had better advertise and both companies finish up making less profit than if they agreed not to advertise at all.

When we looked at pricing we saw that this interdependence gives us a powerful reason for expecting cartels to be formed. Eliminating the uncertainty and agreeing a price means that both firms make more profits. So we have to ask the same question here: why won't these companies do the same thing and form an agreement with respect to advertising budgets? The answer is not difficult to see. There is some hope that each company can see that the other company is keeping to the deal when it comes to pricing. Although we saw that there was the possibility in certain markets of secret price discounts, it will become clear sooner or later if one company is cheating on the deal by cutting prices. It is much harder to ensure that they are not cheating on the deal and increasing advertising. It is much harder for the other company to know whether or not it is finding itself being cheated. There are higher transactions costs policing an agreement on advertising than on pricing. This makes cartels on advertising much less likely. It is more likely that a cartel will establish with an agreement on price, and that companies will agree to compete on non-price variables such as advertising. A further consideration is the difficulty of matching advertising campaigns. A price cut is not only relatively easily detected but it is easily matched also. A good advertising campaign cannot be so easily matched.

This gives another explanation as to why, as we move towards a more concentrated structure, the advertising/sales ratio rises. It is in this kind of oligopolistic interdependency that much wasteful advertising will take place, where each company advertises simply because the other company also advertises. You can understand now why most studies show that at very high degrees of concentration the advertising/sales ratio begins to fall again. When we move to a very high degree of concentration we have moved away from oligopoly and towards a monopoly, and that kind of competitive advertising no longer becomes necessary. A monopolist will still advertise, in the hope of shifting the demand curve and increasing its profitability. But one aspect of advertising behaviour – competitive advertising because your competitors are doing it – no longer applies.

To summarise, we have a number of reasons for thinking that the structure of an industry affects the advertising to sales ratio. We would certainly expect for these reasons that, all other things being equal, increasing concentration leads to a higher advertising to sales ratio at least up to oligopolistic interdependence. It is less certain whether that will hold for very high degrees of concentration as we move towards monopoly.

We briefly consider two studies that confirm what we have been arguing. Both suggest that the relationship between concentration and advertising intensity is the inverted U of Figure 12.1. As the degree of concentration

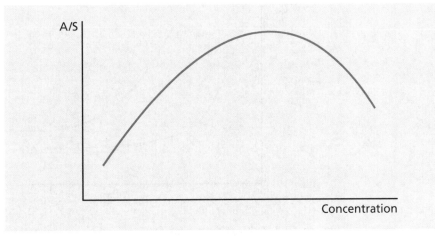

Figure 12.1 Concentration and advertising

in an industry moves from zero, perfect competition towards oligopoly, the advertising/sales ratio increases. At high levels of concentration it falls. Sutton (1974) examined 25 UK industries using the CR5 as a measure of concentration and the familiar A/S ratio as the volume of advertising. His results suggest that A/S peaks at a CR5 of 63.8%. Strickland and Weiss (1976) examined a much larger number of industries. They found the same inverted U with a peak in the CR4 of 57%.

Market structure as a function of advertising

We look now at the possibility of a reverse causal relationship between the advertising/sales ratio and the degree of concentration in industry. However, this time we look at the possibility that the causal relationship is from advertising to concentration because the volume of advertising has an effect upon the industrial structure.

There are two links to explore here. The first is that there is a direct link between advertising and concentration and the second one is a more indirect link through entry barriers. But first there is an argument for saying that the volume of advertising has a direct effect upon the structure of an industry. There are two aspects of this, the first focusing upon economies of scale, the second looking at the effectiveness of advertising in firms of differing size. The first link results from the fact that advertising is a cost that is likely to have scale economies. If a firm engages in a small amount of advertising it is relatively expensive, but as it spends more on advertising some economies of scale in advertising take place. If advertising is a significant item of expenditure it may well mean that minimum efficient scale is at a higher level of output that would otherwise be the case. We can see that from Figure 12.2.

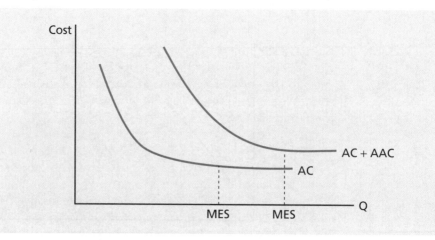

Figure 12.2 Advertising and MES

As output increases, average costs fall until MES – minimum efficient scale. Now suppose that this is an industry where an important part of total cost is advertising costs and advertising costs are also susceptible to economies of scale. Then if we add average advertising costs (AAC) to the non-advertising costs we have all costs. Because there are economies of scale in advertising, the effect of this is that minimum efficient scale is at a larger level of output than before.

This is important because it means that it is likely to lead to a more concentrated industrial structure. Firms will merge until they get the advantage of all the economies of scale available. Now there is a further incentive to merge in order to take advantage of one particular economy of scale, namely advertising. So the fact that economies of scale exist in advertising leads to a more concentrated industrial structure.

There is also the effect that advertising has, in that we think it is likely to be more effective for any given volume of advertising for a large firm than for a small firm. Think about the advertising that you watch on TV that tells you about a new product that you did not know exists. Are you going to buy it or not? By the next morning you have probably forgotten about it, but when you go round the supermarket there is the product on the shelf. Its presence on the shelf reinforces the advertising that you saw the night before. However, if it is a relatively small firm that is advertising it has got a less wide distribution network, the products are available in fewer outlets so the advertising is less effective. Because the number of outlets where the product exists is fewer it is less effective in reinforcing the message of the advertisement. Thus for any given volume of advertising expenditure large firms' advertising is likely to be more effective than that of small firms. Again it means that in those kinds of industries a more concentrated industrial structure is likely as firms get the benefit of that reinforced message by increased firm size.

Those are the main reasons why we think there is a direct link between advertising and concentration. But there is a link of a less direct kind. This is the idea that advertising raises barriers to the entry of new firms. Because it raises barriers to the entry of new firms it makes it more difficult for firms to get into a market and thus protects a relatively concentrated industrial structure. We have already seen that advertising may raise minimum efficient scale and we have seen previously how the higher the level of minimum efficient scale, the harder it is for new firms to get into the market. So advertising raises barriers to the entry of new firms and hence advertising can increase concentration. We explored this idea more fully when we considered Bain's (1956) model of barriers to entry.

That model does not solely relate to advertising. It does, however, give a valuable insight into its potential effects. All three of Bain's key barriers to entry can be raised via advertising. Advertising can sharpen up product differentiation and establish in the mind of the consumer that the product is different. Because there are economies of scale in advertising it can mean that the shape of the long-run average costs curve is one that falls to a fairly large level of output. Thirdly, advertising can build up cost barriers and make it more difficult for new firms to enter the market.

One interesting study was that of Strickland and Weiss (1976), which we mentioned earlier. Their model allowed for the two-way causal relationship between advertising and concentration. They found both to be valid.

Welfare effects of advertising

There is a strong case for saying that advertising can reduce welfare. Even if one discounts the Galbraithian views about the manipulation of consumer preferences, one can argue that the volume of advertising is greater than optimal. In particular, oligopolistic structures, where A/S ratios tend to be highest, lead to wasteful self-cancelling advertising campaigns. Even where there is a monopolist, advertising can be too great. The monopolist maximises private welfare and ignores social welfare. Consumers that would have bought the product unadvertised must still contribute to the advertising costs.

One can argue that under certain circumstances consumers gain welfare by advertising. One illustration of this can be found in the tourists–locals model. In a town there are two types of consumer, the locals and the tourists. Tourists have high search costs. They will only be buying a product once. Locals' search costs are relatively low. They will engage in repeat purchases and will thus be willing to search for the lowest price outlets. Some outlets will charge low prices, selling to locals. Others charge high prices, selling only to tourists who happen to visit them first and for whom the search costs are too high to look elsewhere. Suppose now that the low priced outlets can advertise effectively; some higher priced outlets will be forced to reduce prices and the average price level to consumers is thus reduced. Although this is referred to as a tourists–locals model, it will hold wherever there are consumers with different search costs.

Given the differences in views about advertising's effects upon welfare, one might hope that resorting to empirical evidence might determine the relative weights of the two cases. However, the empirical evidence does not all point in the same direction.

Benham (1972) observed that advertisements for eyeglasses were banned in certain states of the USA. He then compared prices and found that in those states where advertising was permitted prices were substantially lower. Adjusting for differences in income, age etc. he was able to isolate the effect of advertising. He reported that advertising lowered prices by 28%. A further result of this study concerned states banning only the advertising of prices. Other advertising was allowed. The difference in price from those states with no ban at all was not statistically significant. Only where states banned all advertising of eyeglasses were prices significantly higher. The idea that advertising of prices sharpens competition and leads to lower prices is supported elsewhere. Cady (1976) found much the same results in the US pharmaceutical drugs market. However, others such as Arnould (1972) claim that advertising tends to reduce the *quality* of the product.

Advertising and fraud

Since it is difficult to determine the welfare effects of advertising, its control by government is bound to be controversial. One can think of the controversy surrounding the advertising of cigarettes, for example. One aspect of government control that might on the other hand be simple is the control of fraudulent advertising. It is one thing for advertising to make great claims that cannot be disproved – 'The most exciting new product for years'. Claims that are blatantly untrue are of a different order. Most believe that such advertising should be banned and offenders prosecuted. Even here the argument must be treated with caution.

The argument turns upon advertising as information and the way that consumers react to it. If the fraudulent claim is with respect to a search good it is unlikely to be successful. Consumers are aware of its false nature. The problem is where the claim is with respect to an experience good. If the quality is low but claimed to be high, the producer can make a profit even without repeat sales and consumers can be misled. Hence the case for the anti-fraud law.

Now let us consider the degree to which the law should be enforced. Suppose now that the law is rigorously enforced. The enforcement costs may be high relative to the benefits. There is an optimal volume of fraud. Suppose it is generally but not completely enforced. Consumers will know this and will assume that the advertising claims can therefore be trusted. This gives producers an incentive to mislead since consumers are less wary. Suppose that it is not enforced at all. Consumers will place no trust in advertisers' claims unless they believe that it is in the interests of producers to tell the truth. A moderate degree of enforcement may thus be optimal.

Conclusion

We explained why the advertising/sales ratio varies so much between different firms and different industries. The first explanation is the nature of the product itself. Is it a search good or an experience good? Is it a durable or a non-durable good? So part of the answer is in the nature of the product. The second explanation is that it is to do with the structure of the industry in which the product is being sold. Two possibilities may operate here. The first is that the structure of the industry helps to determine the advertising/sales ratio. The second possibility is that the advertising/sales ratio helps to determine the structure of the industry both in a direct way and in an indirect way by raising barriers to the entry of new firms.

The welfare effects of advertising are unclear and are a matter of some controversy.

KEY RESULTS

1 Advertising is a part of marketing.

2 Advertising intensity varies enormously between industries.

3 We can explain such variations partly by the nature of the product and partly by the nature of the industry in which the firm operates.

4 There is a two-way causal relationship between concentration and advertising.

5 The welfare effects of advertising are a controversial subject.

6 Theory suggests that there are an optimal volume of fraudulent advertising and an optimal volume of enforcement that are greater than zero.

Questions

1* Why is it difficult to determine how much advertising is undertaken in an industry?

2* In what sense is advertising an investment for a firm?

3* Why do firms sometimes promote their products with 'money off' coupons rather than with straightforward price cuts? *Hint*: Think about people's search costs and therefore who is most likely to use them.

4 Refer to Box 12.1. To what extent does the article give an empirical rebuttal of the Chicago school view?

5 Refer to Box 12.2. What evidence is there that competition is fiercer than ever? Would you expect an increase in competition to cause an increase in the volume of advertising?

* *Help available at* **http://www.e-econ.co.uk**

BOX 12.2 The optimum volume of advertising

How does the volume of advertising relate to the trade cycle?

The owners of Casa Sanchez, a Mexican restaurant in San Francisco, faced a dilemma. They wanted to advertise, but they could not afford space in a newspaper or an expensive television commercial.

So Martha Sanchez offered free lunches for life to customers prepared to have the Casa Sanchez logo tattooed on their bodies. Now, about 50 people are wandering the streets of San Francisco with pictures of the restaurant's sombrero-topped Corn Man on their biceps, buttocks or thighs.

When people start advertising in weird places, it is a sure sign of an advertising boom. It means traditional media have become so expensive, and so cluttered by the sheer volume of commercials, that advertisers are looking for other ways of making an impact.

The London-based WPP, the world's biggest advertising and marketing group by revenue, estimates that non-traditional media and marketing have already overtaken traditional advertising in terms of global spending, and are showing higher growth rates as advertisers look for alternatives to the saturated conventional media.

One result that few can have failed to notice is the increasing pervasiveness of advertising as marketers push their messages into places that were previously advertisement-free.

Public lavatories and elevators are becoming favoured spots because they give advertisers access to a captive audience, and space is being sold on bus tickets, petrol pump nozzles, delivery trucks, cars, supermarket floors, cash machines and fruit.

Advertisers are also buying their way into public space by striking deals with cash-strapped public authorities. In cities, they are providing bus shelters, benches and kiosks in exchange for the right to advertise on the streets; through sponsorship, they have colonised most artistic, cultural and sporting events; and they are finding their way into schools by sponsoring teaching materials, computers and books.

Conceivably, this is a temporary phenomenon. Advertising is notoriously sensitive to the economic cycle: when times are good, it tends to grow more rapidly than gross domestic product, but at the first whiff of an economic downturn, it plummets.

One reason for its volatility is that advertising is more an act of faith than an investment with a clearly identifiable return. In the short term, it can look suspiciously like a waste of money, in the sense that the cost of most brand advertising almost always exceeds the gross profit derived from any demonstrable increase in sales.

Prof Patrick Barwise of London Business School says a lot of advertising is defensive. 'Most advertising by established brands is done not in the expectation that your sales in one or two years will be higher than they are today, but because if you don't advertise, your sales may be lower, and it will then be more expensive to regain the lost market share.'

Ethereal considerations such as these count for little when budgets are under pressure, and since advertising is often one of the biggest costs on a company's profit and loss account, it is usually the first victim of cuts when an economic downturn looms.

Yet, just as some pundits argue that the economic cycle has been abolished, others are suggesting the advertising cycle has ended – meaning that advertising has entered an era in which it will grow more quickly than gross domestic product, whatever the state of the economic cycle.

Increased competition underpins this argument Generally, the greater the competition, the more companies need to advertise: and most companies are operating in a more competitive environment than at any time in their history.

Overcapacity is rife, and the wide availability of low-cost technology means that it is difficult for any company to maintain a technological lead over its competitors. So marketing and branding have taken over as the main way of differentiating one company's product from another's.

Deregulation and the internet are increasing competition, too, says Leland Chesterfield, an analyst at PaineWebber. 'Washington's deregulation of telecommunications, pharmaceuticals and financial services has produced more competition for consumers, and broadband allows marketers to reach consumers in new ways other than through traditional retailers,' he says.

'I am saying the cycle has been abolished. Growth may moderate, but it will show less violent swings and will continue in excess of GDP growth.'

Much as marketers would like to believe this, few are that optimistic. 'I think you have to be ever cautious,' says Sir Martin Sorrell, WPP's chief executive. 'It's at times like this that you should be examining the reasons why the growth may not continue.'

Source: *Financial Times*, 21 July 2000

Government policy towards industry

We mustn't prejudge the past.

WILLIE WHITELAW

We have seen throughout the book that business decisions are constrained by the operation of markets. In this final chapter we focus on the constraints of government policy.

OBJECTIVES

After reading this chapter you should be able to:

- Appreciate the case for government control of markets.
- Assess the costs and benefits of the privatisation programme.
- Understand the use and limitations of price controls on privatised firms.
- Understand the value of deregulation of privatised firms.
- Appreciate EU and UK attitudes towards dominant firms, mergers and restrictive practices.

Introduction

A key feature of any government policy is its attitude to the allocation of scarce resources, in particular the extent of its reliance upon the price mechanism. There are clear benefits in markets but also problems, particularly the potential for markets to misallocate resources because of the power that lies in the hands of large firms. In this last chapter we draw together some of the material from earlier chapters in order to focus on government behaviour and policy towards industry.

In recent years there has been an increased sense of confidence in the power of markets in many economies. This is not just in the Western world. We have seen in Eastern Europe the collapse of communism and to a considerable extent the embracing of the market mechanism for allocating resources there. This renewed confidence in markets is seen in a number of areas.

The first has been the remarkable decline in international trade barriers. There has been a sharp decline in the extent of protectionism. In the 1960s the average tariff on industrial goods was around 45%, now the average is about 6%.

That decline in international protection of markets has meant that there is far more competition between industries and firms in different countries. However, this change has had its critics. In particular, there are concerns that free trade worsens the distribution of income between rich and poor countries and increases the possibility of exporting externalities in the form of pollution and environmental degradation.

The second area in which one can see the increased sense of confidence of governments in markets has been the decline in the burden of tax within many countries. To some extent this has been reflected in many countries in personal tax rates but it is also true to say that there have been some tax cuts on companies. Tax raises private costs of production and to some extent misallocates resources because market prices are supposed to reflect marginal costs of production. So prices better reflect costs when the burden of taxation placed on companies is lessened. In many countries the reduction has been greater on smaller than on large firms, but overall, company taxation has tended somewhat to decline. Yet this policy also is not without its critics. For example, one of the interesting questions that has to be faced in Europe is the extent of coordination of tax rates, including common business tax rates. The argument is that if one country has a relatively low business tax rate, then firms would tend to relocate towards that lower tax area. So there is some pressure for agreement that tax rates should be common between countries, at least within the European Union. The alternative view is that just as competition is good for firms, so competition is good for governments and competition to get taxes down in order to attract inward investment is part of that process. So if one country's taxes on profits are relatively low and that is drawing resources into that country, it is putting a wholly good pressure on other countries to reduce their tax rates as well. One recent concern about government competition over taxation has been expressed by Hertz (2001). She argues that this 'race to the bottom' in taxation reduces government income and damages the welfare state.

The third area where one sees a growing confidence in markets has been in the move to reduce subsidies to firms, particularly in manufacturing. There was a time when governments saw an industry in financial difficulty and often gave a subsidy as a solution. Subsidies still have a significant effect in many countries, even in Europe. However, it is certainly less than some years ago. This is partly a direct result of an increase in confidence in markets to allocate resources. But there is also an indirect effect because of a macroeconomic change. Something that has been noticeable in the past 20 years has been an increase in the number of governments whose view is that government policy must be to operate a balanced budget. The Keynesian idea that it does not matter if in the short run government expenditure exceeds government income has tended to be less popular. Alongside the classical view of a balanced budget goes a confidence in markets, so as governments have embraced the macroeconomic idea of a balanced budget they have come under increasing pressure to cut government expenditure. One way of doing so is to reduce subsidies given to industry. As in the other areas we considered above, this is not universally popular. In particular, some believe that there is something intrinsically worthwhile about manufacturing output Manufacturing should therefore be protected even when a market solution would be to allow it to decline. Against this background it is not hard to see that government policy towards industries and firms is also controversial.

In this chapter we shall summarise the case for and against active state intervention in firm and industry behaviour. Then we shall analyse policy in three areas, namely *privatisation*, *competition policy* and *industrial policy*.

The basis for government policy towards industry

In earlier chapters we have considered this extensively. Here we draw together the main strands of the argument.

Following the structure–conduct–performance approach, the perfectly competitive structure can be seen as a superior means of allocating scarce resources. Consumer welfare is maximised since price reflects marginal production costs. Monopoly power enables firms to reduce output and raise price, thus reducing welfare. We saw in Chapter 2 some estimates of the size of this deadweight loss. However, the arguments relating to the superiority of perfect competition assume that the level of costs is independent of market type. Some such as Williamson (1968) have argued that monopoly power may result in lower production costs. These benefits may be greater to society than the deadweight allocative loss that monopoly brings. Some other economists such as Liebenstein (1966) have argued that monopoly power enables firms to hide behind entry barriers and have costs greater than the minimum level necessary. This excess he calls X-inefficiency. If this is so, the loss to consumer welfare is even greater under monopoly.

The sources of this potential inefficiency are numerous. Firms may choose to pursue a quiet life. Management may pursue their own goals rather than the goals of the owners. Firms may waste resources protecting their monopoly position. They may erect entry barriers through advertising, predatory pricing behaviour and vertical integration.

Yet the legitimacy of all these criticisms has been challenged. The theory of contestability questions the relevance of the structural approach to markets by suggesting that those firms with monopoly power may be forced to behave like competitive firms. Transactions costs economics can be used to argue that vertical integration is socially efficient since vertically integrated firms save on the transactions costs of engaging in market transactions. The Chicago school has argued that the source of monopoly power is found ultimately only in government behaviour. In the absence of government intervention monopoly profits always draw new resources into an industry. The theoretical superiority of perfect competition is also questioned by the Austrian school. Dynamic efficiency is best achieved by research and development activity that will only come from markets with monopoly power. Given all these conflicting perspectives, it is not surprising that government policy towards industries and firms sometimes lacks coherence.

What we *can* say is that governments leave most resources to be allocated via the price mechanism. However, they do not believe that markets are always an ideal way to allocate resources. In the light of this, we consider three specific areas of government policy. The first is privatisation.

Privatisation policy

Confidence in the power of markets in many countries has in recent years resulted in a very significant shift of resources from state to private ownership. This process is called privatisation. So, for example, in the United Kingdom 30 years ago, gas, electricity, water and telecommunications were in the public sector. All these industries are now in the private sector. Although that process has taken place in the UK, other countries have followed.

What motives have driven governments to transfer resources in this particular way? There are three grounds upon which the case for privatisation most strongly rests. The first case is a belief that there is more cost efficiency in the private sector than in the state sector. The argument goes along the lines that profit is a powerful motivator. So those who work for a state institution do not share in the profits the company makes. They therefore tend not to work so hard and efficiently. But in the private sector where individuals share in the profits that the company makes, there exists an incentive to be cost efficient as part of the process of profit maximisation. So part of the logic of transferring resources from the state to the private sector is superior cost efficiency.

A second ground for believing that resources would be better off in the private sector than the state sector relates to capital markets. When resources are in the state sector and that industry wishes to expand, they have to go to governments and plead for the necessary resources. If the government is under pressure to balance its budget deficit it may well refuse even though it would be allocatively efficient to do so. But if that industry is in the private sector, if it can convince private capital that it is profitable, it will be able to get the appropriate finance. So by putting electricity, gas, water and so on in the UK into the private sector, when those industries want to expand now they can go to the private capital market in the same way that other private companies can and compete for funds there. If the judgement of resource owners is that this is a sensible investment, the funds become available.

A third argument that has been widely used for privatisation has been that wider share ownership is good for a democratic society. In Britain, for example, before the privatisation process really began only a small number of people held shares in private companies on their own account. As a result of the privatisation process millions of people now hold shares in, for example, the electricity, gas and water companies. The government had hoped that once people caught onto the idea of private ownership they would move outside of that limited number of companies and begin to buy shares in other non-privatised British companies. This would be good in that where you have more people owning shares, a larger proportion of people have an interest in the capitalist system. They no longer see profits as something bad but rather as a mark of efficiency. So the argument is that privatisation is helping in the process of encouraging people to be involved in the market system.

There is a fourth claimed benefit of privatisation that is much weaker than it first appears. Some governments think it has the benefit that it increases government revenue. They sell off assets from the state to the private sector in return for revenue which they can then use in the form of lower taxes, or increased spending in other areas of activity. Almost certainly this is not in fact the case. All that the government is doing is transferring revenue from the future to the present. When the government sells shares in an industry, why is anyone prepared to buy the shares? It is because the share represents a claim on the future profitability of an industry. So the government has forsaken that future revenue stream for its present capitalised value. So to the extent that the government sells off state assets, it is not raising government revenue at all, it is simply relocating the timing from the future to the present. Thus it is not enough to say that privatisation increases government revenue. The process must achieve something with respect to efficiency before it can be pronounced a success.

It needs to be recognised that there are trade-offs implicit in these benefits. They cannot all be realised to the full extent. For example, maximising government income means selling the assets unconditionally. But this will enable the purchaser to use its monopoly power to give allocative inefficiency. Widening share ownership requires selling some shares to private investors. Again this may reduce government income. Institutional investors might have been willing to pay more.

If we attempt to measure the success of the privatisation programme we encounter the same problem that we found in measuring the success or otherwise of mergers. It is difficult to isolate what we are trying to measure from changes in other variables. For example, if we look at changes in the profitability of privatised companies, we cannot easily separate the effects of any efficiency improvement from the effects of market power. Perhaps the best attempt to overcome the problem is by Parker and Martin (1995). They examine company performance by considering changes in productivity relative to the rest of the economy. Table 13.1 gives some of their estimates for both labour productivity and total factor productivity. Notice that the results are mixed. Some companies' performance has been decidedly impressive. Others are a considerable disappointment.

Policy towards privatised firms

The largest problem about privatisation is that of allocative efficiency. If the capacity to produce goods and services is transferred into the private sector, there is a danger that resources will be misallocated because there is now a private sector monopoly. Price and output decisions will reflect private rather than social welfare.

Table 13.1 Annual percentage changes in relative productivity: selected privatised firms

Firm	Labour productivity		Total factor productivity	
	Pre-privatisation	Post-privatisation	Pre-privatisation	Post-privatisation
British Airways	8.0	2.2	2.9	6.3
British Airports Authority	−0.2	−2.2	−2.7	−8.0
British Gas	4.1	2.9	−0.5	−2.4
British Steel	8.8	−1.0	2.9	−4.2
Associated British Ports	1.5	12.9	6.0	9.4
BT	4.1	4.9	2.0	4.2

Adapted from Parker and Martin (1995)

Those who are keen on the idea of privatisation say that it need not be a problem. There are means to control such abuse. The two principal ones are *price controls* and *deregulation*.

Privatisation and price controls

We shall examine the use of price controls here but the analysis applies to any monopolistic industry. Price controls are not confined to privatised firms but since that is where they are principally used this is an appropriate place to tackle the problem. Price ceilings in a competitive market are almost always bad. They are either irrelevant if they are set at the price above equilibrium or if they are set at a price that is below equilibrium it simply results in excess demand and a misallocation of resources. So most economists would be of the view that price ceilings are bad in competitive markets. But some would be much more sympathetic where there is some monopoly power, because in principle price ceilings can be used to move firms towards an optimal allocation of resources. We can see that diagrammatically in Figure 13.1.

Left to itself the firm would produce Q_{pm} output because that is where marginal cost equals marginal revenue and they would sell up the demand curve at the price P_{pm}. However, the socially optimal level of output is, in the absence of externalities, where the marginal cost of production reflects the marginal value to society of the output given by the demand curve. So marginal cost = demand gives a socially optimal output, Q_{so}. The appropriate socially optimal price is P_{so}. So the price output decision, which maximises welfare under these conditions, will be at a higher level of output and lower price than the one chosen by the private profit-maximising monopolist.

The logic of the price ceiling is to impose it at P_{so}, the socially optimum price. In order to see from the diagram how a profit-maximising firm would

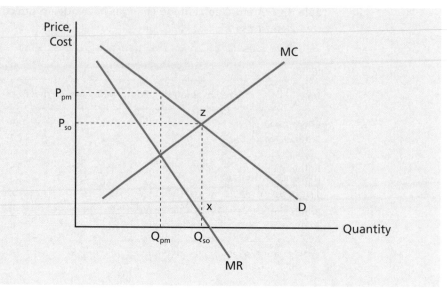

Figure 13.1 Imposition of a socially optimal price ceiling

behave, we need three steps. First, we can see that the effect of a price ceiling is to change the effective demand curve faced by the firm. Then we need to see that if the demand curve faced by the firm has been changed by the price ceiling, the marginal revenue curve faced by the firm has necessarily been altered. Thirdly, we need to see that if the marginal revenue curve has been altered, the profit-maximising level of output will have been altered as well.

First, what does the price ceiling do to the nature of the demand curve? If the price ceiling is set at P_{so}, it prevents the firm using the top part of the demand curve. It cannot produce a small level of output at a higher price. If it produces a small level of output, the highest price it can charge is P_{so}. So the effective demand curve that the firm faces, given the price ceiling, is P_{so}, as far as point Z. Legally the firm, if it made a large level of output, would be allowed to charge as high as the price ceiling. But the market demand conditions are such that it would not be able to do so. For output levels beyond Q_{so} the price ceiling is irrelevant. So the effect of the price ceiling is to change the demand curve to $P_{so}ZD$.

To change the nature of the demand curve faced by the firm is necessarily to change the marginal revenue curve. Over the range from zero to Q_{so} the effective demand curve is perfectly elastic. The price ceiling has made it like a firm in perfect competition. It can always sell another unit of output without lowering price. In consequence, from P_{so} to Z, the marginal revenue curve is the same as the demand curve. The marginal revenue curve is the same as the average revenue curve just as it is for a perfectly competitive firm. Beyond that output level the price ceiling is irrelevant, the old demand curve applies. So then the old marginal revenue curve still applies. The marginal revenue curve is $P_{so}ZXMR$.

The third and last step is to find the price output decision which the profit-maximising firm will now use. It wants to produce where MC = MR, MC equals the new MR at point Z. The profit-maximising firm, given the price ceiling constraint, will produce at Q_{so} with a price at P_{so}. This is the socially optimal price and output.

So, in principle, price ceilings do have a role to play in preventing monopolistic firms from misallocating resources and exploiting consumers. If government imposes a price ceiling at the social optimum it can cause a price output decision which is consistent with consumer welfare maximisation. The above explains why governments use price ceilings as part of their control of firms and industries.

There are important qualifications to that argument above. These qualifications will help us appreciate how price ceilings are used in practice. The first qualification is that the reason why it worked on the diagram is because we made an assumption that this is the way in which firms set prices and output. If we have the correct model of pricing decisions, then the price ceiling will achieve what the government wants. If, however, we don't have the correct model and we believe, for example, that firms are not profit maximisers, then this is not an appropriate model to explain pricing behaviour. Then the conclusion that the price ceiling is an optimum way of handling the problem may not be correct either. The solution is only as good as our analysis of the problem.

There is a second reason why we need to qualify the view that price ceilings are a good mechanism for controlling the monopoly power of firms. If government gets it wrong, and sets a price ceiling lower than the social optimum, then all the problems that occur in a competitive market where a price ceiling is imposed will occur here. It is important to get the price ceiling right. We can see that from Figure 13.2.

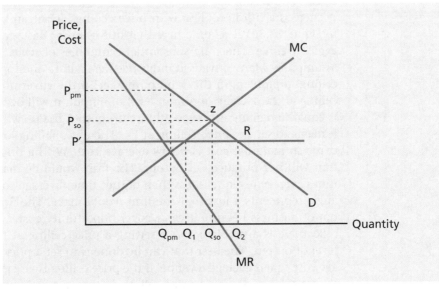

Figure 13.2 A price ceiling below the social optimum

Suppose the government gets the price ceiling wrong and imposes it at P'. We can see what the effect will be; the effective demand curve now faced by the firm is P'RD. The marginal revenue curve is therefore the same as P' until R. Then the profit-maximising decision of the firm will be to produce where marginal cost equals marginal revenue, which is at Q_1 output. Notice that the price ceiling has made the marginal units from Q_1 to Q_{so} unprofitable, so the quantity offered for sale is reduced. But notice also that the lower price causes quantity demanded to expand to Q_2. At a lower price firms will find that consumers wish to buy more. So Q_1Q_2 now represents excess demand: Q_2 is demanded, Q_1 is supplied, and the difference is excess demand. In free markets, wherever there is excess demand the price rises, but the government's price ceiling has taken that possibility away. So a price ceiling that is below the social optimum creates problems of excess demand and also means that we do not get the socially optimal level of output. So it's not simply a question of a government picking a price ceiling and imposing it. For example, if over time inflation takes place it will be necessary to increase the price ceiling along with inflation otherwise the real price ceiling will become more and more severe. This will produce the above problems. Government policy is therefore that privatised monopolistic firms operate under a price ceiling of the form *RPI ± k* where RPI is the retail price index and k is an amount which varies from one industry to another to change the real price over time. For example, for the water companies *k* has been positive. This has allowed them to raise prices in real terms in order to repair crumbling sewer pipes and meet ever-tighter European water purity standards. For BT *k* has been negative. This obliges BT to lower prices over time, thus passing on to consumers the benefit of falling costs associated with improving technology. The details of the controls are worked out through a number of government agencies or offices. For example, the regulatory body for the gas and electricity industries is Ofgem, The Office of Gas and Electricity Markets.

There is a third problem with price ceilings. This can be seen by reference to Figure 13.3. We assume here that this industry has a falling long-run average cost curve. There are substantial economies of scale. This is a reasonable assumption. Many privatised industries were natural monopolies. Why are price ceilings a problem in this kind of market? If the government imposes a price ceiling at the socially optimum level of output, it will be where marginal cost is equal to demand. It is looking for an output of Q_{so}, where MC = D, and so it needs to set the price ceiling at P_{so}. There is a falling long-run average cost curve so marginal cost is below average cost. With a price ceiling at P_{so}, the firm will not produce Q_{so} output. The firm would be making a loss. Output times average revenue is less than output times average cost. The shaded rectangle represents a loss that the firm would make. The firm would simply go out of business because it can't cover opportunity cost.

So there is a problem about setting a price ceiling at the socially optimal level of output. The best that can be done is to set a price ceiling where average cost equals average revenue. If the price ceiling is any lower than that there is zero output. Setting a price ceiling so that average revenue equals average

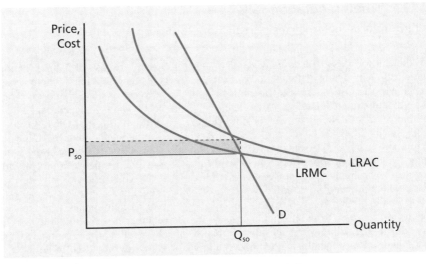

Figure 13.3 Price controls with a declining LRAC

cost is perfectly possible. Remember that this allows a firm to make a normal profit. It will cover opportunity cost. But it is a rejection of the idea of a socially optimal level of output where MC = D. The only way in which one could get the firm to produce where MC = D would be to put the price ceiling lower and then to offer a subsidy to the firm. However, there are problems about doing this. Perhaps the biggest problem is that it is not really socially efficient. The logic of a socially optimum level of output is the idea that the consumer of the marginal unit is paying what it costs society to produce it. Demand is equal to marginal cost. But if subsidies are being paid there is a redistribution of income from the government towards consumers of this product. That is not a socially optimal transfer of income. So whatever is done about a price ceiling there is a problem. As we saw earlier, governments are generally looking for ways to balance their budget. So there is a tendency to look to a price ceiling that allows the industry to make a normal profit, rather than one which requires a subsidy. That problem is not a problem only with respect to privatisation. It is associated with any industry that operates with a falling long-run average cost curve. In practice, though, it is with privatised firms that the problem is most acute.

A fourth problem concerns the nature of *regulatory capture*. Regulation may enhance inefficiency. Regulated firms will be highly organised, more so than their consumers. They may therefore lobby the regulatory body more effectively, such that the government body becomes increasingly more sympathetic to the aims of the firm rather than to the wishes of the consumers.

Finally, a firm may over time lose its incentive to be cost efficient. If it succeeds in reducing costs, only to find that the price control is tightened, it may feel that there is little incentive in the longer term to look for cost savings.

Box 13.1 When regulation fails

John Kay explores the problems of regulatory control.

It is difficult for a regulator to manage a relationship with a single, dominant company. Peter Davis, the first lottery regulator, lost his job for being too close to Camelot. Dame Helena Shovelton, his successor, lost hers for not being close enough.

On one side lies the danger of regulatory capture. Being a regulator is a lonely job. You depend for information on the industry you regulate; the people who work within the industry are the people you see every day. It is easy to understand how regulators come to see the public interest through the eyes of the companies they regulate. That is how airline regulators ended up operating cartels on behalf of the world airline business.

Yet if you escape the danger of capture, there are other pitfalls. You may end up as, in effect, the manager of the business. After all, you have to review the marketing strategies of the contenders for the lottery franchise. You need to make a detailed assessment of whether planned investment in water pipes and sewers is really justified. You have to look at Railtrack's safety record and judge whether it is responsible for late trains. The trouble is that second-guessing commercial decisions is going beyond your job.

Yet if you are to control a business without managing it, you incur the further risk of establishing an adversarial relationship between regulator and regulated. If that happens, regulation is conducted through the media and the courts. This makes lawyers and spin doctors rich, but at the price of undermining the rationality of the regulatory process.

Given that regulating private monopolies is so fraught, we need to avoid it when we can.

Competitive answers are usually better. This is straightforward enough for telecommunications, where the days of natural monopoly are over. The job of a regulator is to achieve a competitive outcome as quickly and as comprehensively as possible and then retire early. The mistake of David Edmonds, head of Oftel, was to believe that such an outcome could be achieved by industry agreement. That is like expecting crime to be managed by negotiations between burglars and their victims.

But you cannot have companies competing to provide a rail network or tap water – they are natural monopolies. And the issue here must be whether it was sensible to pass over ownership of the assets of the industries to a private company. It is increasingly clear in both industries that it would have been better to retain these assets under public control and to transfer responsibility for their operation to competing private companies.

So why need there be a monopoly of the national lottery? If Sir Richard Branson can run a better lottery than Camelot, or people would prefer an operator with more whiskers and less profit, then why should the People's Lottery not get a chance? Equally, why should Camelot have to disconnect its terminals to let him do so? Why should a lottery not be run by anyone who can show that they are respectable and willing to make a suitable contribution to good causes?

There is an argument that a lottery is a natural monopoly. Wouldn't we all rush to the lottery with the biggest prizes? Maybe we would: but football pools survived as a competitive industry for many years, even in the face of legislation that created unnecessary barriers to new entry and innovation.

When it is difficult to choose, it is always worth asking whether you really need to make a choice. And when it is difficult to regulate, it is always worth asking whether competition could do the job instead.

Source: Financial Times, 18 October 2000 **FT**

Privatisation and deregulation

An alternative to using a price ceiling would be what has come to be called deregulation. This means the removal of controls. It goes with bringing competition into an industry in what was formerly a private sector monopoly. Take, for example, the telecommunications industry. In the UK, when the industry was privatised a state monopoly, BT, became a private sector monopoly. Now we have many telephone companies operating in competition with BT. It came about because the government insisted that BT rent its lines out to other companies at cost. So someone competing against BT doesn't require their own set of cables. They simply pay a rental which the government itself controls. An alternative form of deregulation is used in the railway industry. This is franchising, a subject we have already considered. Companies bid for a licence to operate trains on the track owned by Railtrack, part of what was formerly British Rail. Again the purpose is to introduce competition to reduce the need for price controls. However, the process is not without difficulty. There are two in particular. First, since one company may be granted exclusive use of a part of the railway network, one monopoly can be replaced with a number of local monopolies. Secondly, the optimal length of the franchise is difficult to determine. A short franchise discourages a company from making long-term strategic investment decisions. A long franchise makes it harder to replace companies that use their monopoly power to perform poorly. Nevertheless, by introducing competition into an industry, the government may be able partly to overcome the problem that it has transferred a monopoly from the state to the private sector.

There is evidence that deregulation of this kind has been successful, at least in the USA. Table 13.2 shows an attempt by Winston (1993) to measure in a number of different industries the effects of deregulation there. The second column shows the benefits that obtain to consumers as a result of deregulation.

Although there are benefits to consumers, in most cases it does not result in a loss to producers. In many cases producers also gain. The result of deregulation is increased efficiency in production. Resources are more efficiently used and significant gains accrue to both consumers and producers. The benefits are large but, as the estimate in column four shows, the potential for even more benefits is there if the deregulation were to be entirely successful. So even if the evidence of increased efficiency from privatisation is patchy, it appears that deregulation can bring substantial benefits.

Table 13.2 Welfare effects of deregulation, $US billion, 1990

Industry	Consumers	Producers	Total	Additional benefits if deregulation achieves optimality
Airlines	8.8–14.3	4.9	13.7–19.7	4.9
Railroads	7.2–9.7	3.2	10.4–12.9	0.45
Trucking	15.4	−4.8	10.6	0.0
Telecommunications	0.73–1.6	–	0.73–1.6	11.8
Cable television	0.37–1.3	–	0.37–1.3	0.4–0.8
Brokerage	0.14	−0.14	0.0	0.0
Natural gas	–	–	–	4.1
Total	32.6–43.0	3.2	35.8–46.2	21.65–22.05

Adapted from Winston (1993)

Competition policy

Competition policy goes wider than the control of privatised industries. Most western governments are committed to intervening in the market system in order to see that competition prevails in markets. The intervention can either be on a rules basis or on a discretionary basis. The USA favours rules. It establishes criteria, for example, with respect to the market share of companies involved in merger behaviour. The rules approach has advantages. It is relatively inexpensive to administer and firms know clearly where they stand *vis-à-vis* the law. The EU and the UK favour discretion, at least with regard to mergers. Deciding each case on its merits has the advantage of flexibility, although it increases uncertainty for the firms concerned. We consider competition policy under three headings, policy towards market dominance, policy towards mergers and policy towards restrictive practices.

Policy towards market dominance

EU policy towards dominant firms was established in Article 86 of the Treaty of Rome, Article 82 since the Amsterdam Treaty of 1999. This prohibits the abuse of dominant firms where it affects trade between member states. It is not illegal to have a dominant position *per se*. Only its abuse is subject to law. This principle is followed within the UK. The policy is administered by two bodies. The first is the *Office of Fair Trading* (OFT), headed by the Director General of Fair Trading (DGFT). The second is the *Competition Commission*, formerly the Monopolies and Mergers Commission. The activities of both are guided by the Competition Act, 1998.

The Act seeks to prevent dominant firms charging 'excessive' prices. It also bans predatory behaviour. The DGFT's current guidance is that a less than 25% market share would not be sufficient for dominance. More than 40% is likely to be dominant. Within these guidelines any dominant firm can be subject to investigation. The investigation will be undertaken by the Competition Commission. If an abuse of its dominant position is found, the DGFT will seek undertakings that the abuse will be stopped. Powers of enforcement are considerable, including disinvestment.

Policy towards mergers

We have seen that in the view of many economists, as markets become more concentrated, the power to misallocate resources increases. Mergers will tend to cause market concentration to increase, so most governments have the power to prevent large mergers from taking place.

In the USA the 'rules' approach means that if a merger will raise concentration beyond a certain level, the presumption is that it should be stopped. We saw this in Chapter 3. In Europe the discretionary approach means that each case is addressed on its merits. Although there is a fear of the build-up of market power, we have seen the potential benefits of possible economies of scale through mergers. So even though the degree of enforcement of merger legislation will vary between countries, virtually all governments will want to have some control over merger activity.

EU policy towards mergers was established in 1990. The European Commission can examine large cross-border mergers. For the Commission to be able to examine a proposed merger two conditions must be satisfied:

- it must create a combined global turnover of more than €250 million, and
- at least two of the firms involved have an EU-wide turnover of more than €250 million.

Very few mergers meet these criteria. Few of these are investigated. For those that are investigated the key consideration is the effect upon competition. Unlike the UK legislation, any potential efficiency gains cannot be regarded as off-setting the reduction in competition. Few of these mergers are prevented.

In the UK a merger may be referred to the Competition Commission if the merger creates a market share of over 25%. Alternatively it may be referred if the value of the assets involved is greater than some minimum threshold, currently £70m. The Commission must assess whether the merger will be against the public interest. The public interest is not defined but in practice it comes to assessing the potential benefits of scale economies compared with the potential cost of increased market power. Few qualifying mergers are referred. Few of those are prevented. The unstated presumption seems to be in favour of allowing mergers to take place.

Policy towards restrictive practices

Merger policy is an attempt to control the structure within which industries operate. But there is also legislation in most countries that attempts to control the behaviour of firms within it. Most countries have restrictive trade practice legislation. The EU policy is found in what was Article 85 of the treaty of Rome, now Article 81. All agreements and undertakings designed to distort competition are banned. Such agreements can have no status in law. Failure to end such practices can result in fines of up to 10% of company turnover. Powers of search are available to establish the existence of secret agreements. There are exemptions from the general prohibition. In particular, there are exemptions for certain exclusive dealership arrangements such as automobiles. There are also exemptions for agreements on research and development activity. The rationale for such exemptions we have examined in earlier chapters.

In contrast to merger policy, the presumption is against restrictive agreements in the UK. It has become noticeably more rigorous in recent years. Fewer and fewer agreements have been allowed. In 2001 one of the few remaining declared agreements, the setting of minimum prices for over-the-counter pharmaceutical health remedies, was declared illegal.

Powers of search similar to the EU are now available for suspected breaches of the law on restrictive practices. Fines on companies breaking the law are high. There are, however, still doubts as to whether the limited amount of resources available to the OFT and Competition Commission make the legislation entirely credible.

Recently, the UK government has introduced further legislation with the criterion of making the trading environment more competitive. For example, since March 2001 it is possible to jail senior executives of companies engaged in illegal price fixing.

Conclusion

There are significant differences between economists over the relationships between structure, conduct and performance. There are important differences with regard to the ability of the market system to optimise the usage of scarce resources. Thus government policy towards industry will be controversial. Nevertheless, the majority view seems to be that the market mechanism can be improved with judicious state intervention.

However, we should not be tempted to think that the choice is between private sector inefficiency and state efficiency. There is no guarantee that the state itself will be efficient. What we must compare is the possibility of inefficiency in the private sector with the possibility of inefficiency of government control. Governments make mistakes. They may, for example, stop mergers that would be helpful to society. There is also one other possibility. We examined the principal–agent problem and argued that the principal, the shareholder, and the agent, the manager, may not have the same goals. The principal–agent problem may exist between members of society and the government. How can I be sure that the members of the government are acting on my behalf and not on their own behalf? How can I know that they are behaving towards industry in a way that maximises my welfare rather than their own? For these reasons we should not imagine that there is a choice between public efficiency and private inefficiency. Rather we are making a comparison between private inefficiency and public inefficiency.

KEY RESULTS

1 The benefits of government intervention in markets depends upon the model of firm behaviour.

2 In principle, privatisation can improve efficiency, although evidence to support this is limited.

3 Price controls may move firm output closer to the social optimum.

4 Deregulation may be better than price controls but it is difficult to achieve in some markets.

5 EU and UK policy towards dominant firms and mergers is discretionary.

6 UK policy towards restrictive practices has been tighter in recent years.

7 Markets may fail, but so may government intervention.

Questions

1* It is widely believed that the privatisation of the UK railway industry has not been a success. Why might it be difficult to make an objective judgement?

2* UK policy seems to be rules based with respect to restrictive practices and discretionary with respect to mergers. Would you agree? If so, is this sensible?

3* Governments in the EU still offer subsidies to firms, especially in manufacturing industry. Can such a policy be justified?

4 Consider Box 13.1. Do you agree that it would have been better to retain rail and water assets under public control and to 'transfer responsibility for their operation to competing private companies'?

5 Consider Box 13.2. What principles determine the appropriate balance between consumer wants and the freedom of firms?

* *Help available at* ***http://www.e-econ.co.uk***

Box 13.2 The cost of strengthening consumer power
Government initiatives to improve consumer power may have costs.

Where should the legal line be drawn between protecting the interests of consumers and those of companies? This question is about to be tested by two government initiatives – much to the alarm of industry, which fears that companies risk being dragged through the courts for minor red tape infringements. A sharp rise in mass lawsuits brought by pressure groups is also on the cards.

From June 1, a host of consumer protection bodies – including the Office of Fair Trading, trading standards departments and various utility regulators – can apply to the courts for such orders. Businesses deemed to be infringing any one of 10 consumer protection directives will have to stop the offending practice immediately or face unlimited fines and up to two years' imprisonment of directors.

The government has stressed that the initiative is targeted at rogue traders, such as unscrupulous timeshare salesmen and 'international rip-off scams such as dodgy websites that never deliver the goods ordered'.

But industry organisations are not entirely reassured that mainstream companies will escape the effects of the new rules. The areas covered by the orders are extremely broad, including misleading advertising, distance selling, consumer credit and sale of goods. One of the targets cited by the DTI is 'holiday companies that produce brochures that make resorts from hell sound like paradise on earth' – an example that suggests the courts could be asked to intervene in complaints against high street retailers.

The CBI wants the OFT to issue detailed guidelines on how the new orders will work. It also wants the government radically to rethink its second initiative on consumer-driven litigation – representative orders. The Lord Chancellor's Department is consulting on proposals to allow groups representing specific interests – such as consumer organisations, environmental pressure groups and trade unions – to sue companies on behalf of their members.

Lawsuits could be launched – with the court's permission – even in cases where the individuals being represented were not identified. This could include 'all the purchasers of a product or service who had been overcharged . . . for example customers of a public utility company serving a particular area'. It could also cover cases where the individuals represented were 'non-identifiable . . . for example where a consumer group has difficulty finding suitable individuals to run a test case'.

The courts would have the discretion to waive the risk of legal costs, should the lawsuit fail, for groups taking cases in the public interest against the government or a plc. In spite of this, the consultation states that 'it is unlikely that

▶

Box 13.2 continued

businesses will be inundated with representative claims'. Business representatives beg to differ.

Christopher Hodges, of law firm CMS Cameron McKenna, who is chairing the CBI working party on the proposals, cites hard figures to support these reservations. Analysis in his recent book on multi-party claims shows that England and Wales has experienced more of these actions in the past 15 years than any other jurisdiction in Europe.

The cases, mainly in the pharmaceuticals product liability area, are 'notable for the fact that they were overwhelmingly unsuccessful, with 93 per cent of the individual claims failing', Mr Hodges says. He draws a parallel between the 'large number of frivolous, unjustified or disproportionate claims that impose huge costs on industry' produced by class actions in the US and the 'waste of tens of millions of pounds in legal aid' resulting from the poor screening of multi-party claims in England and Wales.

Mr Hodges believes the government could fall into a similar trap with its new proposals, citing the absence of 'any sensible checks and balances to prevent nuisance and speculative claims'.

It remains to be seen whether such arguments convince the government, which believes representative actions are an important tool for increasing individuals' access to justice. But it is clear that industry is far from reconciled to the trend to increased litigation

Source: Financial Times, 23 April 2001   **FT**

Appendix

I hope you feel inspired to read further into the issues raised in this book. If you wish to do so, the most important articles are referenced in the bibliography. Here I give the references to the main specialist books, although only to those that are in print. Some, but not all of these references require a greater knowledge of maths than I have assumed in this book.

Chapter 1

Case, K., Fair, R., Gartner, M. and Heather, K. (1999) *Economics*, Prentice Hall, Chapter 12

Griffiths, A. and Wall, S. (2000) *Intermediate Microeconomics*, 2nd edn, Prentice Hall, Chapter 7

Chapter 2

Lipczynski, J. and Wilson, J. (2001) *Industrial Organisation*, Prentice Hall, Chapter 1

Stead, R., Curwen, P. and Lawler, K. (1996) *Industrial Economics*, McGraw-Hill, Chapter 1

Chapter 3

Lipczynski, J. and Wilson, J. (2001) *Industrial Organisation*, Prentice Hall, Chapter 4

Stead, R., Curwen, P. and Lawler, K. (1996) *Industrial Economics*, McGraw-Hill, Chapter 3

Chapter 4

Griffiths, A. and Wall, S. (2000) *Intermediate Microeconomics*, 2nd edn, Prentice Hall, Chapter 4

Moschandreas, M. (2000) *Business Economics*, 2nd edn, Thomson, 2000, Chapter 6

Chapter 5

Lipczynski, J. and Wilson, J. (2001) *Industrial Organisation*, Prentice Hall, Chapter 8

Stead, R., Curwen, P. and Lawler, K. (1996) *Industrial Economics*, McGraw-Hill, Chapter 10

Cabral, L. (2000) *Introduction to Industrial Organization*, MIT Press, Chapter 16

Chapter 6

Lipczynski, J. and Wilson, J. (2000) *Industrial Organisation*, Prentice Hall, Chapter 10

Stead, R., Curwen, P. and Lawler, K. (1996) *Industrial Economics*, McGraw-Hill, Chapter 9

Chapter 7

Lipczynski, J. and Wilson, J. (2001) *Industrial Organisation*, Prentice Hall, Chapter 9

Cabral, L. (2000) *Introduction to Industrial Organization*, MIT Press, Chapter 11

Griffiths, A. and Wall, S. (2000) *Intermediate Microeconomics*, 2nd edn, Prentice Hall, Chapter 9

Chapter 8

Cabral, L. (2000) *Introduction to Industrial Organization*, MIT Press, Chapter 17

Moschandreas, M. (2000) *Business Economics*, 2nd edn, Thomson, 2000, pp 184–191

Chapter 9

Lipczynski, J. and Wilson, J. (2001) *Industrial Organisation*, Prentice Hall, Chapters 2, 3

Stead, R., Curwen, P. and Lawler, K. (1996) *Industrial Economics*, McGraw-Hill, Chapter 6

Cabral, L. (2000) *Introduction to Industrial Organization*, MIT Press, Chapter 8

Griffiths, A. and Wall, S. (2000) *Intermediate Microeconomics*, 2nd edn, Prentice Hall, G. and W., Chapters 8, 9

Chapter 10

Griffiths, A. and Wall, S. (2000) *Intermediate Microeconomics*, 2nd edn, Prentice Hall, Chapter 2

Chapter 11

Moschandreas, M. (2000) *Business Economics*, 2nd edn, Thomson, 2000, Chapter 10

Griffiths, A. and Wall, S. (2000) *Intermediate Microeconomics*, 2nd edn, Prentice Hall, Chapter 5

Chapter 12

Lipczynski, J. and Wilson, J. (2001) *Industrial Organisation*, Prentice Hall, Chapter 7

Stead, R., Curwen, P. and Lawler, K. (1996) *Industrial Economics*, McGraw-Hill, Chapter 7

Cabral, L. (2000) *Introduction to Industrial Organization*, MIT Press, Chapter 13

Chapter 13

Lipczynski, J. and Wilson, J. (2001) *Industrial Organisation*, Prentice Hall, Chapters 11, 12

Stead, R., Curwen, P. and Lawler, K. (1996) *Industrial Economics*, McGraw-Hill, Chapters 12, 13, 14

Cabral, L. (2000) *Introduction to Industrial Organization*, MIT Press, Chapter 5

Griffiths, A. and Wall, S. (2000) *Intermediate Microeconomics*, 2nd edn, Prentice Hall, Chapter 13

Bibliography

Alexander, D., Flynn, J., and Linkins, L. (1995) 'Innovation and global market share in the pharmaceutical industry', *Review of Industrial Organisation*, 10, 197–207

Angwin, D. and Savill, B. (1997) 'Strategic perspectives on European cross-border acquisitions: a view from top European executives', *European Management Journal*, 15, 4, August, 423–35

Arnould, R. (1972) 'Pricing professional services: a case study of the legal services industry', *Southern Economic Journal*, 38, 495–507

Bain, J. (1956) *Barriers to New Competition*, Harvard University Press

Baumol, W.J. (1959) *Business Behaviour, Value and Growth*, Macmillan

Baumol, W.J. (1961) *Economic Theory and Operations Analysis*, Prentice Hall

Baumol, W.J. (1982) 'Contestable markets: an uprising in the theory of industry structure', *American Economic Review*, 72,1, 1–15

Baumol, W. and Braunstein, Y. (1977) 'Empirical study of scale economies and production complementarities: the case of journal publication', *Journal of Political Economy*, 85, 4, August, 1037–48

Benham, L. (1972) 'The effect of advertising on the price of eyeglasses', *Journal of Law and Economics*, 15, 337–52

Berger, P. and Ofek, E. (1995) 'Diversification's effect on firm value', *Journal of Financial Economics*, 37, 39–65

Blinder, A. (1991) 'Why are prices sticky? Preliminary results from an interview study', *American Economic Review*, 81, 2, May, 89–96

Booth, D., Kanetkar, V., Vertinsky, I. and Whistler, D. (1991) 'An empirical model of capacity expansion and pricing in an oligopoly with barometric price leadership: a case study of the newsprint industry of North America', *Journal of Industrial Economics*, 39, 3, March, 255–76

Bothwell, J. (1980) 'Profitability, risk, and the separation of ownership from control', *Journal of Industrial Economics*, 28, 303–12

Brookes, M. and Wahhaj, Z. (2001) 'The economic effects of business to business Internet activity', *National Institute Economic and Social Review*, 175, Jan., 95–108

Burke, T., Maddock, S. and Rose, A. (1993) 'How ethical is British business?', University of Westminster, Working Paper, Series 2, no 1

Cable, J. and Schwalbach, J. (1991) 'International comparisons of entry and exit', in K. Cowling *et al.* (1980) *Mergers and Economic Performance*, Cambridge University Press

Cady, J. (1976) 'An estimate of the price effects of restrictions on drug price advertising', *Economic Enquiry*, 14, 493–510

Cameron, S. (1998) 'Estimation of the demand for cigarettes: a review of the literature', *Economic Issues*, 3, 2, September, 51–71

Coase, R. (1937) 'The nature of the firm', *Economica*, 1937, New series, IV, 386–405

Coelli, T. and Perelman, S. (2000) 'Technical efficiency of European railways: a distance function approach', *Applied Economics*, 2000, 32, 1967–76

Competition Commission (2000) *A Report on the Supply of Groceries from Multiple Stores in the United Kingdom*, CMD 4842

Contractor, F. and Kundu, S. (1998), 'Modal choice in a world of alliances: analysing organisational forms in the International Hotels sector', *Journal of International Business Studies*, 29 (2), 325–58

Conyon, M. and Gregg, P. (1994) 'Pay at the top: A study of the sensitivity of top directors' remuneration to company specific shocks', *National Institute Economic Review*, August, 83–91

Cowling, K. and Mueller, D. (1978) 'The social costs of monopoly', *Economic Journal*, 88, 727–48

Cowling, K. *et al.* (1980) *Mergers and economic performance*, Cambridge University Press

Cyert, R. and March, J. (1963) *A Behavioural Theory of the Firm*, Prentice Hall

Darby, M. and Karni, E. (1973) 'Free competition and optimal amount of fraud', *Journal of Law and Economics*, 16, 67–88

Davies, S. and Lyons, B. (1982) 'Seller concentration: the technological explanation and demand uncertainty', *Economic Journal*, 92, 903–19

Davis, E. and Kay, J. (1990) 'Assessing corporate performance', *Business Strategy Review*, Summer, 1–16

Demsetz, H. (1969) 'Information and efficiency: another viewpoint', *Journal of Law and Economics*, 12, 1–22

Demsetz, H. (1973) 'Industry structure, market rivalry and public policy', *Journal of Law and Economics*, 16(1), 1–10

Douglas, E. (1984) 'Pricing for economic objectives given search and price adjustment costs', *Journal of Cost Analysis*, 1, Spring, 59–74

Doyle, P. (1994) 'Setting business performance and measuring performance', *European Management Journal*, 12(2), June, 123–32

Drake, L. (1992) 'Economies of scale and scope in the UK building societies; an application of the translog multiproduct cost function', *Applied Financial Economics*, 2, 211–19

Eichner, A. (1987) 'Prices and pricing', *Journal of Economic Issues*, XXI(4), December, 1555–84

European Economy (1988) 'The economics of 1992', 35, March.

Franks, J. and Harris, R. (1986) 'Shareholder wealth effects of corporate takeovers: the UK experience 1955–85', London Business School and University of North Carolina at Chapel Hill, Working Paper

Galbraith, J. (1958) *The Affluent Society*, Houghton Mifflin

Galbraith, J. (1967) *The New Industrial Estate*, Houghton Mifflin

Galbraith, J. (1973) *Economics and the Public Purpose*, Houghton Mifflin

Galbraith, J. (1980) *Annals of an abiding liberal*, André Deutsch

Geroski, P. (1994) *Market structure, Corporate performance and innovative activity*, Oxford: Clarendon Press

Geroski, P. and Scwalbach, J. (eds) (1991) *Entry and Market Contestability: An international comparison*, Blackwell

Gilligan, T. (1986) 'The competitive effects of resale price maintenance', *Rand Journal of Economics*, 17, 544–56.

Goddard, J. and Wilson, J. (1996) 'Persistence of profits for UK manufacturing and service sector firms', *The Service Industries Journal*, 16, 105–17.

Gort, M. (1969) 'An economic disturbance theory of mergers', *Quarterly Journal of Economics*, 82, 624–42

Gregory, A. (1997) 'An examination of the long run performance of UK acquiring firms', *Journal of Business Finance and Accounting*, 24, Sep., 971–1002

Hall, S., Walsh, M. and Yates, T. (1996) 'How do UK companies set prices?', *Bank of England Quarterly Bulletin*, May, 180–92

Harberger, A. (1954) 'Monopoly and resource allocation', *American Economic Review, Papers and Proceedings*, 44, 77–87

Harbison, J. and Pekar, P. (1999) *Smart Alliances: a Guide to repeatable Success*, Booz-Allen and Hamilton

Hennessy, D. (1997) 'Information asymmetry as a reason for vertical integration', in J. Caswell and R. Cotterill (eds) *Strategy and Policy in the food system: Emerging Issues*, Proceedings of NE-165 Conference, Washington DC

Hertz, N. (2001) *The Silent Takeover*, Heinemann

Hitt, M. (1988) *The context of innovation: Investment in R and D and Firm performance*, Technological Innovation and Human Resources series no 1, Berlin and Hawthorne

Hitt, M., Hoskisson, R., Johnson, R. and Moesel, D. (1996) 'The market for corporate control and firm innovation', *Academy of Management Journal*, 39(5), 1084–119

Holl, P. and Pickering, J. (1986) 'The determinants and effects of Actual, Abandoned and Contested Mergers', University of Manchester Institute of Science and Technology, mimeo

Hopenhayn, H. (1992) 'Entry, exit and firm dynamics in long run equilibrium', *Econometrica*, 60, 1127–50

Hornby, W. (1995) 'Economics and business: the theory of the firm revisited: a Scottish perspective', *Management Decision*, 33(1), 33–41

Jacob, R. (2001) 'Plumbing the depths of mutual disdain', *Financial Times*, 28 March

John, G. and Weitz, B. (1988) 'Forward integration into distribution: an empirical test of transaction cost analysis', *Journal of Law, Economics and Organisation*, 4, 337–56

Jovanovic, B. (1982) 'Selection and evolution of industry', *Econometrica*, 50, 649–70

JP Morgan (1998) 'European Mergers-of-equals', unpublished working paper, July

Kaufmann, P. and Lafontaine, F. (1994), 'Costs of control: the source of economic rents for McDonald's's franchisees', *Journal of Law and Economics*, XXXVII, 417–53

Kay, J. (1993) *Foundations of corporate success*, Oxford University Press

Klemm, M., Sanderson, S. and Luffman, G. (1991) 'Mission statements: selling corporate values to employees', *Long Range Planning*, 24(3), 73–8

Krickx, G. (1995) 'Vertical integration in the computer mainframe industry: a transaction cost interpretation', *Journal of Economic Behaviour and Organisation*, 26, 75–91.

Kuehn, D. (1975) *Takeovers and the theory of the firm*, Macmillan

Leibenstein, H. (1966) 'Allocative efficiency versus X-efficiency', *American Economic Review*, 56(3), 392–415

Lieberman, M. (1984) 'The learning curve and pricing in the chemical processing industries', *Rand Journal*, 15, 213–288

Lipczynski, J. and Wilson, J. (2001) *Industrial Organisation, an Analysis of Competitive Markets*, Pearson

Liu, D. and Forker, O. (1988) 'Generic fluid milk advertising, demand expansion and supply response: the case of New York City', *American Journal of Agricultural Economics*, 70, 229–36

Marris, R. (1964) *The Economic Behaviour of Managerial Capitalism*, Macmillan

Maunder, P. (1972) 'Price leadership: an appraisal of its character in some British industries', *The Business Economist*, 4, 132–40

McAfee, P. and Mcmillan, J. (1995) 'Organizational diseconomies of scale', *Journal of Economics and Management Strategy*, 4(3), 399–426

McGahan, A. (2000) 'How industries evolve', *Business Strategy Review*, 11(3), 1–16

Meeks, G. (1977) *Disappointing Marriage: A Study of the Gains to Mergers*, Cambridge University Press

Montgomery, C. and Wernerfelt, B. (1997) 'Diversification, Ricardian rents and Tobin's q', in N. Foss (ed.), *Resources, Firms and Strategies*, OUP

Mueller, D. (1980) 'Mergers, a cross-national comparison of the results', in D. Mueller (ed.), *The determinants and effects of mergers*, Oelgeschlager, Gunn and Hain, Cambridge, Mass

Nelson, P. (1974) 'Advertising as information', *Journal of Political Economy*, 82(4), July–August, 729–54

Newbould, G. (1970) *Management and Merger Activity*, Guthstead

Noulas, A., Ray, S. and Miller, S. (1990) 'Returns to scale and input substitution for large U.S. banks', *Journal of Money, Credit and Banking*, 22(1), February, 94–108

Parker, D. and Martin, S. (1995) 'The impact of UK privatisation on labour and total factor productivity', *Scottish Journal of Political Economy*, 42(2), 201–20

Peteraf, M. (1993) 'The cornerstones of competitive advantage: A resource-based view', *Strategic Management Journal*, 14, 179–91

Porter, M. (1980) *Competitive Advantage*, Free Press, New York

Pratten, C.F. (1988) 'A survey of the economies of scale, Research on the costs of non-Europe, 2.', Office for Official Publications of the European Communities.

Radice, H. (1971) 'Control type, profitability and growth in large firms: an empirical study', *Economic Journal*, 81, 547–62

Rao, R., Bergen, M. and Davis, S. (2000) 'How to fight a price war', *Harvard Business Review*, March–April, 107–15

Resnick, A. and Stern, B. (1977) 'An analysis of information content in television advertising', *Journal of Marketing*, 41, 50–3

Rondi, L., Sembenelli, A. and Ragazzi, E. (1996) 'Determinants of diversification patterns', in S. Davies and B. Lyons (eds) *Industrial Organisation in the European Union*, OUP, Chapter 10

Rumelt, R. (1991) 'How much does industry matter?', *Strategic Management Journal*, 3, March, 167–85

Scherer, F. (1980) *Industrial Market Structure and Economic Performance*, 2nd edn, Rand McNally

Schmalensee, R. (1985) 'Do markets differ much?', *American Economic Review*, 75, June, 341–51

Schumpeter, J. (1942) *Capitalism, Socialism and Democracy*, Allen and Unwin

Schwalbach, J. (1991) 'Entry, exit, market concentration and market contestability', in P. Geroski and J. Schwalbach (eds) *Entry and Market Contestability: An international comparison*, Blackwell

Shipley, D. and Bourdon, E. (1990) 'Distributor pricing in very competitive markets', *Industrial Marketing Management*, 19, 215–24

Simon, H. (1959) 'Theories of decision making in economics', *American Economic Review*, 49, June, 56–65

Spiller, P. (1985) 'On vertical mergers', *Journal of Law, Economics and Organisation*, 1, 285–312

Stigler, G.J. (1958) 'The economies of scale', *Journal of Law and Economics*, 1, October, 54–71

Storey, D., Watson, R. and Winarczyk, P. (1995) 'The remuneration of non-owner managers in UK unquoted and unlisted securities market enterprises', *Small Business Economics*, 7, 1–14

Strickland, A. and Weiss, L. (1976) 'Advertising, concentration and price–cost margins', *Journal of Political Economy*, 84(5), October, 1109–22

Sutton, C. (1974) 'Advertising, concentration and competition', *Economic Journal*, 84, March

Taylor, M. (1988) *Divesting business units: Making the decision and making it work*, Lexington Books

Telser, L. (1964) 'Advertising and competition', *Journal of Political Economy*, 72, 537–62

Vita, G. and Sacher, S. (2001) 'The competitive effects of not-for-profit hospital mergers: a case study', *Journal of Industrial Economics*, XLIX, March, 63–84

Williamson, O. (1964) *The Economics of Discretionary Behaviour*, Prentice Hall

Williamson, O. (1968) 'Economics as an antitrust defence: the welfare trade-offs', *American Economic Review*, 58, 18–31

Williamson, O. (1975) *Markets and Hierarchies: Analysis and antitrust implications: A study in the Economics of Internal Organisation*, New York, Free Press

Williamson, O. (1989) 'Transaction cost economics', in R. Schmalensee and R. Willig (eds), *Handbook of Industrial Organisation*, 1, Amsterdam: North-Holland, Ch. 3

Winston, C. (1993) 'Economic deregulation: days of reckoning for microeconomists', *Journal of Economic Literature*, Sep., 1263–89

Glossary of terms

Absolute cost advantage   The advantage to an incumbent firm because a potential entrant's cost curve is above its own.

Added value   The market value of a firm's output less the cost of inputs, including the opportunity cost of capital. The cost to the economy if the firm were to disappear and its resources were to be used in their next best use.

Advertising/sales ratio   The proportion of sales revenue spent upon advertising.

Agency relationship   One person or firm (the agent) is contracted to act on behalf of another (the principal).

Allocative efficiency   The optimal allocation of scarce resources. For any one firm it requires that its marginal cost is equal to price, assuming no external effects.

Asset specificity   The degree to which a firm's asset is only valuable when it is used in transacting with another specific party. If the asset is entirely asset specific it has no value in an alternative use.

Austrian school   A school of thought that sees competition as a dynamic rather than static process. Profits are the result of innovations that meet society's preferences. They also enable more spending on research and development that fuels economic growth.

Barometric price leadership   One firm in a market takes the lead in setting price levels. In this case the firm is recognised and accepted by other firms as one with good knowledge of the market conditions.

Barriers to entry   Those factors which make it difficult for new firms to establish themselves in the market, thus giving an advantage to the established firms.

Basing point pricing   The practice of setting prices irrespective of transport costs. It facilitates collusive behaviour since any customer will receive the same quote from any company regardless of the location of the customer.

Behavioural theories   Theories which seek to explain firm behaviour largely by the way in which business is organised internally rather than by the structure of the industry in which it operates.

Bounded rationality   In a situation of uncertainty individuals or firms do not consider all possible options, but restrict themselves to a rational choice between a limited number of them.

Cartel   A collusive agreement by firms in an industry to restrict or eliminate competition. The agreement is usually with respect to price.

Chicago school   A school of thought that sees profits as a reward for superior efficiency rather than as the result of monopoly power. Competition will always occur unless governments prevent its development.

Collusive oligopoly   A market dominated by a few large firms who establish agreements, usually on price, in order to reduce the degree of competition between them.

Collusive price leadership (*see* parallel pricing)

Concentration measures Measures of the extent to which economic activity is in the hands of a small number of firms.

Conglomerate A firm engaged in producing a wide variety of different outputs.

Contestable market Markets where there are no costs of entry or of exit. Existing and potential firms face the same cost structure. Such a market allows hit and run behaviour to occur.

Core competencies The distinguishing characteristics of a firm which give it the ability to produce profitably.

Cost-plus pricing The process of determining price by working out costs of production and adding on a mark-up. It might be average variable cost plus, in which case the mark-up must be sufficient to cover fixed costs, or average total costs, in which case it is often called full-cost pricing.

Credence goods Goods whose utility cannot be determined even after purchase and consumption. Consumers lack the information necessary to form an appropriate judgement.

Deadweight loss The loss of welfare that results from the misallocation of scarce resources, most commonly through the exercise of monopoly power.

Deconglomeration A term used to describe the process where diversified companies reduce the spread of their activities to concentrate on core activities.

Deregulation The removal of government control of an industry usually because it is believed that the market is sufficiently competitive to bring about an optimal allocation of resources.

Diversification The process of producing output in a range of different industries.

Dominant firm leadership One firm in a market takes the lead in setting price levels. In this case the firm is the one with the largest market share.

Downstream In the series of steps from raw material to final consumer, activities that are downstream from a firm are those nearer to the final consumer.

Economies of scale Reductions in unit cost as a result of increasing the volume of capital.

Economies of scope Reductions in unit cost as a result of increasing the range of outputs produced.

Exclusive dealerships Arrangements whereby firms will only sell their products to specified suppliers.

Experience goods Goods for which utility cannot be determined until after purchase and consumption

First mover advantage If a game has a series of moves, under some conditions the player making the first move can gain over its rivals.

Foreclosure Refusal to supply downstream firms (or purchase from upstream firms).

Franchising The practice of allocating (to a franchisee) exclusive rights to supply a good or service.

Full-cost pricing The process of determining price by working out average costs of production and adding on a mark-up.

Game theory   A technique for analysing the possible reactions to interdependent rivals' decisions.

Gibrat's law (*see* **the law of proportionate effect**)

Gini coefficient   The area between the Lorenz curve and the line of absolute equality expressed as a proportion of the area of the triangle below (or above) the diagonal. A value of zero represents equality and a value of one complete inequality.

Herfindahl-Hirschmann index   A measure of an industry's concentration found by summing the squares of the market share of each firm. It emphasises the importance of the large firms.

Hierarchy   The organisational structure of a firm that enables decisions to be taken internally on a non-market basis.

Horizontal integration   The acquisition of assets of one or more firms in the same industry.

Hostile takeover   The acquisition of one firm by another where the board of the acquired firm is opposed to the arrangement.

Interdependence   A characteristic of oligopolistic markets. Decisions taken by a firm have a direct effect upon its rivals, usually in terms of demand.

Law of proportionate effect   If the growth of firms is subject to randomness, then over time markets tend to increase in concentration and the number of size classes of firms increases.

Learning effects   The reductions in unit costs as a result of learning from producing the output in previous time periods.

Lerner index   An index measuring the extent to which firms exploit monopoly power. It can be defined as price minus marginal cost divided by price.

Limit pricing   The setting of price by an incumbent firm at a level which deters a potential rival entering the market.

Lorenz curve   A graphical construction showing the cumulative percentage values of two variables, for example the percentage of firms in an industry and the percentage share of the market controlled.

Low-cost price leadership   One firm in a market takes the lead in setting price levels. In this case the firm is the one with the lowest costs so other firms are obliged to accept its lead.

Managerial theories   Theories that assume a divorce of ownership and control. These theories explain management behaviour in terms of its own welfare rather than the welfare of the shareholders.

Mark-up   The difference between average (or average variable) cost and price expressed as a proportion of average (or average variable) cost.

Minimum efficient scale (MES)   The minimum level of output at which it is possible to gain all known scale economies.

Monopoly   A market structure characterised by high entry barriers where one firm produces all of the industry's output.

Multinational (*see* **Transnational**)

Nash equilibrium   A situation in game theory where each player chooses his/her best option in the light of what options he/she thinks other players will choose;

the result is a Nash equilibrium if each player then does as well as possible given the choices made by the other players.

Natural monopoly A market structure where economies of scale are present over such a large level of output that total costs of the industry would be minimised if there were only one firm.

Networks Groups of firms linked by regular contact and relationship.

Neoclassical model The model that makes the assumption that firms maximise profits and that consumers maximise their utility. Demand and cost conditions are known by all parties.

Normal profit The net income to a firm that is just sufficient to cover the opportunity cost of its resources. The minimum that the firm needs to be willing to keep its resources in their current use.

One-shot game Strategic decisions must be made at the outset and cannot be altered during the course of the game.

Opportunity cost (*see also* **normal profit**) The cost of meeting a want expressed in terms of the output of the next most desired alternative that has to be forgone.

Parallel pricing An informal understanding between firms that price changes determined by a leading firm will be matched by the others. Also called collusive price leadership.

Pareto optimality A Pareto optimal state is one in which it is not possible to improve the welfare of one person without making someone else worse off. A Pareto optimal improvement is one which makes at least one person better off without reducing the welfare of anyone else.

Patent The creation by government of an exclusive property right over the development of an application of new knowledge.

Pay-offs The expected values from strategic decisions taken in the context of games theory.

Perfect competition A theoretical market structure in which there are many firms, each of which is too small to influence price and where there are no barriers to exit or entry. Such firms are price takers in that they must take the price determined by the market.

Predation (*see* **predatory pricing**)

Predatory pricing (or predation) The attempt by a large dominant firm to drive a weaker firm from a market, usually by selling at a loss for a period of time.

Price leadership One firm in a market takes the lead in setting price levels and other firms follow. The relationship may be formal or informal and a firm may act as price leader for a variety of reasons.

Price discrimination The charging of different prices to customers for exactly the same product.

Principal–agent problem The separation of ownership from control makes possible a situation in which the agent (manager) can pursue his/her own goals rather than the goals of the principal (owner). The principal is either unaware of or unable to prevent the problem from occurring because the agent is better informed.

Prisoner's dilemma   A game in which both parties could improve their outcomes by cooperation but the nature of the game prevents them from doing so.

Privatisation   The process by which state-owned assets are transferred into private ownership.

Productive efficiency   A firm is productively efficient when it produces a given level of output at the lowest possible cost given the state of technology.

Product differentiation   Making products to be or to appear to be different in the eyes of the consumer. It enables the building of brand loyalty and can act as an entry barrier.

Product life cycle   It has been argued that products go through distinct stages over time, from inception to growth, to maturity and finally to decline.

Regulatory capture   The power of a firm to lobby regulators into changing its behaviour so that it favours the firm rather than the consumer.

Repeated game   A game in which a firm is able to change its strategy over time, usually to allow for strategic decisions made by its rivals.

Resale price maintenance   The practice of fixing the price that downstream customers must charge for the good or service.

Resource-based view   A view that sees the performance of firms being determined by the ownership of unique attributes, or capabilities.

S-curve   A curve that suggests how a typical industry evolves, from being unknown to slow growth, then rapid growth, followed by eventual decline.

Satisficing   Seeking to produce a satisfactory outcome for all parties within a firm rather than seeking outcomes that maximise the welfare of one group or that of just a few.

Schumpeterian view   The view that monopoly profits are good for society in that they enable firms to engage in R&D activity.

Search goods   Goods for which utility can be determined before purchase and consumption.

Stochastic process   A random, chance process.

Strategic alliances   Cooperative agreements between firms, usually of a long-term nature, in such areas as franchising and R&D activity.

Structure–conduct–performance paradigm   An approach to industrial economics that sees the performance of firms being dependent upon their behaviour, and that behaviour being determined by the structure of the market in which those firms operate.

Survivor technique   A method used for inferring the shape of a long-run cost curve by observing which size category of firm best survives over time.

Tobin's q   The ratio of the market value of a firm to the replacement cost of capital. It would equal one in a perfectly competitive market but one would normally expect it to exceed one where there is monopoly power.

Transactions costs   Those costs which arise as a result of the exchange process such as time spent negotiating prices and checking that agreements have been adhered to.

Transnational   A firm that owns or effectively controls productive capacity in more than one country.

Upstream In the series of steps from raw material to final consumer, activities that are upstream from a firm are those nearer to the raw material stage.

Value added The market value of output less the cost of inputs from other industries.

Vertical integration Carrying out activities at different stages of the production process.

Workable competition The best form of market structure of those that are feasible.

X-inefficiency The extent to which actual production costs are above the minimum possible costs given the current state of technology.

Zero-sum game A game in which gains to any party are exactly offset by losses to some other party.

Index